SpringerBriefs in Geography

For further volumes:
http://www.springer.com/series/10050

Barney Warf

Global Geographies
of the Internet

Springer

Barney Warf
Department of Geography
University of Kansas
Lawrence, KS
USA

ISSN 2211-4165   ISSN 2211-4173   (electronic)
ISBN 978-94-007-1244-7   ISBN 978-94-007-1245-4   (eBook)
DOI 10.1007/978-94-007-1245-4
Springer Dordrecht Heidelberg New York London

Library of Congress Control Number: 2012941426

Printed on acid-free paper

Springer is part of Springer Science+Business Media (www.springer.com)

Contents

Chapter 1
Introduction

In December, 2011, more than 2.25 billion people used the internet, making it a tool of communications, entertainment, and other applications accessed by roughly 32 % of the world's population (www.internetworldstats.com/stats.htm). For most users these uses extend well beyond email, the most common internet use, to include: bill payments and electronic banking; job and housing searches; stock trading; "e-tail" shopping; searching for health information and news; online classes; digital gambling; online videogames; Voice Over Internet Protocol telephony; hotel and airline reservations; chat rooms; electronic tax payments; downloading television programs, movies, digital music, and pornography; and popular sites and services such as YouTube, Facebook, and Google. In all these ways, and more, cyberspace offers profound real and potential effects on social relations, everyday life, culture, politics, and other social activities. Indeed, for rapidly rising numbers of people around the world, the "real" and the virtual have become thoroughly interpenetrated. In this light, access to cyberspace is no longer a luxury, but a necessity. As its applications have multiplied, the internet is having enormous impacts across the globe, including interpersonal interactions and everyday life, identity formation, retail trade and commerce, governance, and is affecting the structure and form of cities, in the process generating round upon round of non-Euclidean geometries in the context of a massive global wave of time–space compression.

By now, digital reality and everyday life for hundreds of millions of people have become so thoroughly fused that it is difficult, if not impossible, to disentangle them. In this context, simple dichotomies such as "off-line" and "on-line" fail to do justice to the diverse ways in which the "real" and virtual worlds for hundreds of millions are interpenetrated. Yet for many others—the familiar litany of the poor, the undereducated, ethnic minorities, and the socially marginalized— the internet remains a distant, ambiguous world. Denied regular access to cyberspace by the inability to purchase a personal computer, the technical skills necessary to log on, or public policies that assume their needs will be magically addressed by the market, the information have-nots living in the economically

B. Warf, *Global Geographies of the Internet*, SpringerBriefs in Geography,
DOI: 10.1007/978-94-007-1245-4_1, © The Author(s) 2013

advanced world are deprived of many of the essential skills necessary for a successful or convenient life. While those with regular and reliable access to the internet drown in a surplus of information—much of it superfluous, irrelevant, or unnecessary—those with limited access have difficulty comprehending the opportunities it offers, the savings in time and money it allows, and the sheer convenience, entertainment value, and ability to acquire data from bus schedules to recipes to global news.

1.1   Conceptions and Misconceptions About Information Systems

There exists considerable confusion about the real and potential impacts of telecommunications on urban structure, in part due to the long history of exaggerated claims made in the past, particularly by those subscribing to "post-industrial" theory (e.g., Toffler 1970). Often such views, which are widespread among many academics and planners, hinge upon a simplistic, utopian technological determinism that ignores the complex, often contradictory, relations between telecommunications and local economic, social and political circumstances.

A cottage industry of geographers has artfully charted the origins and growth of cyberspace, its uneven social and spatial diffusion, and its multiple impacts, ranging from cyber communities to digital divides to electronic commerce (Dodge and Kitchin 2000; Castells 2001; Kellerman 2002; Crampton 2003; Zook 2005a, 2005b; Malecki and Moriset 2008). Such authors typically embed the internet within post-Fordist capitalism, and, drawing on the literature in critical cartography, view it as a power/knowledge constellation with decisive social roots and consequences. Zook and Graham (2007) note the internet's "core and periphery" structure, as exemplified by the dominant role played by search engines such as Google, and voice concerns over the privatization of the digital commons. This literature offers a valuable means for spatializing the internet, demonstrating its rootedness in social relations and changing geographic relations of proximity, and serves as a necessary antidote to many prevailing utopian and technocratic interpretations such as those that proclaim the ostensible "death of distance" (Cairncross 1997), the "end of geography" (O'Brien 1992), and a "flat world" (Friedman 2005).

Often such views hinge on a simplistic, utopian technological determinism that ignores the complex relations between telecommunications and local economic, social, and political circumstances. Technological determinism is a widespread but erroneous interpretation of how new innovations are related to social structures: it portrays technologies as the driving force behind change, and thus having an autonomous, independent status, and views society as the passive recipient. This line of thought, which is alarmingly popular in analyses of the internet, often leads to simplistic erroneous interpretations of spatial change.

For example, repeated predictions that telecommunications would allow everyone to work at home via telecommuting, dispersing all functions and spelling the obsolescence of cities, have fallen flat in the face of the persistent growth in densely inhabited urbanized places and global cities. In fact, telecommunications are usually a poor substitute for face-to-face meetings, the medium through which most sensitive corporate interactions occurs, particularly when the information involved is irregular, proprietary, and unstandardized in nature. Most managers spend the bulk of their working time engaged in face-to-face contact, and no electronic technology can yet allow for the subtlety and nuances critical to such encounters. It is true that networks such as the internet allow some professionals to move into rural areas, where they can conduct most of their business online, gradually permitting them to escape from their long time reliance on large cities where they needed face-to-face contact. Yet the full extent to which these systems facilitate decentralization is often countered by other forces that promote the centralization of activity. For this reason, a century of telecommunications, from the telephone to fiber optics, has left most high-wage, white-collar, administrative command and control functions clustered in downtown areas. In contrast, telecommunications are ideally suited for the transmission of routinized, standardized forms of data, facilitating the dispersal of functions involved with their processing to low-wage regions. In short, there is no particular reason to believe that telecommunications inevitably lead to the dispersal or deconcentration of functions; by allowing the decentralization of routinized ones, information technology actually enhances the comparative advantage of inner cities for nonroutinized, high-value-added functions that are performed face to face. Thus, telecommunications facilitate the simultaneous concentration and deconcentration of economic activities.

Thus, popular notions that "telecommunications will render geography meaningless" are simply na. While the costs of communications have decreased, as they did with transportation, other factors have risen in importance, including local regulations, the cost and skills of the local labor force, government policies, and infrastructural investments. Economic space, in short, will not evaporate because of the telecommunications revolution. Exactly how telecommunications are deployed is a contingent matter of local circumstances, public policy, and local niche within the national and world economies.

1.2 The Rise of the Networked Society

One of the most fruitful interpretations of the internet, which avoids technological determinism, arises from the works of Manuel Castells (1996, 1997), who famously came up with the notion of the network society. Castells distinguished earlier *information* societies, in which productivity was derived from access to energy and the manipulation of materials, from later *informational* societies that emerged in the late 20th century, in which productivity is derived primarily from knowledge and information. In his reading, the time–space compression of post-modernism was manifested in the global "space of flows," including the three "layers" of transportation and communication infrastructure, the cities or nodes that occupy strategic locations within these, and the social spaces occupied by the global managerial class:

> Our societies are constructed around flows: flows of capital, flows of information, flows of technology, flows of organizational interactions, flows of images, sounds and symbols. Flows are not just one element of social organization: they are the expression of the processes dominating our economic, political, and symbolic life.... Thus, I propose the idea that there is a new spatial form characteristic of social practices that dominate and shape the network society: the space of flows. The space of flows is the material organization of time-sharing social practices that work through flows. By flows I understand purposeful, repetitive, programmable sequences of exchange and interaction between physically disjointed positions held by social actors (1996:412).

He notes, for example, that while people live in places, postmodern power is manifested in the linkages among places and people, that is, their interconnectedness, as personified by business executives shuttling among global cities and using the internet to weave complex geographies of knowledge invisible to almost all ordinary citizens. This process was largely driven by the needs of the transnational class of the powerful employed in information-intensive occupations; hence, he writes (1996, p. 415) that "Articulation of the elites, segmentation and disorganization of the masses seem to be the twin mechanisms of social domination in our societies." Flows thus consist of corporate and political elites crossing international space on transoceanic flights; the movements of capital through telecommunications networks; the diffusion of ideas through organizations stretched across ever-longer distances; the shipments of goods and energy via tankers, container ships, trucks, and railroads; and the growing mobility of workers themselves. In this light, the space of flows is a metaphor for the intense time–space compression of contemporary capitalism. Through the space of flows the global economy is coordinated in real time across vast distances, i.e., horizontally integrated chains rather than vertically integrated corporate hierarchies. In the process, it has given rise to a variety of new political formations, forms of identity, and spatial associations.

For Castells (1996), the space of flows and the new geometries that accompany it wrap places into highly unevenly connected networks, typically benefiting the wealthy at the expense of marginalized social groups. Ruggie (1993, p.141) likens such networks to the "economic equivalent of relativity theory." However, the global space of flows is far from randomly distributed over the earth's surface: rather, it reflects and reinforces existing geographies of power concentrated within specific nodes and places, such as global cities, trade centers, financial hubs, and corporate headquarters. Indeed, because the implementation of fiber lines reflects the powerful vested interests of international capital, these systems may be seen as "power-geometries" (Massey 1993) that ground the space of flows within concrete historical and spatial contexts.

1.3 Outline of this Volume

Given the enormity and rapid growth of the internet, there is no feasible way this slim volume can capture every detail of its geography and implications. Rather, it attempts to sketch some of the fundamental contours that define the internet, primarily at the global level. Much of the focus is on countries in which the internet is most heavily deployed, i.e., the economically developed world, although studious attempts are made to address its mounting implications in the developing regions of Asia, Africa, and Latin America. Central to the arguments presented here is the uneven geographical significance of the internet: if we are to avoid simplistic technological determinism, a social and spatial contextualization is necessary, which escapes the aspatial "one-size-fits-all" view so common in popular discourse.

Chapter 2 notes the origins and development of the internet and its contemporary global geographies. Because its history has been abundantly explicated elsewhere (Hafner and Lyon 1996), there is no need to recapitulate this story in depth here. Rather, it begins with the infrastructure that makes the internet possible, the world's grid of fiber optics and satellites. Then it turns to the rapid growth in internet users and their uneven distribution around the world. It delves into the complex issue of the digital divide, in which social inequalities are replicated in cyberspace. Finally, it offers a regional overview of internet usage around the world in the hopes of demonstrating that its geography cannot be understood independently of the varied local and national contexts in which it is embedded.

Chapter 3 focuses on the political limitations of cyberspace, i.e., internet censorship, a topic that has received woefully inadequate attention (Warf 2010). Governments around the world vary greatly in the extent to which they limit freedom to access information over the web, ranging from North Korea, where it is essentially illegal, to almost unfettered access in Western Europe and North America. Because the internet is as much a political as it is an economic and social phenomenon, appreciating the nature and extent of censorship is vital to understanding its geography and uneven growth. It ends with the argument that the internet offers the possibility of a Habermasian free speech situation, one in which truth claims are adjudicated on the basis of persuasion and consensus rather than power.

Chapter 4 looks at the economic implications of the internet in the form of electronic commerce, or e-commerce. Although the internet's origins were largely military and academic in nature, it has become thoroughly commercialized. From "e-tailing" to the decentralization of back office functions, from web-based universities to Voice Over Internet Protocol, the internet has revolutionized how business is done, lowering transactions costs, enhancing competitiveness, accelerating product cycles, and facilitating the globalization of small businesses. The chapter also offers a region-by-region overview of the uneven geography of e-commerce around the world.

Chapter 5 turns to electronic governance, or e-government. As with the market, the internet has helped to usher in a broad restructuring of the state. From simple on-line procurements of government documents and official information to the interactive facilities of web 2.0, e-government offers numerous possibilities to change the interactions between citizens and the state. As with e-commerce, and internet use and growth more broadly, e-government varies geographically. The chapter thus highlights regional differences in e-government in many domains across the planet.

Chapter 6 concludes the volume with a survey of social media. With cell phones, e-mail, and sites such as Facebook, more people are more connected to one another today than at any time in human history. What does this process mean for the nature of the self in the digital age? After charting the geographies of mobile phones and Facebook, the chapter concludes that a new, deeply relational self is gradually displacing the traditional Western model of the subject, i.e., the autonomous Cartesian individual devoid of social roots and origins. The chapter concludes with a plethora of examples about how social media been harnessed to further progressive political movements.

Throughout the volume, emphasis is placed on regional and national variations in internet access and usage, government censorship, commerce, and e-govern-ment. There are no doubt large and important variations within countries as well, although we know much less about them. The point of this regional emphasis is to demonstrate that place still matters, that the internet hardly floats in some neth-erworld independent of real world politics, culture, and economics, and that any realistic understanding of cyberspace must take into consideration its geographic variations. These vignettes are not intended to be comprehensive: rather, they should be seen as indicators that all the world's enormous social diversity is recapitulated in the digital realm, with widely varying incentives, opportunities, constraints, and impacts of internet usage.

References

Cairncross, F. (1997). *The death of distance: How the communications revolution will change our lives*. Boston: Harvard Business School Press.

Castells, M. (1996). *The information age, volume I: The rise of the network society*. Oxford: Blackwell.

Castells, M. (1997). *The information age, volume II: The power of identity*. Cambridge: Blackwell.

Castells, M. (2001). *The internet galaxy*. Oxford: Oxford University Press.

Crampton, J. (2003). *The political mapping of cyberspace*. Edinburgh: Edinburgh University Press.

Dodge, M., & Kitchin, R. (2000). *Mapping cyberspace*. London: Routledge.

Friedman, E. (2005). The reality of virtual reality: The internet and gender equality advocacy in Latin America. *Latin American Politics and Society, 47*(3), 1–34.

Hafner, K., & Lyon, M. (1996). *Where wizards stay up late: The origins of the internet*. New York: Simon and Schuster.

Kellerman, A. (2002). *The internet on Earth: A geography of information*. Hoboken: John Wiley.

Malecki, E., & Moriset, B. (2008). *The digital economy: Business organisation, production processes, and regional developments*. London: Routledge.

Massey, D. (1993). Power-geometry and a progressive sense of place. In J. Bird (Ed.), *Mapping the futures: Local cultures, global change* (pp. 59–69). New York: Routledge.

O'Brien, R. (1992). *Global financial integration: The end of geography*. New York: Council on Foreign Relations Press.

Ruggie, J. (1993). Territoriality and beyond: Problematizing modernity in international relations. *International Organisation, 47*, 139–174.

Toffler, A. (1970). *Future shock*. New York: Random House.

Warf, B. (2010). Geographies of global internet censorship. *GeoJournal, 76*(1), 1–23.

Zook, M. (2005a). *The geography of the internet industry*. Oxford: Wiley-Blackwell.

Zook, M. (2005b). The geography of the internet. *Annual Review of Information Science and Technology, 40*, 53–78.

Zook, M., & Graham, M. (2007). The creative reconstruction of the internet: Google and the privatization of cyberspace and digiplace. *Geoforum, 38*(6), 1322–1343.

Chapter 2
Origins, Growth, and Geographies of the Global Internet

To appreciate the complexity, implications, and geography of the internet, it is vital to understand where it came from and how it came to be. Toward this end, this chapter sketches the broad outlines of the world's internet in several stages. It opens with an overview of the seminal technologies that make the internet possible, fiber optics and satellites, which together comprise the infrastructure of cyberspace. Second it traces some of the highlights of the internet's history, from its origins with the U.S. military to its explosive growth and commercialization today. In the process, it charts the uneven geographies of growth over time and space. The third section addresses the digital divide, or sociospatial inequalities in internet usage, which are found to one extent or another across the planet. Finally, the chapter concludes with a brief regional survey of internet usage in various world regions to highly the spatially uneven character of its deployment and implications.

2.1 Fiber Optic Networks and Satellites

Two technologies—satellites and fiber optic lines—form the primary technologies deployed by the global telecommunications industry, including the internet. Although they overlap to a great extent, satellite and fiber optics carriers exhibit market segmentation. Economically, both reflect the typical cost structure of telecommunications, i.e., high fixed costs and barriers to entry and low marginal costs. However, firms offering these services serve overlapping, but slightly different markets: satellites overwhelmingly dominate mass media transmission, although fiber carriers have recently begun to invade this market (e.g., cable television). Fiber carriers are heavily favored by large corporations for data transmissions and by financial institutions for electronic funds transfer systems, in part because of the higher degrees of security and redundancy this medium offers.

The world's network of satellites and earth stations comprise a critical, often overlooked, element in the global telecommunications infrastructure. Since the late

B. Warf, *Global Geographies of the Internet*, SpringerBriefs in Geography, DOI: 10.1007/978-94-007-1245-4_2, © The Author(s) 2013

1950s, the world has launched more than 5,500 satellites, the vast majority of which were sent into orbit by the U.S. and the USSR/Russia. In addition to military applications, satellites are used extensively by telecommunications companies, multinational corporations, financial institutions, and the global media to link far-flung operations, including international data transmissions, electronic funds transfer systems, telephone networks, teleconferencing, and media sales of television and radio programs. Satellites in orbit appear in a variety of sizes and degrees of technological sophistication. Large satellites capable of handling international traffic sit 35,700 km (22,300 miles) high in geostationary orbits, which are by far the most valuable orbital slots because only in that narrow sliver of space do satellites and the Earth travel at the same speed relative to each other, making the satellite a stable target for signals transmitted upward from earth stations. Because such orbital arcs are a scarce resource, their distribution is strictly controlled through international organizations. The cost of launching satellites and the fuel needed to maintain them in their proper orbit are also constraints to their economic viability. Satellites typically have a 10 year life span, primarily because they exhaust their available fuel, necessitating their eventual replacement by a new, frequently much improved, generation. From its vantage point, a broad-beam geostationary satellite can transmit to (i.e., leave a "footprint" over) roughly 40 % of the earth's surface, creating instantaneous time–space convergence, so that only three or four are sufficient to provide global coverage. Because the cost of satellite transmission is not related to distance, it is commercially competitive in rural or low density areas (e.g., remote islands), where high marginal costs often dissuade other types of providers, particularly fiber optics providers (Warf 2006, 2007).

The terrestrial counterpart of the satellite is the earth station. There are tens of millions of earth stations located worldwide, ranging in size from one-half meter to 30 m. The vast majority, however, can only receive information, not transmit it (i.e., downlink only). When microwave signals are sent over great lengths and become broadly diffused, earth stations require large, powerful antennas to receive them. The distribution of the world's 483 publicly-owned earth stations designed for international traffic (Fig. 2.1) reveals they are concentrated in the largest and wealthiest countries, particularly the U.S., which, with 70, has vastly more than any other state. Countries without these facilities (e.g., Afghanistan), or those with an insufficient number to satisfy domestic demand, must rely upon leased connections to other nations.

Although satellites are used for internet access in some parts of the world, increasingly the technology has been marginalized by the growth of fiber optics. Fiber optics are long, thin, flexible, highly transparent rods of quartz glass (or less commonly, plastic) about the thickness of a human hair that can transmit light signals through a process of internal reflection, which retains light in the core and transforms the cable into a waveguide. They can transmit voice, video, or data traffic at the speed of light (299,792 km/s); because light oscillates much more rapidly than other wavelengths (200 trillion times per second in fiber cables v. 2 billion per second in a cellular phone), such lines can carry much more information than other types of telecommunications. Modern fiber cables contain up to 1,000

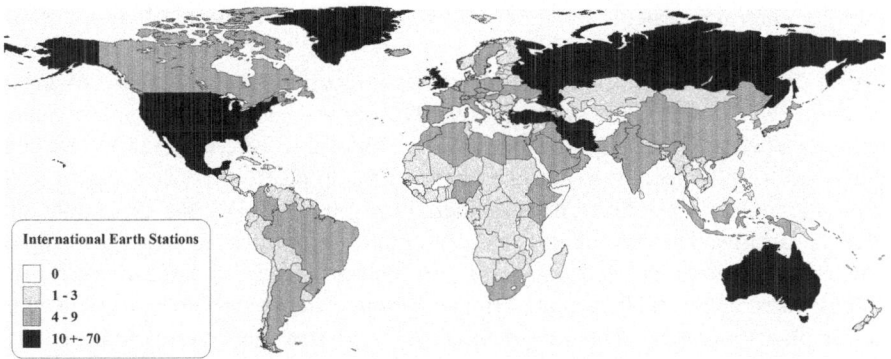

Fig. 2.1 Distribution of earth stations capable of international traffic. *Source* Compiled by author from CIA Factbook, http://www.odci.gov/cia/publications/nsolo/factbook

fibers each and are ideal for high-capacity, point-to-point transmissions. Moreover, fiber cables do not corrode or conduct electricity, which renders them immune to electromagnetic disturbances such as thunderstorms. The transmission capacities of fiber optics grew rapidly in the late twentieth century as the microelectronics revolution unfolded. Financial and producer services firms were at the forefront of the construction of a vast, seamless integrated network of fiber cable because they allowed the deployment of electronic funds transfer systems, which comprise the nervous system of the international financial economy, allowing banks to move capital around a moment's notice, arbitrage interest rate differentials, take advantage of favorable exchange rates, and avoid political unrest (Warf 1995). Fiber carriers are heavily favored by large corporations for data transmissions and by financial institutions for electronic funds transfer systems, in large part because of the higher degrees of security and redundancy this medium offers. Although their transmission costs have also declined, satellites have failed to match the latest leaps in fiber optics capacity and can compete with transoceanic submarine cables only with great and mounting difficulty; today, 94 % of all international tele-communications is transmitted via cables (Warf 2006). As their competitive edge has eroded, satellite providers have been steadily forced to serve markets in low-density regions, relatively low-profit arenas compared to the lucrative high-volume, corporate data transmissions market.

Large fiber networks are generally owned and operated by consortia of firms. Until the 1990s, all commercial fiber lines were built, used, and paid for by a handful of monopoly carriers such as AT&T, British Telecom, Japan's Kokusai Denshin Denwa (KDD), known informally in the industry as "The Club." The Club system allowed telecommunications carriers to construct and own undersea cables and to serve as their users or vendors. Typically, landing facilities are owned by carriers from the country in which the facility is located but the "wet links" (undersea cables) are jointly owned by club members. Under the club system, AT&T, for example, ventured aggressively into the international fiber optics market as it globalized in the face of declining market share in the U.S., often by entering strategic alliances that stretched across national borders. Similarly, Sprint affiliated with France Telecom and Deutsche Telekom to form Global One in 1996, and AT&T and British Telecom acquired a 30 % share of Japan Telecom. Under the Club system, capacity was allocated and payments made before or during construction of the network. Members were required by national regulators to sell capacity to non-members on a non-discriminatory basis close to cost. Allegations arose that Club members discriminated against new entrants by offering disadvantageous conditions of membership, such as capacity prices. However, as deregulation encouraged new entrants into the cable markets, the Club system began to fragment. Private systems, in which carriers invite non-carrier investors such as banks, emerged as an alternative system, and recently, non-carrier systems have also appeared.

The network of fiber lines linking the world constitutes the nervous system of the global financial and service economy, linking cities, markets, suppliers, and clients around the world, and the backbone of internet traffic (Fig. 2.2). The geography of global fiber networks centers primary upon two distinct telecommunications markets crossing the Atlantic and Pacific Oceans, connecting two of the major engines of the world economy, North America and East Asia. In 1988, in conjunction with MCI and British Telecommunications, AT&T initiated the world's first trans-oceanic fiber optic cable, Trans-Atlantic Telecommunications (TAT-8), which could carry 40,000 telephone calls simultaneously. The trans-Atlantic line was the first of a much broader series of globe-girdling fiber lines that AT&T erected in conjunction with a variety of local partners. Because large corporate users are the primary clients of such networks, it is no accident that the original and densest web of fiber lines connects London and New York, a pattern that extends historically to the telegraph and telephone (Hugill 1999). The next generation, TAT-9 and TAT-10, which began in 1992, could carry double the volume of traffic of TAT-8. The third generation, TAT-11 to TAT-13, was the first to use EDFA rather than older repeaters. Newer generations of cable were even more powerful. Starting with the Trans-Pacific Cable (TPC-3) in 1989 connecting New York and Tokyo, a growing web of trans-Pacific lines mirrored the rise of East Asian trade with North America, including the surging economies of the Newly Industrialized Countries. In 1996, the first all-fiber cable across the Pacific, TPC-5, was laid. In 2006, a consortium including Verizon and five Asian providers announced plans to lay an 11,000 mile U.S.–China link that would support 1.28 terabits of information—60 times the capacity of the next largest cable—in time for the Beijing Olympics in 2008. In 2007, Google announced the purchase of large quantities of trans-Pacific fiber cable with the aim of launching a multi-terabit Unity service in 2009.

The complex interplay of deregulation, globalization, and technological change increased the international transmission capacities and traffic volumes for fiber optics carriers explosively. Between 1988 and 2003, for example, trans-Atlantic fiber optic cable capacity increased from 43,750 voice paths to 45.1 billion (103,000 %), while across the Pacific Ocean, cable carriers' capacity rose from 1,800 voice paths to 1.87 billion (an astonishing 1.6 billion %).

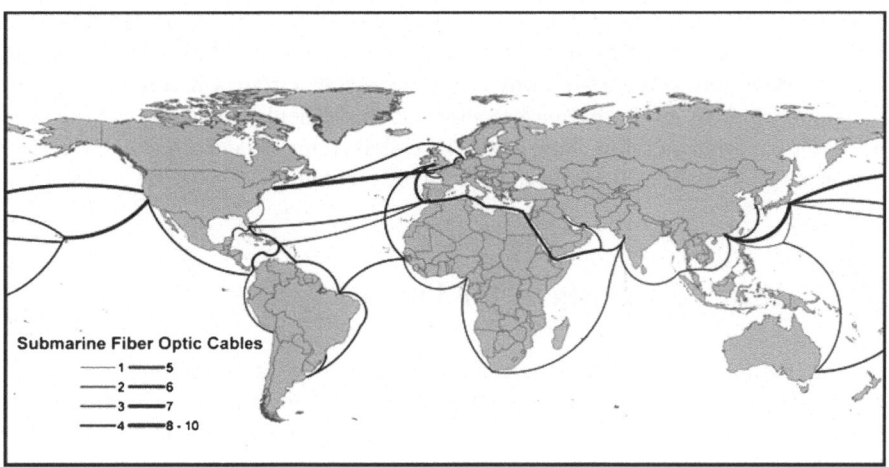

Fig. 2.2 The world's major fiber optic cables. *Source* After Staple (2007)

In addition to the two major markets, fiber lines have extended into several newer ones. In 1997, AT&T, NYNEX and several other firms (including, for the first time, non-telecommunications firms) opened the self-healing Fiberoptic Link Around the Globe (FLAG), a system that eventually expanded to 55,000 km connecting Europe and Southeast Asia. The world's longest submarine telecommunications network, FLAG, the world's longest submarine telecommunications cable, filled a void in undersea cable capacity between Europe, the Middle East, and Asia. It also hooked into regional systems such as the Asia Pacific Cable Network, a 12,000 km system linking Japan, South Korea, Taiwan, Hong Kong, the Philippines, Thailand, Vietnam, and Indonesia, as well as the Caribbean Fiber System (i.e., the Eastern Caribbean Fiber System, Antillas 1, Americas 1, and Columbus 2). Unlike earlier systems, FLAG allowed carriers to purchase capacity as needed, rather than compelling them to purchase fixed quantities.

Although they overlap to a great extent, satellite and fiber-optic carriers exhibit market segmentation. Fiber is heavily favored by large corporations for data transmission and by financial institutions for electronic funds transfer systems. Satellites tend to be used more often by international television carriers. Telephone and internet traffic use both. These two types of carriers are differentiated geographically as well: Because their transmission costs are unrelated to distance, satellites are optimal for low-density areas (e.g., rural regions and remote islands), where the relatively high marginal costs of fiber lines are not competitive. Fiber-optic carriers prefer large metropolitan regions, where dense concentrations of clients allow them to realize significant economies of scale in cities where frequency transmission congestion often plagues satellite transmissions. Satellites are ideal for point-to-area distribution networks, whereas fiber-optic lines are preferable for point-to-point communications, especially when security is of great concern. Historically, the primacy of each technology has varied over time. From

1959 to 1980 (i.e., before the widespread adoption of fiber optics), satellites enjoyed limited competition from transoceanic copper cable lines with low capacity rates. From the 1970s onward, the microelectronics revolution allowed fiber-optic lines to erode the market share of traffic held by satellites. New techniques of data transmission, such as the so-called frame delay format, raise speeds of transmission nearly 30-fold over the 1990s technology.

2.2 Origins and Growth of the Internet

The internet originated in the 1960s under the U.S. Defense Department's Agency Research Projects Administration (ARPA), which designed it to allow computers to communicate with one another in the event of a nuclear attack. Much of the durability of the current system is due to the enormous amounts of federal dollars dedicated toward research in this area (Hafner and Lyon 1996; Murphy 2002). ARPA grouped together several young, ambitious computer scientists, including Paul Baran, who invented packet switching, and related innovations such as neural networks, queuing theory, adaptive routing, and file transfer protocols. In the process, ARPA gave birth to a network quite different from the centralized system of the telephone company (i.e., AT&T), which relied on analogue information: rather, digitization facilitated a decentralized, then distributed network, which subsequently became a model for rhizomes, a popular trope in poststructuralist analyses. The nucleus of what would become ARPANET initially connected universities such as Stanford, UCLA, the University of California at Santa Barbara, and the University of Utah. The initial military goals were soon supplemented by civilian ones. In 1972, Ray Tomlinson adapted computer messages for personal use, inventing email.

From 1984 to 1995, the internet was administered by the National Science Foundation, which deployed it to connect academic supercomputers in a select series of campuses across the country. Simultaneously, some of the world's first cybercommunities began to take route, such as the WELL (Whole Earth Lectronic Link) in San Francisco. The famous European Particle Physics Lab (CERN) developed hypertext and Universal Resource Locators (URLs), the system of addresses used on what would become the World Wide Web, including file transfer protocol (FTP) and specifications of pages fetched using the HTTP protocol.

In the 1990s internet control was privatized via a consortium of telecommunications corporations. The internet emerged on a global scale through the integration of existing telephone, fiber-optic, and satellite systems, which was made possible by the technological innovation of packet switching, TCP/IP (Transmission Control Protocol/Internet Protocol), and Integrated Services Digital Network (ISDN), in which individual messages may be decomposed, the constituent parts transmitted by various channels, and then reassembled, virtually instantaneously, at the destination. In the 1990s, graphical interfaces developed in Europe greatly simplified the use of the internet, leading to the creation of the World Wide Web. Tim Berners-Lee, often called the "father of the World Wide Web," played a key role in this process. Soon thereafter private web browsers sprouted like mushrooms, including Netscape, Internet Explorer, and Firefox. The number of websites grew exponentially, from roughly 1 million in 1990 to more than 4 billion in 2011.

The microelectronics revolution initiated enormous decreases in the cost of computers and exponential increases in their power and memory. Of these, the continued decline in the price of personal computers (PCs) looms large. Following Moore's Law, which speculates the cost of computers falls in half every 1½ years, PCs have become increasingly ubiquitous in many countries, and relatively fast, low-end machines are readily available for relatively modest sums. Indeed, fiber optics arguably transformed the internet from a communications to a commercial system, accelerating the pace of customer orders, procurement, production, and product delivery (Malecki 2002). Spurred by declining costs, deregulation, and an increasingly tech-savvy public, the growth of the internet has been phenomenal; indeed, it is arguably the most rapidly diffusing technology in world history. Global access to the internet is deeply conditioned by the density, reliability, and affordability of national telephone systems, which form the heart of the architecture of cyberspace. For this reason, the distribution of internet hosts also mirrors the enduring legacy of the superpower bifurcation during the Cold War: Soviet-backed regimes distrusted the telephone, which allows two-way communication, and preferred television, which allows only one-way flows of information.

With rapid declines in the cost of computer technology, a glut of fiber optics that led to dramatic falls in communications prices, easy-to-use graphical interfaces, and the clear potential for all sorts of as-yet unheard of applications, it is no wonder that internet usage worldwide began to grow exponentially. The number of users soared from roughly 10 million in 1990 to more than 2.25 billion in December, 2011 (Fig. 2.3), an average rate of increase of almost 14 % per year. The distribution of the world's internet users in 2011 (Fig. 2.4) reflects the size of different national populations and their internet penetration rates. Four countries—China, the U.S., India, and Japan—had more than 100 million users each, although with more than 513 million users China exceeds the next three largest countries combined. With other countries with significant pools of users such as South Korea and Indonesia, approximately 922 million internet users were located in Asia, or almost half of the world's total (Table 2.1). In contrast, the world's poorest region, sub-Saharan Africa, had relatively small populations of netizens. These broad regional differentials were reflected in the linguistic structure of the internet as well (Table 2.2). While English remains the premier tongue used today on the Web—the digital lingua franca of 536 million people—Chinese, spoken by 445 million netizens, is the second-most heavily used language, and growing rapidly, followed by Spanish (153 million users). Other languages such as Japanese, Portuguese, German, Arabic, French, and Russian are also significant.

Internet use ("penetration") rates varied considerably by country in 2011 (Fig. 2.5). Whereas the vast bulk of the populations in economically developed countries use it, including near-universal rates in Scandinavia, penetration rates are markedly lower in the developing world (but growing by leaps and bounds).

Fig. 2.3 Growth in world internet users, 1990–2011. *Source* internetworldstats.com

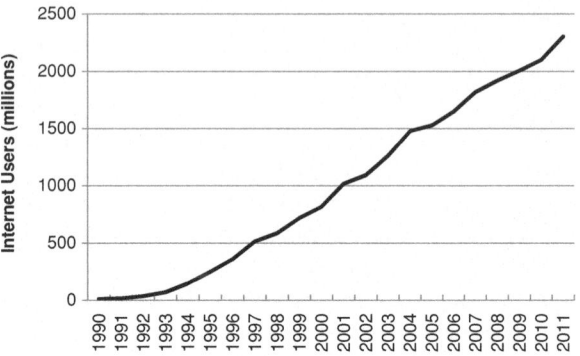

Internet penetration rates (percentage of people with access) among the world's major regions, ranging from as little as 0.2 % in parts of Africa to as high as 96 % in Scandinavia. By the end of 2011, penetration was 77 % of the U.S. population. Inequalities in access to the internet internationally reflect the long-standing bifurcation between the First and Third Worlds. While no country is utterly without internet access, the variations among and within nations in accessibility are huge. Given its large size, the United States—with more than 245 million users—dominates when measured in terms of absolute number of internet hosts. The world's highest penetration rates (Table 2.3) are found in Iceland (97.8 %), followed by Norway (97.2 %), Sweden (92.9), and Luxembourg (91.4 %); Eastern Europe lags considerably behind, and in Russia only 44 % of the population uses the internet. In Asia, access is by greatest in South Korea (82.7 %) and Japan (80 %); about 38 % of China is hooked up, although the numbers there are growing rapidly, and already amount to more than 513 million users. In Latin America, the largest numbers of users are found in Brazil (79 million, or 39 %) and Mexico (42 million, 36.9 %). The internet in the African continent is largely confined to South Africa, although it is growing explosively there. In all cases, per capita incomes are the key; the internet can only be used by people with resources sufficient to own computers and learn the essential software. Variations in the number of users is also reflected in the geography of internet flows (although flow data are much harder to come by than are place-specific attribute data): 75 % of all international traffic on the internet is either to or from the United States, fueling fears among some people that the internet is largely a tool for the propagation of American culture.

The most salient feature about the internet may be its exceedingly rapid rate of growth. Very few technologies in world history, with perhaps the exception of the mobile phone, have exhibited such explosive rates of adoption. As penetration rates soared around the planet, millions of new users have been brought on line. Figure 2.6 portrays national differentials in the growth of internet usage. Explosive growth is readily evident in sub-Saharan Africa and the Middle East, where growth rates between 2000 and 2011 exceeded 10,000 % (and sometimes reach absurdly high rates such as 182,900 %, albeit from a very small base). In contrast, growth

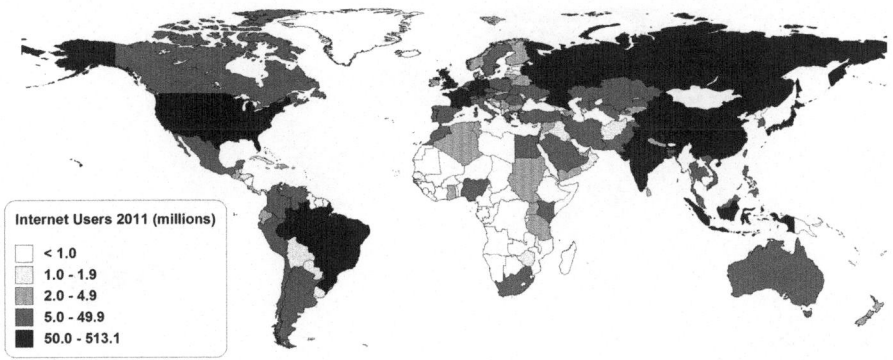

Fig. 2.4 Distribution of world's internet users, December 2011. *Source* internetworldstats.com

Table 2.1 Internet users by major geographic region, December 2011 (millions)		
Asia	922.3
Europe	476.2
North America	272.1
Latin America	215.9
Africa	110.9
Middle East	68.6
Oceania	21.3

Source Internetworldstats.com

Table 2.2 Largest languages used on the Internet, December 2011 (millions)		
English	536.6
Chinese	444.9
Spanish	153.3
Japanese	99.1
Portuguese	82.5
German	75.2
Arabic	65.4
French	58.8
Russian	59.7
Korean	39.4

Source Internetworldstats.com

rates in the entire Western Hemisphere, Europe, Russia, Japan, and Oceania were relatively modest by comparison. Thus, while the internet was largely confined to the developed world early in its history, it is growing the most rapidly in the developing world today, particularly in Africa and Asia. This growth brought 1.325 billion new users on-line during this period, who were unevenly distributed

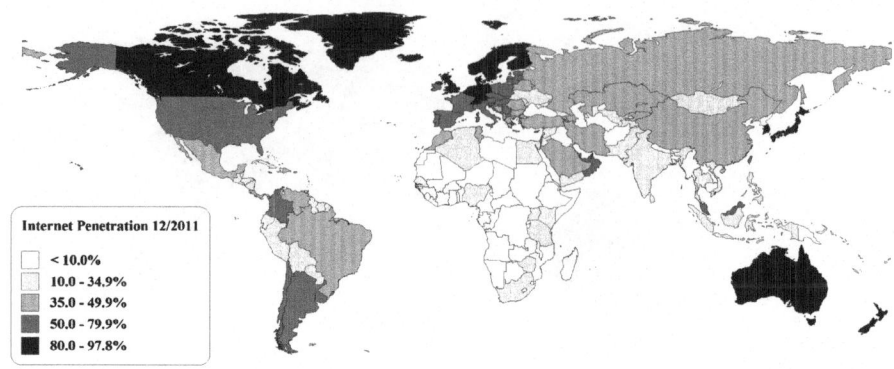

Fig. 2.5 Map of internet penetration rates, December 2011. *Source* internetworldstats.com

Table 2.3 Internet penetration rates for 20 best-connected countries, December, 2011		
	Iceland	97.6
	Norway	94.8
	Sweden	92.5
	Netherlands	88.6
	Denmark	86.1
	Finland	85.3
	Luxembourg	85.3
	United Kingdom	82.5
	South Korea	81.1
	Australia	80.1
	New Zealand	79.7
	Germany	79.1
	Japan	78.2
	Singapore	77.8
	Belgium	77.8
	Canada	77.7
	United States	77.3
	Switzerland	75.3
	Estonia	75.1
	Austria	74.8
	Israel	71.6

Source internetworldstats.com

across the face of the planet (Fig. 2.7). Most (59 %) of the world's netizens, therefore, are relatively recent additions to the world's population of internet users. In China, for example, more than 490 million of its netizens, or 96 %, began after 2000, and the same proportion in India witnessed 116,000 new internet users log-in.

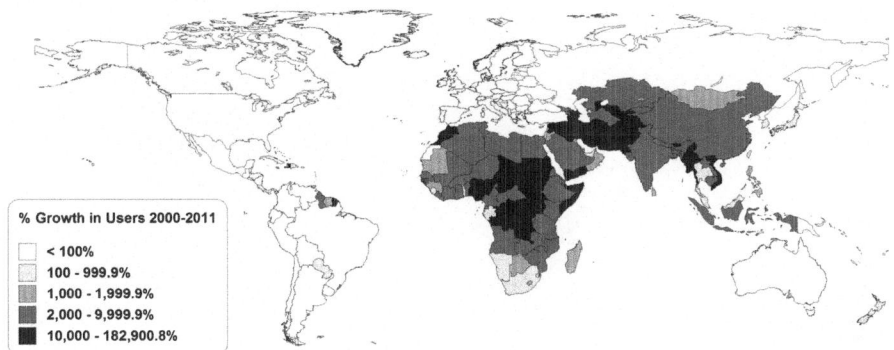

Fig. 2.6 Map of growth in internet users, 2000–2011. *Source* internetworldstats.com

2.3 Digital Divides

Clearly internet usage is highly uneven among and within countries. The digital divide, or social and spatial differentials in internet access, has been the subject of a growing body of literature (Norris 2001; Korupp and Szydlik 2005; Warf 2001), revealing how digital communications are enfolded in relations of wealth and power in ways that reproduce inequalities in cyberspace. Howard et al. (2010, p. 111) point out, "The causes and consequences of the digital divide have become a contested area of research. Understanding the digital divide is crucial to understanding the role of the Internet in contemporary social development." Fundamentally this question is about who has access and can use the internet and who does not. "Access" and "use" are admittedly vague terms, and embrace a range of meanings, including the ability to log-on at home, school, cybercafé, or work (DiMaggio et al. 2001). Rather than a simple access/non-access dichotomy, it is more useful to think of a gradation of levels of access, although data of this subtlety rarely exist. Thus, it is increasingly common to speak of "digital differentiation" rather than a divide (Selwyn 2002, 2004).

The digital divide is a complex, changing, and multi-dimensional phenomenon that reflects the diverse channels through which social inequalities are reinscribed in cyberspace. Everywhere, class markers such as income and education are strongly correlated with internet access and use. Everywhere, age plays a key role: the elderly are inevitably the least likely to adopt the internet. In many places, gender is important too: in North America the gendered divide has disappeared, but in Europe it persists, and in the developing world it is pronounced. The digital divide is also a geographical phenomenon. Everywhere, large urban centers tend to exhibit higher rates of connectivity than do rural areas (Mills and Whitacre 2003; Warf 2001).

As the uses and applications of the internet have multiplied, the costs sustained by those denied access rise accordingly. At precisely the historical moment that contemporary capitalism has come to rely upon digital technologies to an

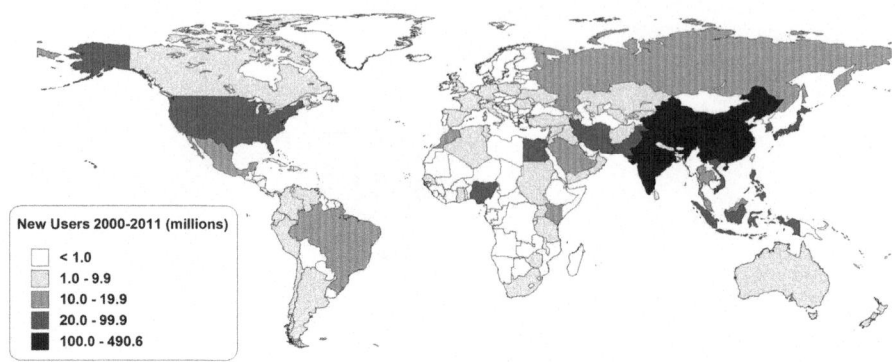

Fig. 2.7 Distribution of new internet users, 2000–2011. *Source* internetworldstats.com

unprecedented extent, large pools of the economically disenfranchised are shut off from cyberspace. As the internet erodes the monopolistic roles once played by the telephone and television, and as the upgrading of required skill levels steadily render information technology skills necessary even for lower wage service jobs, lack of access to cyberspace becomes increasingly detrimental to social mobility. Indeed, those excluded from the internet may be more vulnerable to social forces they do not and often cannot perceive than ever before.

Because personal computer ownership rates are relatively low in much of the developing world, and because Internet Service Provider (ISP) individual access charges are often high, many users rely upon privately-owned internet cafés for access rather than individual ISP accounts. Cafés are particularly important for those who lack dial-up access at home or at work or who simply cannot afford personal computers of their own. In the developing world, internet cafes tend to be most commonly found in commercial districts frequented by tourists, exhibit a range of ownership structures from sole proprietorships to international chains, and charge access prices that vary widely among and within countries. In addition to for-profit cybercafés, many non-profit and non-governmental organizations have established networks of neighborhood telecenters, which have played catalytic roles in community development in many areas.

In addition to international discrepancies in access, internet usage also reflects the power-geometries *within* countries (Massey 2005) through which the poor, elderly, ethnic minorities, and rural areas enjoy markedly less access (Chakraborty and Bosman 2005; Mills and Whitacre 2003). Unfortunately, relatively little is known about this issue, in large part due to lack of data on the topic. However, the enormous growth rates of the internet mean that digital divides are rapidly changing, and as access improves for many hitherto marginalized groups, may slowly decline over time.

The latest frontier in the digital divide is unquestionably the arena of broadband delivery services, which varies widely in availability among the world's countries (Fig. 2.8). Broadband applications include digital television, business-to-business linkages, internet gaming, telemedicine, videoconferencing, and internet

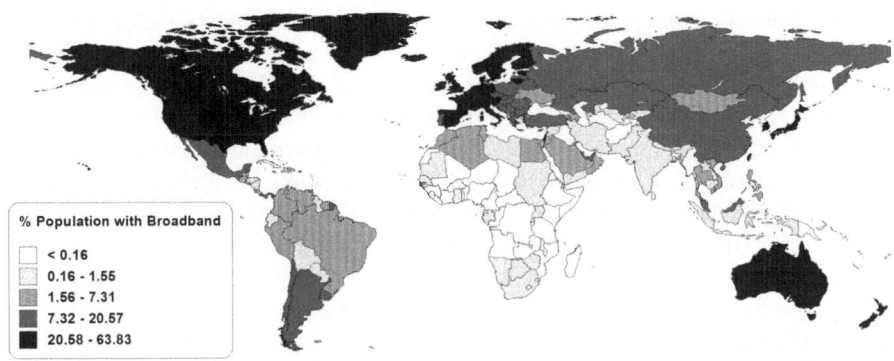

Fig. 2.8 Map of broadband penetration per 100 inhabitants, 2010. *Source* International Telecommunications Union. *Note* Because an Internet subscription may be shared by many people, the penetration rate will not reflect the actual level of access to broadband Internet of the population

telephony. With large, graphics-intensive files at the heart of most internet uses today (e.g., downloading forms, reading on-line newspapers), broadband has become increasingly imperative for Web browsing. However, the geography of broadband access replicates the globe's geographies of wealth and power—it is largely confined to the economically developed world. There are strong reasons to believe that far from eliminating the digital divide, broadband reproduces it, gives it new form, and in some cases, accentuates it.

Claims that access to the internet is readily available to all, and therefore its effects cannot help but be beneficial and democratic, must be viewed with great skepticism. Technologies, including telecommunications, are never socially or spatially neutral in their impacts. There is a persistent and continuing need to link the understanding of cyberspace with very real spaces of class and power. All the existing social categories of wealth and power are replicated in cyberspace, at least in terms of access to the equipment and technical know-how necessary to gain entree. At the global level, the internet is likely to reinforce or even deepen existing divisions between the haves and have-nots, between the developed and developing worlds, as much as it is likely to eliminate them, connecting a global digerati with increasingly disconnected from the local environments of their own cities and countries. Castells (1997, p. 351) likens cyberspace to Athenian democracy:

> While a relatively small, educated, and affluent elite in a few countries and cities would have access to an extraordinary tool of information and political participation, actually enhancing citizenship, the uneducated, switched off masses of the world, and of the country, would remain excluded from the new democratic core, as were slaves and barbarians at the onset of democracy in classical Greece.

Thus, the internet represents the Athenian vision of democracy writ large, an issue that figures prominently in debates about internet censorship (Chap. 3).

Rosy and premature predictions that the internet would unleash human potential in low income communities, level hierarchies and blur the lines of authority have given way to more realistic assessments that point to the exacerbated social and economic tensions that accompany the diffusion of this technology in many communities, enhancing the divisions between the information "haves" and "have nots." This division mirrors the increasing polarization of Western societies in general, noting the disintegration of the public sphere and the commodification of private ones. In an age in which social life is not only increasingly mediated through computer networks but fundamentally altered by them, the annihilation of public spaces and their reconstruction around the increasingly commodified, privatized spaces of cyberspace has disturbing implications for those without the wealth and power to gain access to the internet. Participation in electronic communities reflects the social contexts that shape the adoption and diffusion of internet technology; thus, the definition of "access" must be broadened from simply owning a computer and logging into the internet to include the institutional and cultural forces that entice and encourage people to remain digitally connected. As the internet has diffused through progressively broader tiers of Western society, albeit unequally, new users frequently resemble the general population with greater frequency; fears that the "digital divide" will remain in perpetuity, therefore, may be exaggerated.

Lastly, it is abundantly evident that geography still matters. Access to the internet is deeply conditioned by where one is, which is in turn a reflection of relations of wealth and power. Long standing categories of core and periphery are all too apparent within cyberspace, such as the divisions between developed and less-developed nations or cities and rural areas. Thus, electronic systems simultaneously reflect and transform existing topographies of class, gender, money, and ethnicity, creating and recreating hierarchies of places mirrored in the spatial architecture of computer networks. Far from eliminating differences among places, systems such as the internet allow their differences to be exploited. As both a site of fixed investments and a space of flows, the internet in an age of hypermobile capital must be judged as much in terms of equality of access as efficiency of use, by the ways it generates benefits to those who need it most as well as to those who use it heavily.

2.4 Regional Geographies of the Global Internet

Despite some proclamations that cyberspace is spaceless, that distance is dead, or that we live in a flat earth, the reality of internet usage is that it is thoroughly interpenetrated with regional, national, and local political systems, economies, and cultures. Thus, the geography of the internet is deeply conditioned by, and in turn shapes, the spatiality of the world's socioeconomic systems. To shed more light on this topic, this section offers a brief tour of the regional dimensions of the internet in the world's major regions.

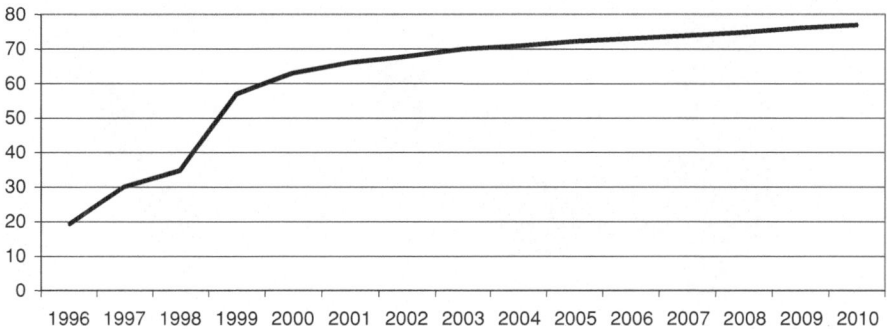

Fig. 2.9 U.S. internet penetration rates, 1996–2010. *Source* Calculated by author from internetworldstats.com

2.4.1 North America

U.S. penetration rates have grown steadily over time (Fig. 2.9), reaching 78 % in 2011. However, internet use was highly uneven across the country (Fig. 2.10), and was typically highest in wealthier, better educated states in the West and Northeast and lower in the South. Although internet penetration rates in the U.S. are not as high as Scandinavian nations, they remain higher than many other urbanized, industrialized countries, and Americans as a whole still constitute the largest and most influential national bloc of internet users in the planet. Several factors have conspired to accelerate internet usage in the U.S. among and within different social groups. Almost 80 % of Americans use a PC once or more per week either at work or at home, the vast bulk of which are networked. Because the value of a network rises proportional to the square of the number of users, the internet and the PC made each other increasingly powerful and attractive. Simultaneously, the rise in user-friendly graphics interfaces greatly facilitated internet access for the parts of the population lacking in sophisticated computer skills. Moreover, as the number of applications of the internet has grown, the hours of usage have increased steadily to more than 9 per week. The rise in PC ownership has been a central claim of those who argue the digital divide will disappear on its own accord.

Throughout the 1995–2011 period, growth in internet use among various socio-demographic groups was rapid, often spectacular (Table 2.4). Average internet penetration rates—including access at home, work, or school—more than quadrupled, from 14 to 77 %; by 2011, 245 million Americans were using the internet regularly. The innovation, the most rapidly diffused technology in world history, went from a tool or toy of a minority to an essential implement used by the vast majority. Every social group, as differentiated by age, gender, race/ethnicity, educational level, or household income, experienced marked gains. Thus, to the extent that the digital divide persists in the U.S. (and other economically advanced countries), it must be understood within the context of this sustained and rapid increase in the number of users and proportion of the population.

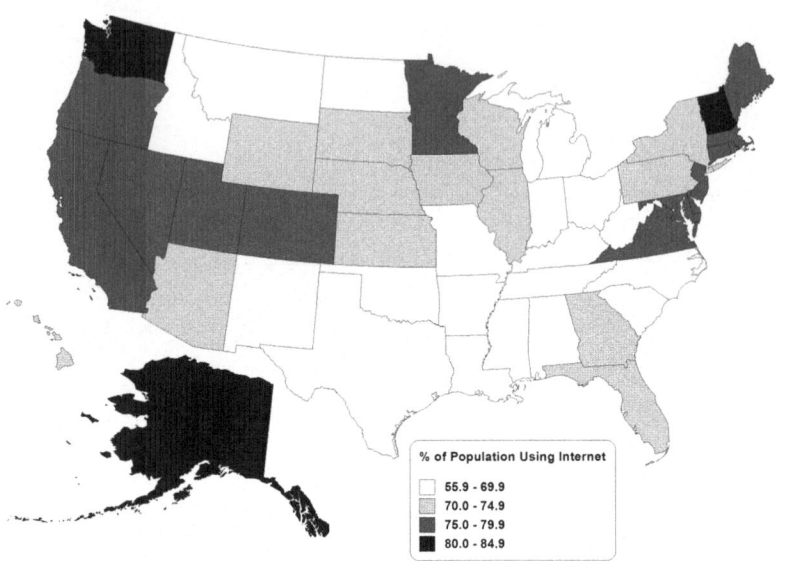

Fig. 2.10 Map of proportion of U.S. adults using the Internet, 2010. *Source* Author, using data from www.census.gov/compendia/statab/cats/information_communications.html

This growth, however, did not occur at identical rates among all social categories. Take, for instance, age. The young (i.e., under 30 years of age) steadily exhibited the highest internet penetration rates, reaching 83 % in 2011. For many children who grow up surrounded by digital technologies, the internet is hardly mysterious. In contrast, in both benchmark years, the elderly experienced the lowest rates of internet usage (a mere 2 % in 1995 v. 33 % in 2011), as well as the slowest rate of increase in users. Many elderly find new technologies to be difficult or intimidating, do not appreciate the potential benefits, and are easily frustrated by their lack of technical skills. The digital divide, therefore, is closely wrapped up with generational differences.

One dimension of the U.S. digital divide that has drawn the most serious scrutiny concerns racial or ethnic differences. Given the profound inequalities in U.S. society in terms of income, educational opportunities, and employment that exist between whites and ethnic minorities, it is not surprising that this gap is manifested in terms of access to cyberspace, i.e., i.e., much of the racial ravine in digital access is due to income discrepancies. In 1997, for example, white internet usage rates were more than double that of Latinos/Hispanics (37.7 v. 16.6 %), and roughly double that of African–Americans (19.0 %). In 2011, internet access rates for whites remained well above those for minorities or the national average. There are signs, however, that this dimension of the digital divide is slowly, if hesitantly, diminishing. Today, the majority of ethnic minorities uses the internet, and the relative difference between them and the white population has declined significantly. There are important differences within minority populations, however. Among African-Americans, internet usage tends to be concentrated among the young and the college-educated,

Table 2.4 Growth in adult U.S. internet users, 1995–2010

	On-line (%)		Growth in percentage
	2010	1995	
Age			
18–29	88	21	67
30–49	87	18	69
50–64	78	9	71
65+	42	2	40
Total	77	14	63
Sex			
Men	78	18	60
Women	77	10	67
Race/Ethnicity			
White	78	21	57
Black	66	11	55
Latino/Hispanic	84	14	72
Education			
<High school	47	2	45
High school graduate	67	8	59
Some college	89	20	69
College graduate	94	29	65
Household income			
<$30,000	56	8	48
$30,000–$49,000	82	15	67
$50,000–$75,000	93	23	70
>$75,000	95	32	63

Source http://www.census.gov/population/socdemo/computer/2007/tab02.xls and http://www.
census.gov/compendia/statab/2010/tables/10s1121.xls

particularly women. Likewise, the Latino population is far from heterogeneous, and significant discrepancies in internet access and usage remain among various subgroups; usage rates tend to be much higher among bilingual Latinos than those who speak only Spanish. Indeed, among English-dominant Latinos, internet usage rates are identical to Whites. Generally, Mexican-Americans and those with origins in Central or South America had lower rates of access than do Cuban-Americans or Puerto Ricans. In short, while racial or ethnic discrepancies in internet access and usage remain, all groups have experienced significant growth in uses and the relative differences between them have declined.

Persistently underlying the digital divide in the United States are vast socio-economic differences, particularly education and household income, which effectively serve as markers of class. Although populations at all of four broad educational levels (less than high school, high school graduate, some college, college graduate) exhibited gains in internet access, profound differences remain. Among college-educated Americans, internet usage is almost universal (91 %); those with a high school education or less are users witnessed a growth from

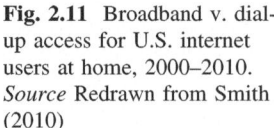

Fig. 2.11 Broadband v. dial-up access for U.S. internet users at home, 2000–2010. *Source* Redrawn from Smith (2010)

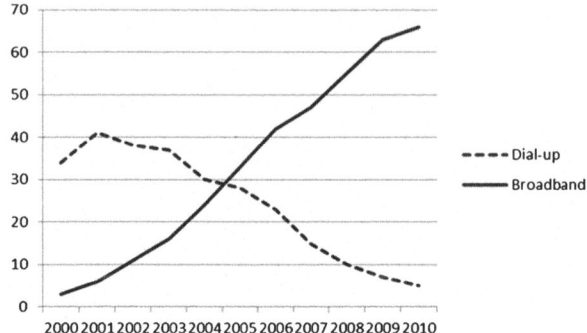

2 % in 1995 to 35 % in 2011. Educational level, therefore, is a prime predictor of who is on-line and who is not. Similarly, income remains a useful measure of who has access and who does not, particularly at home. In 1995 roughly one-third of upper-income households (over $75,000 annually) used the internet; by 2006, this share had risen to 93 %. Rapid growth rates also occurred among those of more modest means, although less than a majority (45 %) of poor households (less than $30,000 annually) were users in 2011. Thus, as with race/ethnicity and educational level, absolute discrepancies persist but relative differences declined as internet usage rates advanced most rapidly among those with hitherto the least access.

Schools remain perhaps the most important arena in which the digital divide is manifested and reproduced. In an age in which the acquisition of skills to participate in advanced producer services is key to upward social mobility, this issue assumes special importance. Inequalities in school funding are mirrored in the prevalence of the internet in public classrooms: while 99 % of schools offer children access to networked PCs in one way or another, these rates vary significantly in terms of quality of access. After home and school, public libraries are the third-most common point of internet access for children, especially for lower income minorities; however, libraries have limited hours and often lack high-speed connections. Not surprisingly, the digital divide in schools has strongly racialized overtones: white students are much more likely than are minorities to use the internet in the classroom or school library.

In 2011, roughly 44 % of the U.S. population used broadband technologies of one sort or another, and dial up access declined proportionately (Fig. 2.11). This proportion is relatively low compared to most of the economically developed world; indeed, under the Bush Administration, the U.S. slipped from third to 13th place internationally in terms of relative access to broadband services, and Americans pay 10–20 times as much per megabit over broadband as do their counterparts in Korea and Japan. Broadband accessibility closely mirrors that of the internet as a whole: it tends to be most prevalent among the young, whites, the well-educated, and rises monotonically with household income. Moreover, broadband is unevenly distributed spatially among U.S. states (Fig. 2.12). Broadband technologies have been slow to reach rural America: whereas 86 % or

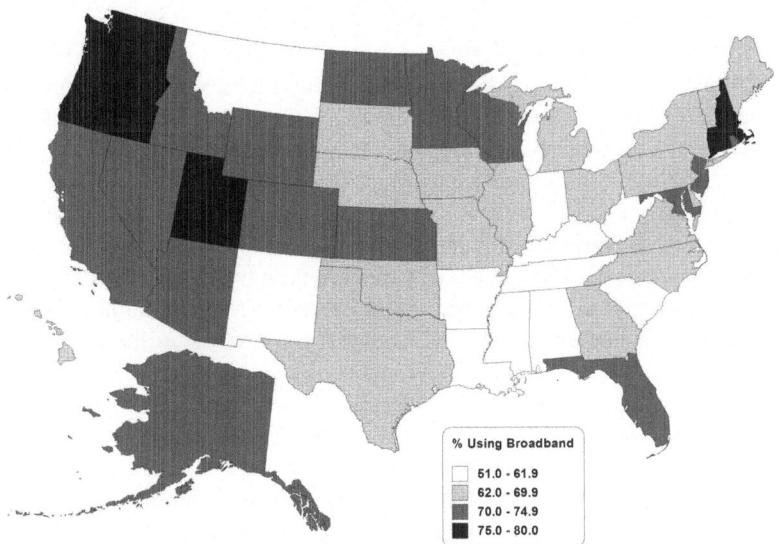

Fig. 2.12 Map of U.S. broadband Internet usage rates, 2010. *Source* Author, using data from http://www.census.gov/compendia/statab/cats/information_communications.html

residents in cities with more than 100,000 residents have access to DSL, very few in towns with less than 10,000 people do so.

Canada also faces a digital divide (Sciadas 2002; Howard et al. 2010), with, for example, markedly lower rates of use in Atlantic Canada, which tends to be poorer, more rural, and demographically older than the rest of the country. Unlike the U.S., however, the Canadian government has aggressively promoted broadband services in rural areas and free internet access in public libraries and community centers.

2.4.2 Europe

Europe provides a panoply of internet use that ranges from the exceptionally high to the very low. In 2011, 345 million netizens lived in the continent (excluding Russia), with an average penetration rate of 73 %. However, rates of usage varied widely, and were typically much higher in Northern and Western Europe than in the eastern and southern parts, reflecting long-standing socioeconomic differentials. There is thus a significant digital divide among, as well as within, European countries (Demoussis and Giannakopoulos 2006). Indeed, Orviska and Hudson (2009) argue that internal variations in internet usage exceed those among countries. While income is important in explaining internet access and use, age seems to be a major variable everywhere, as the young are invariably the most likely to log into cyberspace (Brandtzæg et al. 2011).

Germany, with 67 million netizens (82.7 %), has the largest national population of users in Europe. Despite a relatively egalitarian social structure and government policies aimed at ameliorating discrepancies in internet access, the German digital divide persists. Younger residents are more likely to be users than older ones. A schism remains entrenched between urban and rural areas for reasons that include structural differences and individual characteristics (Schleife 2010). Regional discrepancies also persist: whereas Berlin exhibits much higher usage than the national average, Bavaria and the states of former East Germany lag behind.

France was relatively slow to adopt the internet, in part because of the legacy of its older Minitel system and a lag in deregulating its telecommunications market from the France Telecom monopoly. Today it harbors 50 million users, with a penetration rate of 77 %. In the 2000s, marked discrepancies in internet access were evident by income as well as between the largest metro areas and rural regions. The French government tackled that country's digital divide aggressively, including a program to offer 1.2 million of its poorest citizens a free PC with internet connection (Sayer 2006) as well as a subsidy to reduce PC costs to "1 € per day" for university students. In contrast to the laissez faire attitude of the U.S., the French also implemented street cyberkiosks, an annual internet festival, and subsidies for technicians to help with home internet installment. Nonetheless, broadband usage has been delayed there, and is roughly the same as the median rate of the EU.

In Britain the internet diffused rapidly, and today includes 84 % of the population. The British digital divide follows the familiar contours of age, income, education, and urban location, reflecting and reinforcing sociospatial differentials in opportunities for learning (Eynon 2009). British internet use was amplified by a national policy encouraging broadband use was adopted in 2003, when the technology rapidly grew in popularity to include 85 % of the country's netizens. British residents under age 25 were three times as likely as those over 65 to use the web (Helsper et al. 2008). Unlike the U.S. and Scandinavian countries, in which women are the largest pools of users, the digital divide in Britain is characterized by heavier male usage. As in all industrial countries, mobile internet access is growing rapidly in popularity. Non-internet users in Britain report they do not engage with cyberspace because they are "not interested," find the technology confusing, or cannot afford access, pointing to a mixture of digital choice and digital divide (Reisdorf 2011).

The European Union has adopted a series of telecommunications policies designed to promote internet access, particularly the diffusion of broadband. In 2005, the European Commission launched i2010, an initiative promoted to enhance internet access across the continent. This goal was explicitly articulated in the Lisbon Strategy of 2010, which was implemented with the broader aim of accelerating the continent's shift into a knowledge-based economy. The European Digital Agenda stipulates that by 2013 all EU citizens should have access to broadband internet, a goal unlikely to be met.

In all the Scandinavian nations, including Iceland, a well-educated "leisure class" (Florida 2004) has become adept at using information technology for a wide variety of purposes. In part due to sustained and aggressive promotion by their respective national governments, Scandinavian states are well known to exhibit some of the world's best developed internet infrastructures, including broadband and wireless internet services, and exceptionally high levels of usage. Indeed, penetration rates in all Scandinavian nations exceed 90 %, often reaching as high as 96 %. Thus, what is essentially universal access to the internet has thus essentially eliminated the digital divide in Scandinavian states, in marked contrast to the highly unequal state of affairs in the United States. This state of affairs reflects a wealthy, highly educated populace as well as liberal government programs that aggressively promoted internet and other forms of telecommunications usage. In Sweden and Canada, for example, a steady convergence of internet, telephony, and video services has occurred, blurring once separate markets and reducing costs to consumers (Wu 2004). Finland in particular has had exceptional success in providing wireless services, a reflection of that nation's lead in mobile and cellular telephony (e.g. Nokia) for more than a generation (Palmberg 2002; Steinbock 2001). In Scandinavia, as in most of the world, internet usage has been particularly popular among the young. Given that schools in Scandinavia actively promote learning of information technologies, the widespread popularity of such devices among the young is not surprising. Indeed, an adolescent blogosphere has formed in which views are expressed, identities shaped, and connections forged (Bjanason et al. 2010; Kaare et al. 2007). Generally, information technologies in Scandinavia, as elsewhere, reinforce communities forged through face-to-face contacts rather than generate new ones (Thulin and Vilhelmson 2005).

In Southern Europe, where internet use lags behind that in the northern parts of the continent, the internet still plays an important role in the lives of Italians, Spaniards, and Portuguese. In Italy, its use predictably follows the long-standing north–south divide. Fiber connections and broadband were until recently largely confined to prosperous metropolitan areas such as Rome and Milan. Thus, while penetration rates in the Piedmont resemble those of Northern Europe, the Mezzogiorno, home to one-third of the population, has less than one-quarter of its netizens, although this gap appears to be declining. Italy also faces a tremendous age barrier in internet use: 79 % of Italians under age 30 use the web, but only 7 % of those over 65 do so. The Spanish case is similar, with Madrid and Barcelona dominating the country's internet connectivity. Rural areas such as Extremadura and Castilla y León lag well behind. PC ownership in Spain and Portugal lags well behind the EU average, and both countries exhibit a pronounced gender bias in favor of males. The Spanish government responded with a series of subsidized *telecentros* in rural areas, but dropped the program in 2006. Most regional governments adopted complementary programs, including subsidized wifi access in parks and public buildings.

Eastern Europe lags well behind the west in internet access. Typically, poorer countries have worse digital divides than do wealthier ones, and in Europe Greece and Bulgaria exhibit some of the worst regional differentials (Vicente and López 2011). In the Czech Republic, one of the region's better-connected countries, widening income differentials have been manifested in an enlarging, not diminishing, digital divide (Lupač and Sladek 2008). With assistance from the United Nations, Poland launched Internet Republic, a project aimed at facilitating internet access in rural areas. Broadband in the country, roughly 17 %, is among the lowest in Europe. Hungary's urban–rural schism is the dominant feature of its digital divide, and the government's eHungary Program, launched in 2003, trumpeted internet access in the schools and 3,000 public access points.

2.4.3 Russia

In Russia, the internet began in the early 1990s to serve large financial institutions; the growth in individual and residential users occurred only after the banking crisis of the late 1990s, when a series of regional data transmission nets popped up (Perfiliev 2002). However, in the mid-1990s, O'Lear (1996) found Russian environmentalists using e-mail to network and share information. By 2011, with a 44 % penetration rate, roughly 61.5 million netizens lived in the country. Access to the internet, however, is socially and spatially uneven, often slow, and subject to severe political oversight. In Russia, many inter-city communications networks still rely heavily on copper cable wires, when most of the world's telecommunications traffic has moved decisively into fiber optics cable. As in many countries, Russian internet use has been concentrated in the largest cities, particularly Moscow and St. Petersburg. A persistent rural–urban divide remains however: "Private providers have not developed outside of large cities not only because of the lack of advanced telecommunications infrastructure and high construction costs, but also because potential markets of regular internet users remain very small" (Perfiliev 2002, p. 419).

In a country where newspapers, television, and radio stations are already under tight government control, the Russian internet has emerged as the last bastion of relatively uncensored speech. The Putin government gradually sought to extend its influence over the internet, essentially following the Chinese model of granting the secret service extensive monitoring powers, ostensibly on the grounds of fighting corruption (Troianovski and Finn 2007). As Russia's penetration rate increased, threatening to broaden the sphere of public debate and give rise to autonomous voices, the administration responded by purchasing independent websites, promoting pro-government websites, and fostering a network of government-friendly bloggers. Russia's internet surveillance law, the System for Operational-Investigative Activities, allows state security services unfettered physical access to internet service providers and requires them to report statistics about users.

2.4.4 Central Asia

In Central Asia, privatization and deregulation of telecommunications have occurred much more slowly than in most of the world, and are often handicapped by governments fearful of losing control over a vital means of information control. In 2007, the Kazakh operator Kazakhtelecom was the region's first state-owned company to actually offer its shares for sale, but only 4.1 % have been sold. The Kyrgyz government has gradually liberalized its telecommunications sector, which improved the affordability of internet access there and made use of cyberspace more attractive and profitable; however, as OpenNet Initiative (2010a) points out, "Kyrgyzstan is an effectively cyberlocked country dependent on purchasing bandwidth from Kazakhstan and Russia." Some governments cling to the older model of state-owned telecommunications, such as Afghanistan and Uzbekistan, in which UzbekTelecom retains a legal monopoly status even as it is being privatized. In 2001, following a brief window of privatization that opened with independence in 1991, Turkmenistan granted a monopoly over data services to TurkmenTelecom, driving several smaller internet service providers (ISPs) out of business.

As in most of the world, the most active Central Asian netizens tend to be young and well educated, including students, government employees, and those working for large corporations. In Kyrgyzstan, one-half of users are students and 75 % are under age 30. Ninety percent of Uzbeki users have a post-secondary education (Wei and Kolko 2005). Not surprisingly, often elites situated in urban areas tend to exhibit the highest rates of connectivity. In Uzbekistan, for example, 85 % of netizens live in urban areas (Wei and Kolko 2005), 70 % of whom are concentrated in Tashkent (Privacy International 2003; OpenNet Initiative 2010c). In Kyrgyzstan, 77 % of internet users are located in Bishkek. In Turkmenistan, 95 % of users are in the capital, Ashgabat (OpenNet Initiative 2010b). In Kyrgyzstan, the majority of Internet users depend on cafes (Privacy International 2003; Srinivasan and Fish 2009). In Uzbekistan, roughly 40 % of users do so from their homes, 40 % use their place of work, but 30 % use cybercafés (OpenNet Initiative 2010c). In Kazakhstan, half of users have internet access from their homes. In Afghanistan, cybercafés are essentially confined to the airport in Kabul and a few luxury hotels. In Tajikistan, a network of 400 cafes are the dominant points of entry into cyberspace; the average café costs $US 0.73/h, compared to the national minimum salary of $US 7.00 per month. However, strict licensing requirements have reduced the number of Tajik cybercafés. In Turkmenistan, private internet cafes are illegal, although the government monopoly TurkmenTelecom operates 15 cafes in the country (OpenNet Initiative 2010b). Prices in these cafes in 2007 averaged $US 4/h (compared to an average income of $US 100/month), although after President Berdymukhamedov reprimanded the Minister of Communications for such high charges they dropped to $US 2/h. In 2008 TurkmenTelecom began to offer dial-up home access, but at such high prices it is unaffordable to most residents, an implicit form of censorship designed to limit internet access (Lambroschini 2011). Clark and Gomez (2011, p.8), however, argue that rather than fees, it is the technical skills of staff that make cybercafés accessible to unskilled users. Throughout Central Asia, internet cafes tend to be clustered in commercial districts frequented by tourists, particularly business districts, hotels, and airports. Cybercafes are also major points of government control over the internet: those in which customers attempt to access banned websites are routinely closed, and customers who access pornography typically face steep fines. However, as internet penetration rates climb, including more access at home, the importance of cybercafés is likely to diminish.

2.4.5 East Asia

Chinese internet use, of course, stands in a class by itself. China's first international internet connection began in 1987, when the country was linked to Germany (Jing 2007). Today its largest ISPs are China Netcom and China Telecom. Large numbers of Chinese rely on internet cafes, where they are subject to strict censorship (Chap. 3). Domestically-produced portals tend to be highly popular, including Sina.com and 163.com, as well as home-grown search engines such as Baidu. Indeed, only 6 % of Chinese computers have internet linkages outside of the country (Crampton 2007). From modest beginnings, and in the context of sustained, explosive economic growth, Chinese internet use has grown rapidly (i.e., 20-fold between 2000 and 2011). With more than 513 million users in 2011, China forms the largest single national pool of netizens in the world, with a penetration rate of 38.4 %. Indeed, Chinese has become the second-most heavily used language in cyberspace today (Table 2.2). The Chinese blogosphere, with 20 million blogs and counting, has become an increasingly important force in politics, giving voice to critics of government corruption and dissident groups such as Falun Gong.

Enormous social and spatial inequalities typify the Chinese internet (Song 2008; Guo and Chen 2011). As in many developing countries, Chinese internet users are disproportionately male (55 %) and unmarried (58 %), and include numerous students and those with above-average incomes. Two-thirds of China's netizens earn 6,000 yuan or more per year, well above the national average. Because internet access is relatively expensive in China, many low wage workers find the internet simply unaffordable, even at internet cafes. In 2005, China had more than 110,000 internet cafes, which employed 1 million people: of their users, 70 % were between ages 18 and 30, 90 % were male, half held a university degree, and the most common usage was to play computer games. Users tend to be heavily concentrated in urban areas, particularly along the prosperous eastern third of the country. Thus, whereas 50 % of Beijing's residents log in, as do 50 % of Guangdong, only 3.8 % of the population of rural Guizhou does so. One-fifth of China's netizens live in either Beijing or Shanghai. Whereas 700 million Chinese live in rural areas, they form only 27 % of the country's netizens. As elsewhere, this urban–rural digital divide largely reflects the government's emphasis on urban areas as motors of economic growth and the unwillingness of China's ISPs to invest in lower-income, and often lower-density, rural areas.

The Japanese internet included roughly 101 million users in 2011, with a penetration rate of 80 %. Unlike China, but similar to the U.S. and Europe, the bulk of Japanese access the web via personal computers at home; as a result, internet cafes are less common. As with other Asian countries, Japan has invested heavily in broadband applications: internet access speeds are 30 times faster than in the U.S., and considerably cheaper, which have greatly facilitated cable television and the government's efforts to promote e-commerce and telecommuting (Harden 2007). Moreover, Japan has seen its mobile internet usage surge to the world's highest rate, which has surpassed the use of landlines (Ishii 2004). Despite these investments, Japan, too, exhibits a digital divide, with a disproportionate concentration of users in the greater Tokyo-Yokohama and Osaka metropolitan areas. The blogosphere is exceptionally popular in Japan: 80 % of the country's netizens visit a blog once a month or so.

South Korea, among the world's most hard wired countries, has a remarkably well developed internet infrastructure. (In contrast, in North Korea the internet is all but forbidden, with the exception of a handful of government officials). With 40 million users in 2011, South Korea has a penetration rate of 82.7 %, the highest in Asia (and higher than the U.S.). Seoul, the country's primate city, captures a large proportion of the country's internet users (Hwang 2004), and its netizens deploy the web to a wider range of purposes than do those outside of the capital. To mitigate the country's digital divide, the Korean government established a series of "information model villages" or e-villages. Many Koreans enjoy one of the 20,000 "PC bangs," local slang for internet cafes; computer gaming is enormously popular (Schiesel 2006), and games such as *Starcraft* have become a national obsession, with professional players. Korean *Starcraft* champions such as Lim Yo-Hwan or Hong Jin-Ho are national celebrities. The Korean government initiated and supports the Korean Games Development and Promotion Institute, an agency charged with encouraging and facilitating the gaming industry as a key strategic industry within that country.

2.4.6 Southeast Asia

Southeast Asia exhibits enormous contrasts in internet use, ranging from hyperconnected Singapore to Myanmar, in which 0.2 % are logged in. With highly uneven rates of economic and population growth, as well as different national policies toward internet adoption, this region exhibits some of the most marked contrasts in internet use in the world. While all countries there experience digital divides, their governments have consistently sought to address the issue through a variety of policies with varying degrees of success (Tipton 2002; Evers and Gerke 2004).

Singapore, in which 77 % of the population has internet access, is one of Asia's best-connected countries, with connectivity levels rivaling those in North America and Western Europe, which is perhaps no surprise given the long commitment to telecommunications made by Singapore's government (Corey 1991). Singapore has aggressively positioned itself as a regional, and increasingly, global center of telecommunications and information services. In this vein, Singapore Telecommunications initiated a series of high speed fiber linkages with India in 2001, Bangladesh in 2002, and Thailand and Indonesia in 2003. Today, 90 % of the island enjoys high-speed broadband connections. Affluence and widespread internet access have created a critical mass of web users, who routinely apply the internet to banking and shopping. The Singaporean state retains tight control over the island's internet content, with some of the region's strictest censorship.

In Thailand, with 18 million users (24.7 %) in 2011, the by-now familiar pattern of a bifurcation between cosmopolitan, internet-savvy youth clustered in the primate city and less connected people in rural areas is prominent. Thus, while 68 % of the population lives in rural areas, only 16 % of Thai netizens do so. Facebook is particularly popular here, and has been used in protests against the ruling monarchy.

Malaysia's digital divide largely reflects the pronounced differences between the country's peninsular portion and the poorer provinces of Borneo. Socially, the country's elderly and Indian population was the least likely to be connected. The government's proactive policy, Vision 2020, which seeks to catapult the state into a knowledge-based economy by that year, has had significant impacts in encouraging Malays to participate in cyberspace, including incentive programs such as "One Home, One PC" and a systematic roll-out plan to facilitate broadband adoption (Nair et al. 2010). The Malaysian government's Multimedia Super Corridor (MSC) has integrated information technology at the core of its Vision 2020 Master Plan (Mohan et al. 2004), and generated 17,000 jobs, of which 80 % were knowledge-intensive. Part of this effort includes the Multimedia University in Cyberjaya, owned by the privatized Telekom Malaysia which has established collaborative linkages with 37 companies and 29 universities around the world.

Indonesia's internet straddles more than 17,000 islands, an environment more economically conducive to satellites, with low marginal costs, than fiber optics. With 55 million users (22 %) in 2011, the country forms one of the world's larger pools of netizens. Indonesia was the world's first developing nation to use satellites for domestic connectivity, launched several generations of its Palapa ("Unity") satellites to provide internet services to all 27 provinces; PalapaNet recently began to sell services to neighboring ASEAN countries as well. The government has spent tens of millions of dollars, including foreign aid, to promote broadband connectivity in 72,000 rural villages (Jumaat 2010). With low PC ownership, many users rely on one of the country's 2,000 cybercafes, or *warung internet* (often abbreviated to *warnet*) which are overwhelmingly clustered in cities all over Java (Furuholt and Kristiansen 2005). *Warnet* have become increasingly important foci of social and political transformation (Lim 2003).

Although it lags behind its more economically developed neighbors, the internet has diffused rapidly in Vietnam as well (Lam et al. 2004). Its 30 million users represent one-third of the country, and are predominantly clustered in Ho Chi Minh City and Hanoi (Moi 2009). As with most totalitarian countries, the government severely censors the Vietnamese net. Invoking dependency theory, Surborg (2009) argues that in the context of Vietnam's *doi moi* reforms, the internet represents the intrusion of the global capitalist ruling class into the country.

Finally, the Philippines, with almost 30 million netizens (29 %), also exhibits a pronounced digital divide with, of course, Manila at the core. Despite this discrepancy, cyberspace is becoming woven into Filipino society in multiple ways. Filipinos are particularly fond of text messaging, and have the highest per capita rate of use in the world. The slow diffusion of the internet there has led to the adoption of distance-learning courses to the advantage of outlying rural islands.

2.4.7 South Asia

The world's third largest national group of internet users—121 million people in 2011—are found in India, a mere 10 % of the population. However, the Indian internet is expanding rapidly, particularly among the growing middle class accustomed to cyberspace. Between 2000 and 2011, 116 million new users (96 % of the country's netizens) came on-line, a growth rate of almost 34 % annually. The halting deregulation of the Indian telecommunications sector, a hidebound bureaucracy, and insufficient investment in rural electrification have kept this growth from being even higher, however.

Despite its reputation for a booming economy centered on software and information technology, centered on cities such as Bangalore that are by far the best connected places in the country, in reality access to the Indian internet is very uneven (Keniston and Kumar 2004). The Indian digital divide is dominated by its sharp urban–rural contrasts: thus, while 12 % of urban Indians logged on in 2008, only 1.2 % of those in rural areas do so (Singh 2010). In large cities, users can take advantage of the 12,200 cybercafes present in 2005 (Rao 2005). Outside of cities, major obstacles include poverty, illiteracy, gender discrimination, and the lack of a well developed telephone system. Nonetheless, with the gradual diffusion of the internet to the county's innumerable villages, in which 70 % of the population lives, many farmers are using cyberspace to obtain real-time information about crop prices, access health care information, and access land ownership records (Devraj 2002; Cecchini and Scott 2003; James 2004). India's digital divide is also characterized by sharp gender inequalities, with women comprising only 17 % of the country's netizens (Dhawan 2012). Lower caste Indians, especially the *dalits*, or untouchables, face the most difficult obstacles accessing cyberspace (Thirumal and Tartakov 2011). The government has initiated programs to address these discrepancies by promoting wireless internet usage, community-owned intranets, and satellite services (Rao 2005).

Outside of India, South Asia contains much smaller pools of users in Pakistan (29 million users, or 15 % penetration) and Bangladesh (5 million users, or 3.5 %). In both countries, patriarchal barriers and gender roles firmly limit women's access to cyberspace. Despite the Pakistani government's rhetoric about closing the country's digital divide, enhancing human capital, promoting exports, and attracting foreign information technology investment, very little has been done in practice. Karachi and Islamabad remain the best-connected points in the country, termini of international fiber optic cables. Rural Pakistanis, however, live in an endemic state of information poverty (Ameen and Gorman 2009). While internet use has grown rapidly (59 % annually), the infrastructure has had difficulty in keeping up with the surge in demand. A few government-sponsored telemedicine clinics operate in rural areas, and some universities have established distance-learning programs (Mujahid 2002). Bangladesh fares even worse, with a very low telephone density, high illiteracy, acute shortages of computer skills, and virtually no broadband, problems compounded by the relative lack of Bengali content on the web.

2.4.8 Arab World

Roughly 320 million Arabs comprise about 5 % of the world's population. With an average Internet penetration rate of 25 % in 2011, or 79 million users, the Arab world lags behind the world average, particularly industrialized regions. There exist to date remarkably few systematic attempts to understand the Arab world's internet geography (see Warf and Vincent 2007). Understanding the nature and impacts of the internet in the Arab world is made difficult in part by the widespread Orientalist misconceptions about Arabic culture and society found in the West: like all societies in the age of intense and rapid globalization, Arab societies are complex mixtures of the traditional, the modern, and the postmodern (Fandy 1999). Considerable diversity may be found among Arab states in terms of internet usage. Typically, Arab states with the best-developed internet systems are those that have diversified their economies from petroleum, have competitive telecom-munications markets, relatively equalized gender roles, numerous cybercafes, and high rates of wireless phone usage.

In 2011, roughly 79 million people in Arab countries (including non-Arabs, e.g., Berbers and foreign nationals) logged on. In absolute terms, the largest numbers were found in Egypt, by far the most populous Arab country, which had 21.7 million users, Morocco (15.6 million), and Saudi Arabia (11.4 million). Penetration rates were highest in the Persian/Arabian Gulf states, particularly the UAE and Qatar, which, with 69 %, rivaled the rates found in many countries of Europe. Like many Gulf states, the UAE has a large immigrant population from South and Southeast Asia; Privacy International (www.privacyinternational.org)

estimates that 60 % of that country's users are Asian. Among the seven emirates that constitute the UAE, Dubai and Abu Dhabi have taken the lead in facilitating internet growth (Kalathil and Boas 2003). More impoverished Arab countries, in contrast, exhibited much lower rates, ranging as low as 9 % in Sudan and 4 % in Iraq.

Because personal computer ownership rates are relatively low in the Arab world, and because ISP access charges are often high, most Arab internet users rely upon internet cafes for access rather than individual ISP accounts (Wheeler 2004). Their popularity varies among Arab countries. Jordan made the *Guinness Book of World Records* for the largest local concentration of internet cafes anywhere: more than 200 are clustered on a single street in Irbid (Wheeler 2006). Cafes are also popular in Algeria and Morocco, which have more than 3,000 and 2,120 of them, respectively. Cafes are particularly important for those who lack dial-up access at home, and as Wheeler (2004) notes, they constitute "informal communities, where users come and go, activities are not measured and monitored, where the effects of internet use are difficult to assess." Users spend an average of 12 h per week on-line, often in chat rooms. An important alternative to cybercafes is publicly-funded internet community access points such as Tunisia's Publinet centers and Jordan's Knowledge Stations (Wheeler 2006).

2.4.9 Sub-Saharan Africa

The global space of flows and "information highway" seem to have largely bypassed the African continent. By virtually any measure, the region remains the least connected in the world, the bottom-most tier of the global digital divide. Whereas 32 % of the world's people used the internet at the end of 2011, in sub-Saharan Africa the average internet penetration rate was only 11 %; home to 850 million people, 12 % of the world, Africa has less than 5 % of its internet users. Hobbled by widespread poverty, economic stagnation, illiteracy, an inadequate telecommunications infrastructure, often unreliable electrical systems, lack of technical skills, and frequently indifferent governments, Africa was late to join the digital revolution, and the internet is still relatively uncommon on the continent. However, despite these obstacles, cyberspace on the continent is still growing by leaps and bounds. Like other information technologies, the internet has diffused unevenly across the African continent (Wilson and Wong 2003; Oyelaran-Oyeyinka and Lal 2005), simultaneously reflecting and transforming long-standing regional inequalities. Thus, South Africa has long been the most prominent member of Africa's information revolution. Throughout Africa, great social and spatial inequalities in internet access exist within each country: telephones tend to be concentrated in urban areas, where companies derive economies of scale in service provision, although in many African countries the bulk of the population lives in rural ones. In South Africa, for example, only 8 % of the country's internet users are blacks, although they comprise 79 % of the total population (Brown and Licker 2003).

African internet cafés are commonly found in commercial districts frequented by (typically young) tourists, students, and business executives; exhibit ownership structures ranging from sole proprietorships to international chains; and charge access prices that vary widely among and within countries (Mutula 2003; Esharenana et al. 2003). Because many cafés derive a substantial share of their profits from non-Africans, their fees are often too high to make them accessible to low income people. Based on observations of cybercafés in Uganda, Mwesige (2003) argues that because they are affordable only to the relatively well-off, they may be accentuating, not decreasing, the digital divide within countries. However, as the prices of internet connectivity have fallen, cybercafés are sprouting up in some African slums as well, and are most Africans' primary means of access. Some African governments have promoted the growth of cybercafés in slums, such as South African's Universal Service Agency efforts in the Khayaletsha slum near Cape Town (Mancebo 2003). In addition to for-profit cybercafés, many non-profit and non-governmental organizations have established networks of neighborhood telecenters (Mayanja 2003), which have played catalytic roles in community development. Ghana, for example, has a well-developed system (Falch 2004). In Tanzania, state-subsidized telecenters have complicated the geographies of inclusion and exclusion that normally arise from market forces (Mercer 2006).

2.4.10 Latin America and the Caribbean

At the close of 2011, 234 million people in Latin America and the Caribbean used the internet. The region exhibits a mean penetration rate of 40 %, higher than the world average but considerably lower than the economically developed world. Penetration rates varied considerably, with the highest consistently found in the Caribbean, the wealthiest and best-connected region. In many respects, the most well-connected parts of the greater Latin American region lay in the Caribbean, including Puerto Rico but also places such as Antigua (with a rate penetration greater than that of the U.S.), Barbados, and St. Lucia. In the 2000–2011 period, more than 6.3 million Caribeños joined the global on-line community. Outside of the Caribbean, Argentina leads Latin American penetration rates (with 67 %); closely following are Chile (59.4 %), Uruguay (56 %), and Colombia (55.9 %). Conversely, countries with the lowest penetration rates tend to be poor, including the hemisphere's lowest, in Nicaragua (11.7 %), as well as Honduras (13.1 %), and Cuba (15.4 %). Long marginalized ethnic minorities and impoverished residents of rural areas or urban barrios are unlikely to have access to the internet or benefit much from its usage. For example, Friedman (2005, p. 12) quotes the director of a network of rural women who notes "peasant women do not use computers and many do not know that this technology exists." The lines of digital inclusion and exclusion are therefore often drawn on the same boundaries that divide class, gender, ethnicity, and political and economic power. Nonetheless, fuelled by falling prices of computer hardware and software, growing computer literacy (especially among the young), and slowly, if unevenly, rising incomes, Latin American internet usage grew explosively between 2000 and 2011. The region as a whole witnessed a growth rate in users of 32 %, which was considerably slower than states in Africa and Central Asia.

Many Latin Americans rely on internet cafes, which tend to be clustered in commercial districts frequented by tourists, exhibit a range of ownership from sole proprietorships to chains such as PapayaNet, and have access charges that vary widely among and within countries (Rao 1999). In countries with growing middle classes, however, home-based internet access is more likely. In addition to for-profit cybercafés, many non-profit and non-governmental organizations have established networks of telecenters, which have played catalytic roles in community development in many areas (Hunt 2001). For example, Somos@telecentros, a network of telecenters, allows diverse groups to share experiences and collaborate in the acquisition of information resources.

Within the world of Latin American broadband, local wireless applications have gained ground quickly, generally among commercial establishments. For example, the title of the "world's first WiFi-linked e-payments network" is claimed by The Mall of San Marino in Guayaquil, Ecuador (Burger 2004). Because wireless internet access is generally confined to a few "hotspots" such as coffee houses or airports, most users must utilize a landline in order to access cyberspace. Thus, whereas 15 % of Americans use the wireless internet, in Brazil, only 2.6 % do so, and Brazil leads the region in this respect (Nielson Mobile 2008). However, as wireless technologies proliferate, and as have surged well ahead of landlines, Latin America may enjoy the potential to leapfrog old technologies (Davison et al. 2000).

2.5 Conclusions

Contrary to the hyperbole that continues to swarm around the internet, multiplying even faster than do viruses and webpages, cyberspace reflects all of the inequalities and social divisions that permeate the non-virtual world. Far from constituting some mythologized world of unfettered individualism, as some advocates portrayed it, cyberspace in fact is thoroughly shot through with relations of class, gender, ethnicity, and other social categories. Theorizations of the digital divide must of necessity take these dimensions into account to avoid the overly optimistic, technologically-determinist, and often conservative perspectives that deny their ongoing existence and significance to understanding the internet. When viewed in social terms, the virtual and real worlds are mutually constitutive: discrepancies in access to the internet both mirror and constitute inequalities in the world outside of cyberspace.

It is important to emphasize the dramatic growth of the internet, which the world over is expanding by leaps and bounds. Growth rates vary, of course, and tend to be highest in countries with small populations of netizens in 2000. In 11 years, 1.3 billion new netizens were brought on-line, or 120 million (8.5 %) annually. Overall, the internet is growing more rapidly in the developing world than in the economically advanced one, in which saturation levels have been effectively reached. In some African states, growth rates are explosive. Such observations mean that any statistics on internet use will soon be out of date. They also imply that while the digital divide remains a pressing issue, it is gradually ameliorating among and within countries.

Contextualizing the internet—embedding it in economic, political, and cultural relations—inevitably means comprehending it in spatial terms. There is no one, unified network, but a loose assemblage of different networks. Many factors combine to produce the uneven spatiality of the internet, including differences in income, literacy, demographic composition (notably age), gender relations, tele-communications policies, and government censorship, generating a geography of cyberspace that is inescapably multiscalar in nature. As this chapter has demonstrated, for example, the digital divide varies markedly in severity, causes, and outcomes in different countries. Moreover, the internet helps to produce the spatial unevenness that it simultaneously reflects: in some countries, it has democratized discourse, empowered marginalized groups, and spurred economic growth; in others, it has reinforced existing hierarchies of wealth and power, notably patri-archal ones, by producing enormous information asymmetries. Such considerations should lead us to be wary of viewing the internet in teleological terms, as some omnipotent force inevitably destined to emancipate humanity. Rather, its consequences are contingent, ever-changing, and locally-specific. Such a perspective is necessary as a sobering antidote to the overly optimistic, technologically determinist utopianism that pervades much popular wisdom about this topic.

References

Ameen, K., & Gorman, G. (2009). Information and digital literacy: a stumbling block to development? A Pakistan perspective. *Library Management, 30*(1/2), 99–112.

Bjanason, T., Gudmundsson, B., & Olasfsson, K. (2010). Towards a digital adolescent society? The social structure of the Icelandic adolescent blogosphere. *New Media and Society, 12,* 1225–1243.

Brandtzæg, P., Heim, J., & Karahasanović, A. (2011). Understanding the new digital divide—A typology of internet users in Europe. *International Journal of Human-Computer Studies, 69*(3), 123–138.

Brown, I., & Licker, P. (2003). Exploring differences in internet adoption and usage between historically advantaged and disadvantaged groups in South Africa. *Journal of Global Information Technology Management, 6*(4), 6–26.

Burger, A. (2004). Broadband wifi spreads in Latin America. *E-Commerce Times,* 16 June 2004. http://www.ecommercetimes.com/story/34517.html

Castells, M. (1997). *The information age, volume II: The power of identity.* Cambridge: Blackwell.

Cecchini, S., & Scott, C. (2003). Can information and communications technology applications contribute to poverty reduction? Lessons from rural India. *Information Technology for Development, 10,* 73–84. http://itd.ist.unomaha.edu/archives/1.pdf

Chakraborty, J., & Bosman, M. (2005). Measuring the digital divide in the United States: Race, income, and personal computer ownership. *Professional Geographer, 57*(3), 395–410.

Clark, M., & Gomez. R. (2011). The negligible role of fees as a barrier to public access computing in developing countries. *Electronic Journal of Information Systems in Developing Countries, 46*(1), 1–14.

Corey, K. (1991). The role of information technology in the planning and development of Singapore. In S. Brunn & T. Leinbach (Eds.), *Collapsing space and time* (pp. 217–231). New York: HarperCollins.

Crampton, J. (2007). The biopolitical justification for geosurveillance. *Geographical Review, 97*(3), 389–493.

Davison, R., Vogel, D., Harris, R., & Jones, N. (2000). Technology leapfrogging in developing countries—An inevitable luxury? *Electronic Journal on Information Systems in Developing Countries, 1*(5), 1–10. http://www.ejisdc.org.

Demoussis, M., & Giannakopoulos, N. (2006). Facets of the digital divide in Europe: Determination and extent of internet use. *Economics of Innovation and New Technology, 15*(3), 235–246.

Devraj, R. (2002). India's digital divide: An ever-widening chasm. http://unpan1.un.org/intradoc/groups/public/documents/apcity/unpan005099.pdf

Dhawan, H. (2012). Digital divide: IT boom in India left women behind, finds study. *Times of India* (March 8). http://articles.timesofindia.indiatimes.com/2012-03-08/india/31135572 _1_internet-users-mobile-phones-gender-gap

DiMaggio, P., Hargittai, E., Newman, W., & Robinson, J. (2001). Social implications of the internet. *Annual Review of Sociology, 27,* 307–336.

Esharenana, E., Okiy, R., & Ruteyan, J. (2003). A survey of cybercafés in Delta State, Nigeria. *Electronic Library, 21*(5), 487–495.

Evers, H., & Gerke, S. (2004). Closing the digital divide: Southeast Asia's path towards a knowledge society. Center for East and Southeast Asian Studies, Lund. http://www.genus.lu.se/images/Syd_och_sydostasienstudier/working_papers/evers_gelke.pdf

Eynon, R. (2009). Mapping the digital divide in Britain: Implications for learning and education. *Learning, Media and Technology, 34*(4), 277–290.

Falch, M. (2004). Tele-centers in Ghana. *Telematics and Informatics, 21*(1), 103–114.

Fandy, M. (1999). Cyberresistance: Saudi opposition between globalization and localization. *Comparative Studies in Society and History, 41,* 124–147.

Florida, R. (2004). *The rise of the creative class.* New York: Basic Books.

Friedman, E. (2005). The reality of virtual reality: The internet and gender equality advocacy in Latin America. *Latin American Politics and Society, 47*(3), 1–34.

Furuholt, B., & Kristiansen, S. (2005). Information dissemination in a developing society: Internet café users in Indonesia. *Electronic Journal on Information Systems in Developing Countries, 22*(3), 1–16. http://www.ejisdc.org

Guo, Y., & Chen, P. (2011). Digital divide and social cleavage: Case studies of ICT usage among peasants in contemporary China. *China Quarterly, 207,* 580–599.

Hafner, K., & Lyon, M. (1996). *Where wizards stay up late: The origins of the internet.* New York: Simon and Schuster.

Harden, B. (2007). Japan's warp-speed ride to internet future. *Washington Post* (August 29). http://www.washingtonpost.com/wp-dyn/content/article/2007/08/28/AR2007082801990.html

Helsper, E., Dutton, W., & Gerber, M. (2008). *To be a network society: A cross-national perspective on the internet in Britain.* Oxford Internet Institute, Research Report No. 17. Oxford.

Howard, P., Busch, L., & Sheets, P. (2010). Comparing digital divides: Internet access and social inequality in Canada and the United States. *Canadian Journal of Communication, 35*, 109–128.

Hugill, P. (1999). *Global Communications since 1844: Geopolitics and technology*. Baltimore: Johns Hopkins University Press.

Hunt, P. (2001). True stories: Telecentres in Latin America and the Caribbean. *Electronic Journal on Information Systems in Developing Countries, 4*(5), 1–17. http://www.ejisdc.org

Hwang, J. (2004). Digital divide in internet use within the urban hierarchy: The case of South Korea. *Urban Geography, 25*, 372–389.

Ishii, K. (2004). Internet use via mobile phone in Japan. *Telecommunications Policy, 28*, 43–58.

James, J. (2004). Reconstruing the digital divide from the perspective of a large, poor, developing country. *Journal of Information Technology, 19*, 172–177. http://arno.uvt.nl/show.cgi?fid=52153

Jing, X. (2007). Caught in the net. *Beijing Review, 50*, 18–20.

Jumaat, D. (2010). Indonesia reveals plan to bridge digital divide. *Asia Pacific FutureGov*. http://www.futuregov.asia/articles/2010/may/13/indonesia-reveals-plans-bridge-digital-divide/

Kaare, B., Brandtzaeg, P., Heim, J., & Endestad, T. (2007). In the borderland between family orientation and peer culture: The use of communication technologies among Norwegian tweens. *New Media & Society, 9*(4), 603–624.

Kalathil, S., & Boas, T. (2003). *Open networks, closed regimes: The impact of the internet on authoritarian rule*. Washington, DC: Carnegie Endowment for International Peace.

Keniston, K., & Kumar, D. (2004). *IT experience in India*. London: Sage.

Korupp, S., & Szydlik, M. (2005). Causes and trends of the digital divide. *European Sociological Review, 21*, 409–422.

Lam, D., Boyman, J., & Martin, B. (2004). Internet diffusion in Vietnam. *Technology in Society, 26*(1), 39–50.

Lambroschini, A. (2011). No Twitter revolt for Central Asia's closed regimes. http://Physorg.com (Feb. 24). http://www.physorg.com/news/2011-02-twitter-revolt-central-asia-regimes.html.

Lim, L. (2003). The internet, social reform, and networks in Indonesia. In N. Couldry & J. Curran (Eds.), *Contesting media power: Alternative media in a networked world* (pp. 273–288). Lanham, MD: Rowman and Littlefield.

Lupač, P., & Sladek J. (2008). The deepening of the digital divide in the Czech Republic. *Cyberpsychology: Journal of Psychosocial Research on Cyberspace* 2(1). http://www.cyberpsychology.eu/view.php?cisloclanku=2008060203

Malecki, E. (2002). The economic geography of the Internet's infrastructure. *Economic Geography, 78*, 399–424.

Mancebo, F. (2003). Cybercafe. In K. Christensen & D. Levinson (Eds.), *Encyclopedia of community: From the village to the virtual world* (pp. 368–371). River Edge, NJ: World Scientific Publishing.

Massey, D. (2005). *For space*. London: Sage.

Mayanja, J. (2003). *The African community telecentres: In search of sustainability*. Washington, DC: World Bank Institute.

Mercer, C. (2006). Telecentres and transformations: Modernizing Tanzania through the internet. *African Affairs, 105*(419), 243–264.

Mills, B., & Whitacre, B. (2003). Understanding the non-metropolitan–metropolitan digital divide. *Growth and Change, 34*(2), 219–243.

Mohan, A., Omar, A., & Aziz, A. (2004). ICT clusters as a way to materialize a national system of innovation: Malaysia's multimedia super corridor flagships. *Journal on Information Systems in Developing Countries, 16*(5), 1–8. http://www.ejisdc.org

Moi, A. (2009). Environmental governance through information: China and Vietnam. *Singapore Journal of Tropical Geography, 30*(1), 114–139.

Mujahid, Y. (2002). Digital opportunity initiative for Pakistan. *Electronic Journal on Information Systems in Developing Countries, 8*(6), 1–14. http://www.ejisdc.org/Ojs2/index.php/ejisdc/article/viewFile/45/45

Murphy, B. (2002). A critical history of the Internet. In G. Elmer (Ed.), *Critical perspectives on the Internet* (pp. 27–45). Lanham, MD: Rowman & Littlefield.

Mutula, S. (2003). Cyber café industry in Africa. *Journal of Information Science, 29*(6), 489–497.

Mwesige, P. (2003). Cyber elites: A survey of internet café users in Uganda. *Telematics and Informatics, 21*(1), 83–101.

Nair, M., Han, G., Lee, H., Goon, P., & Muda, R. (2010). Determinants of the digital divide in rural communities of a developing country: The case of Malaysia. *Development and Society, 39*(1), 139–162.

Nielson Mobile. (2008). Critical mass: The worldwide state of the mobile web. http://www.nielsenmobile.com/documents/CriticalMass.pdf.

Norris, P. (2001). *Digital divide: Civic engagement, information poverty, and the internet worldwide*. Cambridge: Cambridge University Press.

O'Lear, S. (1996). Using electronic mail (e-mail) surveys for geographic research: Lessons from a survey of Russian environmentalists. *Professional Geographer, 48*, 209–217.

OpenNet Initiative. (2010a). Kyrgyzstan. http://opennet.net/sites/opennet.net/files/ONI_Kyrgyzstan_2010.pdf

OpenNet Initiative. (2010b). Turkmenistan. http://opennet.net/research/profiles/turkmenistan

OpenNet Initiative. (2010c). Uzbekistan. http://opennet.net/sites/opennet.net/files/ONI_Uzbekistan_2010.pdf

Orviska, M., & Hudson, J. (2009). Dividing or uniting Europe. Internet usage in the EU. *Information Economics and Policy, 21*(4), 279–290.

Oyelaran-Oyeyinka, B., & Lal, K. (2005). Internet diffusion in sub-Saharan Africa: A cross country analysis. *Telecommunications Policy, 29*(7), 507–527.

Palmberg, C. (2002). Technological systems and competent procurers: The transformation of Nokia and the Finnish telecom industry revisited? *Telecommunications Policy, 26*, 129–148.

Perfiliev, Y. (2002). Development of the internet in Russia: Preliminary observations on its spatial and institutional characteristics. *Eurasian Geography and Economics, 43*(5), 411–421.

Privacy International. (2003). Silenced—Costa Rica. http://www.privacyinternational.org/article.shtml?cmd[347]=x-347-103752

Rao, M. (1999). Bringing the net to the masses: Cybercafés in Latin America. *On the Internet.* http://www.isoc.org/oti/articles/0199/rao2.html

Rao, S. (2005). Bridging digital divide: Efforts in India. *Telematics and Informatics, 22*, 361–375.

Reisdorf, B. (2011). Non-adoption of the internet in Great Britain and Sweden. *Information, Communication & Society, 14*(3), 400–420.

Sayer, P. (2006). France picks fight with digital divide. *Infoworld.* http://www.infoworld.com/t/networking/france-picks-fight-digital-divide-214

Schiesel, B. (2006). Land of the video geek. *New York Times*, October 8, p. 1. http://www.nytimes.com/2006/10/08/arts/

Schleife, K. (2010). What really matters: Regional versus individual determinants of the digital divide in Germany. *Research Policy, 39*(1), 173–185.

Sciadas, G. (2002). *The digital divide in Canada.* Ottawa: Statistics Canada.

Selwyn, N. (2002). 'E-stablishing' an inclusive society? Technology, social exclusion and UK government policy making. *Journal of Social Policy, 31*(1), 1–20.

Selwyn, N. (2004). Reconsidering political and popular understandings of the digital divide. *New Media & Society, 6*(3), 341–362.

Singh, S. (2010). Digital divide in India: Measurement, determinants and policy for addressing the challenges in bridging the digital divide. *International Journal of Innovation in the Digital Economy, 1*(2), 1–24.

Smith, A. (2010). Home broadband 2010. http://www.pewinternet.org/~/media//Files/Reports/2010/Home%20broadband%202010.pdf

Song, W. (2008). Development of the internet and digital divide in China: A spatial analysis. *Intercultural Communication Studies, 8*(3), 20–43. http://www.uri.edu/iaics/content/2008v17n3/03%20Wei%20Song.pdf

Srinivasan, R., & Fish, A. (2009). Internet authorship: Social and political implications withinKyrgyzstan. *Journal of Computer-Mediated Communication, 14*(3), 559–580.

Staple, G. (2007). *Telegeography 2007: Global telecommunications traffic statistics and commentary.* Washington, DC: Telegeography, Inc.

Steinbock, D. (2001). Assessing Finland's wireless valley: Can the pioneering continue? *Telecommunications Policy, 25,* 71–100.

Surborg, B. (2009). Is it the 'development of underdevelopment' all over again? Internet development in Vietnam. *Globalizations, 6*(2), 225–247.

Thirumal, P., & Tartakov, G. (2011). India's Dalits search for a democratic opening in the digital divide. In P. Leigh (Ed.), *International exploration of technological equity and the digital divide: Critical, historical and social perspectives* (pp. 20–39). London: IGI Global Press.

Thulin, E., & Vilhelmson, B. (2005). Virtual mobility of urban youth: ICT-based communication in Sweden. *Tijdschrift voor Economische en Social Geografie, 96*(5), 477–487.

Tipton, F. (2002). Bridging the digital divide: Pilot agencies and policy implementation in Thailand, Malaysia, Vietnam, and the Philippines. *ASEAN Economic Bulletin, 19*(1), 83–99.

Troianovski, A., & Finn, P. (2007). Kremlin seeks to extend its reach in cyberspace. *Washington Post,* October 28, p. 1. http://www.washingtonpost.com/wp-dyn/content/article/2007/10/27/AR2007102701384_pf.html

Vicente, M., & López, A. (2011). Assessing the regional digital divide across the European Union-27. *Telecommunications Policy, 35*(3), 220–237.

Warf, B. (1995). Telecommunications and the changing geographies of knowledge transmission in the late 20th century. *Urban Studies, 32,* 361–378.

Warf, B. (2001). Segueways into cyberspace: Multiple geographies of the digital divide. *Environment and Planning B: Planning and Design, 28,* 3–19.

Warf, B. (2006). International competition between satellite and fiber optic carriers: A geographic perspective. *Professional Geographer, 58,* 1–11.

Warf, B. (2007). Geopolitics of the satellite industry. *Tijdschrift voor Economische en Sociale Geografie, 98,* 385–397.

Warf, B., & Vincent, P. (2007). Multiple geographies of the Arab internet. *Area, 39,* 83–96.

Wei, C., & Kolko, B. (2005). Resistance to globalization: Language and internet diffusion patterns in Uzbekistan. *New Review of Hypermedia and Multimedia, 11*(2), 205–220.

Wheeler, D. (2004). The internet in the Arab world: Digital divides and cultural connections. http://www.riifs.org/guest/lecture_text/internet_n_arabworld_all_txt.htm

Wheeler, D. (2006). Empowering publics: Information technology and democratization in the Arab world—Lessons from internet cafes and beyond. Oxford Internet Institute research report no. 11. http://www.oii.ox.ac.uk/research/publications.cfm

Wilson, E., & Wong, K. (2003). African information revolution: A balance sheet. *Telecommunications Policy, 27*(1–2), 155–177.

Wu, I. (2004). Canada, South Korea, Netherlands and Sweden: Regulatory implications of the convergence of telecommunications, broadcasting and Internet services. *Telecommunications Policy, 28,* 79–96.

Chapter 3
Global Internet Censorship

Of all of the innumerable myths that swarm around cyberspace, one of the most insidious is that the internet is an inherently emancipatory tool, a device that necessarily and inevitably promotes democracy by giving voice to those who lack political power, and in so doing undermines authoritarian and repressive governments. President Ronald Reagan, for example, asserted that "The Goliath of totalitarianism will be brought down by the David of the microchip" (quoted in Kalathil and Boas 2003, p. 1), while the chair of Citicorp, Walter Wriston (1997, p. 74) argued that "the virus of freedom ... is spread by electronic networks to the four corners of the earth." Oh that such optimistic proclamations were true. Drawing on modernizationist theories of development, in which rising education levels and information access led inexorably to a liberalization of the public sphere via a well informed, rationale public that asserts itself politically, prevailing discourses about the politics of the internet tend to be couched in an unrealistic utopianism rooted in technological determinism and a silence regarding the perpetuation of inequality. Such visions appeal widely to Western policy makers, who may exaggerate the extent and power of ostensibly freedom-loving cyberdissidents. Closely associated with this idea is that the global community of netizens is a self-governing one in which the state has become largely irrelevant (Goldsmith and Wu 2006).

The reality, unfortunately, is more complex and depressing, and the necessary corrective calls for a state-centered approach. As Lake (2009) notes, "the Web is not nearly the implacable force for freedom that some of its champions have portrayed. The world's authoritarians have shown just as much aptitude for technology as their discontented citizens." Many governments across the planet aggressively limit access to the internet, and as Kalathil and Boas (2003) demonstrate, internet opposition to censorship and political activism is typically confined to small groups of educated individuals, often diasporas, and has relatively little impact among the masses of their. "Censorship," of course, means many things and takes many different forms: parents who restrict their children's access to pornography or corporations that monitor their employees at work are examples. The focus here, however, is on government restrictions on internet access.

B. Warf, *Global Geographies of the Internet*, SpringerBriefs in Geography,   45
DOI: 10.1007/978-94-007-1245-4_3, © The Author(s) 2013

Internet accessibility reflects, *inter alia*, the willingness of governments to allow or encourage their populations to log-into cyberspace. Repressive governments often fear the emancipatory potential of the internet, which allows individuals to circumvent tightly controlled media. Theorizations of internet censorship can draw fruitfully on contemporary geographic discussions of the state, power, and discourse. Foucauldian perspectives loom large in this regard. Critical analyses of cyberspace, for example, point to geosurveillance, invasions of privacy, and the formation of digital panopticons (Crampton 2007; Dobson and Fisher 2007). Such work has demonstrated that clearly the internet can be made to work against people as well as for them. Far from being innately emancipatory in nature, cyberspace can be used to reinforce hegemonic powers, cultivate a climate of fear, and prevent or minimize dissent.

3.1 Motivations and Mechanisms of Internet Censorship

There are multiple motivations for internet censorship, and thus several forms and types, including political repression of dissidents, human rights activists, or comments insulting to the state (e.g., in China, Iran, Burma/Myanmar); religious controls to inhibit the dissemination of ideas deemed heretical or sacrilegious (as found in many Arab states); protections of intellectual property, including restrictions on illegally downloaded movies and music; or cultural restrictions that exist as part of the oppression of ethnic minorities (e.g., refusal to allow government websites in certain languages) or sexual minorities (i.e., gays and lesbians). Typically, governments that seek to impose censorship do so using the excuse of protecting public morality from ostensible sins such as pornography or gambling, although more recently combating terrorism has emerged as a favorite rationale. Deliberately vague notions of national security and social stability are typically invoked as well. Other proponents hold that some degree of censorship is needed to combat "cyberanarchy" (Goldsmith 1998) or to prevent crime (Katyal 2001).

Governments face a choice in the degree of censorship, including its *scope* (or range of topics) and *depth* (or degree of intervention), which ranges from allowing completely unfettered flows of information (e.g., Denmark) to prohibiting access to the internet altogether (e.g., North Korea); most opt for a position between these two poles. Thus, the conflict between internet free speech and national territorial laws speaks to the notion that the "power container" of the nation-state has sustained mounting "leakages" to and from the world-system. Most frequently, interventions to limit access or shape the contents of cyberspace reflect highly centralized power structures, notably authoritarian one-party countries concerned with an erosion of legitimacy. As Villeneuve (2006) points out, countries seeking sovereignty over their cyber-territories often generate unintended consequences to censorship (e.g., diminished innovation, negative publicity that may lead to pariah status, reduced tourism, or offended corporations), results that policy makers rarely anticipate or acknowledge when putting such systems into place.

Essentially, censorship involves control over internet access, functionality, and contents (Eriksson and Giacomello 2009). Precise filtering is almost impossible, but there is a wide variety of methods are used to control the flow of digital information, including requiring discriminatory ISP licenses, content filtering based on keywords, redirection of users to proxy servers, rerouting packets destined for a specific IP address to a blacklist, website blocking of a list of IP addresses, tapping and surveillance, chat room monitoring, discriminatory or prohibitive pricing policies, hardware and software manipulation, hacking into opposition websites and spreading viruses, denial-of-service (DOS) attacks that overload servers or network connections using "bot herders," temporary just-in-time blocking at moments when political information is critical, such as elections, and harassment of bloggers (e.g., via libel laws or invoking national security). Content filtering often relies on keyword matching algorithms that evolve as the Internet's lingo changes, and filtering may occur at the levels of the ISP, the domain name, a particular IP address, or a specific URL. Most forms of filtering are difficult to detect technically: the user may not even know that censorship is at work. Most ISPs lack the ability to block transmission to an individual IP address or URL, so governments undertaking this task in volume frequently purchase foreign (usually American) software for this purpose. Filtering mechanisms suffer the risk of overblocking, or "false positives," i.e., blocking access to sites that were not intended to be censored, and underblocking, or "false negatives," i.e., allowing access to sites that were intended to be prohibited (Murdoch and Anderson 2008). Most common and particularly important is self-censorship, as the bulk of casual internet users well understand the boundaries of politically acceptable use within their respective states. Often cultivating a persuasive, hegemonic view of dominant powers is more efficient than outright force. Typically both persuasion and coercion are combined as local contexts demand. Once formal censorship is initiated, no matter how benign or transparent, the temptation to enlarge its scope, or what Villeneuve (2006) calls "mission creep," is always there.

The institutions used to enforce such policies, which are typically outgrowths of older media regulatory regimes concerned with newspapers, radio, and television, are usually government ministries of information and communication. The degree of centrality in the management of internet censorship varies considerably. Because the state is not a monolithic entity but composed of diverse agencies, sometimes working at cross-purposes, rather than view censorship as the simple repression of oppositional discourses it is more instructive to think of it in terms of multiple, sometimes contradictory authorities that invoke diverse strategies of suppression of various groups and individuals for a broad array of reasons and motivations. Adding to this complexity is the rapidity with which the internet has grown and changed technologically; often government censors have difficulty keeping up-to-date with changing technologies (e.g., text messaging) or slang terms used to communicate hidden meanings.

The degree and type of internet censorship obviously varies widely and reflects how democratic and open to criticism different political systems are. Reporters

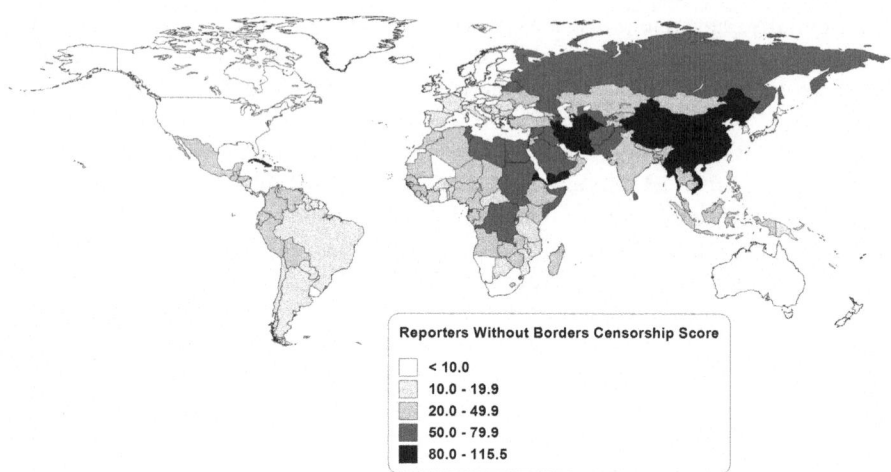

Fig. 3.1 Map of Reporters Without Borders internet censorship rankings, 2011. *Source* data drawn from http://en.rsf.org/press-freedom-index-2011-2012,1043.html

Without Borders, an NGO headquartered in Paris and one of the world's preeminent judges of censorship, ranks governments across the planet in terms of the severity of their internet censorship (Fig. 3.1; see also Quirk 2006). Their index of internet censorship is generated from surveys of 50 questions sent to legal experts, reporters, and scholars in each country. Thus, countries in northern Europe, the U.S. and Canada, Australia and New Zealand, and Japan exhibit minimal or no censorship (scores < 10). Conversely, a rogue's list of the world's worst offenders, including China, Vietnam, Burma/Myanmar, Iran, and Turkmenistan, exhibit the planet's most severe and extensive restrictions (scores > 80). In North Korea, internet access is illegal, although the government uses it to send messages to the outside world (Hachigian 2002). In between these extremes lies a vast array of states with modest to moderate forms of internet censorship that reflect their diverse systems of governance, the presence or absence of civil liberties, and the ability of various groups to resist limitations on their ability or right to use the internet in whatever manner they so prefer. Using the categories of Fig. 3.1, Table 3.1 summarizes the distribution of the world's population and internet users according to the level of severity of censorship. Thus, only 13 % of the world's people, but a third of internet users, live in countries with minimal censorship; conversely, roughly one-quarter of the world's people and internet users live under governments that engage in very heavy censorship (the vast bulk of whom are located in China).

Internet penetration rates—the proportion of the population with regular access to cyberspace at home, school, or work—also shape the contours of censorship geography. Penetration rates have important implications for state attempts at control. In impoverished states, in which penetration rates are low and users rely heavily on cybercafes, censorship is relatively easy and resistance is futile. However, falling prices for personal computers, expansion of home ownership,

Table 3.1 Global population and internet users by severity of internet censorship, 2011

RWB[a] Score	Population (000s)	%	Internet Users (000s)	%
0–9	912,137	13.4	629,208	31.9
10–19	743,610	10.9	320,059	16.2
20–49	2,826,536	41.5	400,853	20.3
50–79	732,971	10.8	139,775	7.1
80–115	1,602,751	23.5	480,462	24.4
Total	6,818,006	100.0	1,970,357	100.0

[a] Reporters without borders
Source Calculated by author

and rising technological prowess of users generate a population that is more difficult to monitor and discipline. Moreover, rising incomes, literacy rates, and technical skills often lead to modernizing elites that actively resist censorship through organized means. Indeed, unlike traditional media such as newspapers and television, whose centralized structures make them amenable to state control, the decentralized, rhizomic, interactive structure of the internet makes it much more difficult for state authorities to manipulate. Nonetheless, it should be remembered that "it is actually easier for a government to computer search vast quantities of E-mail than to open regular mail or monitor tapped telephones" (Dunn 2000, p. 467). There is no guarantee, however, that censorship measures succeed. As Hachigian (2002, p. 41) points out, "The subtle choices regimes make about how to treat the Internet are designed to reinforce their broader strategies for retaining power, and those choices do not predict regime viability in a clear way."

However, internet censorship should be seen as part of a more complex array of contested relations in cyberspace: the Web is not simply a tool a tool of government control, but an arena of conflict. Thus, the internet also serves a variety of counter-hegemonic purposes, including human rights groups and ethnic or political movements in opposition to governments (Warf and Grimes 1997; Kreimer 2001; Crampton 2003). Attempts at censorship are often resisted, sometimes successfully, by local cyberactivists, such as through the use of anonymizing proxy servers in other countries that encrypt users' data and cloak their identities. Today, numerous groups in civil society use the medium to connect isolated once-invisible populations (e.g., gays and lesbians), unite and empower women's movements, give voice to human rights activists, and allow political minorities to promote their own agendas. Thus, internet usage both reflects and in turn shapes prevailing political orders. In authoritarian regimes with relatively weak civil societies, opposition to state-control is often weak and ineffectual; in more democratic states, opposition can be organized, vociferous, and effectual. When seen as a contested terrain of political struggle, the interactions between government internet censors and the various groups that resist such impositions resembles a cat-and-mouse game that continually evolves over time. As the context of internet censorship changes, including rising penetration rates, deregulation of telecommunications providers, and new geopolitical circumstances (e.g., openness to foreign investment), both government authorities and their opponents resort to changing tactics. Overt control over cybercafés, for example, may give way to government blockages of dissident websites, while opposition groups may utilize foreign proxy servers, anonymizing software, or texting by cell phones to circumvent such obstacles. The outcome of such contestations is inevitably path dependent, contingent, and unpredictable.

In this light, a rough sequence of stages of internet censorship summarizes the major forms of state political intervention as they vary over time. Generally, authoritarian governments in countries with low internet penetration rates resort to relatively crude measures, such as restricting public access through licenses and monitoring of cybercafes. A national, sanitized intranet may be offered as a substitute for the global internet. Cuba, Vietnam, and Burma/Myanmar exemplify this approach. As more people move on-line, including rising home personal computer ownership rates, a more complex, expensive, and cumbersome set of censorship mechanisms is called for, including firewalls and blocking or filtering web-site access. Arrests and imprisonment of cyberdissidents may be common. China, Kazakhstan, and Saudi Arabia are prime exemplars of these tactics. A third stage involves widespread internet access, in which "soft" censorship tactics are the norm, particularly self-censorship and encouraging ISPs to police their users. Singapore and Russia illustrate this type and degree of government intervention. Finally, at least in the hopes of many optimistic observers, widespread internet usage can overwhelm the state's capacity to control dissent, as in northern Europe and the U.S. and Canada.

3.2 Regional Configurations of Internet Censorship

There is a highly uneven topography of internet censorship around the globe, one that reflects the geographies of the world's diverse political systems, the extent of internet penetration rates, the social, cultural, and economic constitutions of various societies, and the degree of political opposition. Such complexity means that patterns of internet censorship do not lend themselves readily to pat characterizations but require a more detailed, case-by-case analysis. The uneven landscapes of internet censorship reflect the complex intersections between the growth of cyberspace and a large variety of regional, national, and local political and cultural contexts. Decisions of whether and how to regulate internet access reflect the degree of centralization of political control, cultural attitudes toward dissent, and geopolitical concerns, particularly for states seeking to attract foreign investment. For example, countries seeking to promote development of an information technology sector or international exports of services (e.g., Malaysia), including tourism, are often concerned that internet censorship can diminish the revenues from such efforts. This section explores internet censorship in various world regions to illustrate that like other aspects of cyberspace, including e-commerce and e-governance, the dynamics of censorship are intimately enfolded in regional and national political structures.

3.2.1 China

In a country with more than 513 million internet users in December, 2011, Chinese internet censorship is arguably the world's most severe (Kahn 2002). The Communist Party of China has long exerted strict, centralized control over flows of information within and across the nation's borders, largely through the Ministry of Information Industry (MII), although internet policing is conducted primarily through the Ministry of State Security. The state has encouraged internet usage, but only within an environment that it controls, and cyberspace in China remains relatively free compared to the traditional media. In the early phases of internet development, the state did little to regulate cyberspace, but as chat rooms and blogs pushed the boundaries of allowable dissent with a steady stream of criticism of government officials, it began to tighten control significantly after 2000 (Bi 2001). Indeed, for the first decade the internet likely strengthened the government's control, although as China's population of netizens grew explosively, it increasingly became a vehicle for challenges to the state's authority (Hachigian 2001), leading to increasingly harsh repression. In 2005, the OpenNet Initiative (2005) declared that "China operates the most extensive, technologically sophisticated, and broad-reaching system of internet filtering in the world." The Chinese government has been blunt in its justification for censorship, asserting its necessity to maintain a "harmonious society."

The government deploys a vast array of measures collectively but informally known as the "Great Firewall," which includes publicly employed monitors and citizen volunteers, screens blogs and email messages for potential threats to the established political order. There are numerous components to the Great Firewall that operate with varying degrees of effectiveness. International internet connections to China are squeezed through a selected group of state-controlled backbone networks. Popular access to many common Web services, such as Google and Yahoo!, is heavily restricted (MacKinnon 2008; Paltemaa and Vuori 2009). The national government hires armies of low-paid commentators, commonly called by the derogatory term the "five-mao party," (slang for the cash amount of 50 cents), to monitor blogs and chat rooms, inserting comments that "spin" issues in a light favorable to the Chinese state. Some municipal governments take censorship into their own hands: Beijing, for example, uses 10,000 volunteer internet monitors (Wines 2010). However, a large share of censorship occurs via internet companies themselves (MacKinnon 2009), which monitor chat rooms, blogs, networking services, search engines, and video sites for politically sensitive material in order to conform to government restrictions. Websites that help users circumvent censorship like anonymizer.com and proxify.com are prohibited. Users who attempt to access blocked sites are confronted by Jingjing and Chacha, two cartoon police officers who inform them that they are being monitored. Instant messaging and mobile phone text messaging services are heavily filtered, including a program called QQ, which is automatically installed on users' computers to monitor communications. Blogs critical of the government are frequently dismantled, although for the most part the government out-sources this function to blog-hosting companies (MacKinnon 2008). In 2006, for example, Microsoft's MSN Spaces blog-hosting site agreed to conform to government "guidelines" in return for freedom from censorship at the ISP level. The popular service Sina Weibo, with 300 million microbloggers, uses a point system to monitor politically objectionable comments: after an initial allocation of 80 points, users have points deducted until they reach zero, when their blog is terminated (Wines 2012). In June, 2009, the government attempted to require manufacturers to install filtering software known as Green Dam Youth Escort on all new computers, but retreated in the face of a massive popular and corporate outcry (LaFraniere 2009), a lawsuit from a California firm, Cybersitter, alleging that China stole its software (Crovitz 2010), and the fact that Green Dam inadvertently jammed government computers (Lake 2009). In response, Falun Gong released a program to circumvent it called Green Tsunami.

The Great Firewall system began in 2006 under an initiative known as the "Golden Shield," a national surveillance network that China developed with the aid of U.S. companies Nortel and Cisco Systems (Lake 2009) and extended beyond the internet to include digital identification cards with microchips containing personal data that allow the state to recognize faces and voices of its 1.3 billion plus inhabitants. The envy of authoritarian governments worldwide, the Golden Shield has been exported to Cuba, Iran, and Belarus. Indeed, in many respects, China's state-led program of internet development serves as a model for other authoritarian governments elsewhere.

The Chinese government has periodically initiated shutdowns of data centers housing servers for websites and online bulletin boards, disrupting use for millions. Email services like Gmail and Hotmail are frequently jammed; before the 2008 Olympics, Facebook sites of critics were blocked. In 2007, the State Administration of Radio, Film and Television mandated that all video sharing sites must be state owned. Police frequently patrol internet cafes, where users must supply personal information in order to log on, while web site administrators are legally required to hire censors popularly known as "cleaning ladies" or "big mamas" (Kalathil and Boas 2003).

At times government censorship can generate problems with foreign investors. The government for years blocked access to *The New York Times*, until its editors complained directly to President Jiang Zemin, but left the web site for *USA Today* unmolested (Hachigian 2002). In the Chinese case, Google, the world's largest single provider of free Internet services, famously established a separate, politically correct (by China's government standards) website, Google.cn, which censors itself to comply with restrictions demanded by the Chinese state, arguing that the provision of incomplete, censored information was better than none at all (Dann and Haddow 2008). In early 2010, responding to the ensuing international criticism, Google announced it would no longer cooperate with Chinese internet authorities and withdrew from China. Untroubled, the Chinese government promotes its home-grown search engines such as Baidu, Sohu, and Sina.com, which present few such difficulties.

Finally, the Chinese state has arrested and detained several internet users who ventured into politically sensitive areas. Although it cannot monitor all websites in the countries, the state pursues the intimidation strategy popularly known as "killing the chicken to scare the monkeys" (Harwit and Clark 2001). Reporters Without Borders reported in 2008 that China had incarcerated 49 cyberdissidents, the most in the world. For example, cyberjournalist Hu Jia, winner of the European Sakharov Prize for Freedom of Thought, was sentenced to 3½ years in prison in 2008 for "inciting subversion of state power." Human rights activist Huang Qi received a similar sentence that same year for posting criticisms of the Sichuan earthquake relief efforts. Librarian Liu Jin received 3 years for downloading information about the organization Falun Gong, which China treats as terrorists. China's best known blogger, Zhou Shuguang, was prohibited from traveling to Germany to judge an international blogging competition. Others have been prosecuted for posting or downloading information about Tibetan independence, Taiwanese separatism, or the Tiananmen Square massacre. No avenue exists to repeal censorship decisions.

Such measures have helped to limit the use of the web by democracy and human rights advocates, Tibet separatists, and religious groups such as Falun Gong. They also help proactively to sway public opinion in favor of the state. However, given the polymorphous nature of the web, such restrictions eventually fail sooner or later. By accessing foreign proxy servers, a few intrepid Chinese netizens engage in *fanqiang*, or "scaling the wall" (Stone and Barboza 2010). Using its programmers in the U.S., Falun Gong has developed censorship-circumventing software called Freegate, which it has offered to dissidents elsewhere, particularly in Iran (Lake 2009). Chinese censorship and its resistance thus form a continually change front of strategies and tactics: As one Chinese blogger put it, "It is like a water flow—if you block one direction, it flows to other directions, or overflows" (quoted in James 2009).

3.2.2 Russia, Ukraine, and Belarus

The archipelago of countries consisting of Russia and neighboring states—a region long known for many governments that resist transparency, abuse human rights, and rely on state-controlled media—exhibits numerous attempts to restrict access to the internet as well as govern its contents. In Russia, where the conventional media are already under tight government control, the Putin government gradually sought to extend its influence over the internet, essentially following the Chinese model of granting the secret service extensive monitoring powers, ostensibly on the grounds of fighting corruption (Troianovski and Finn 2007). As Russia's penetration rate increased, threatening to broaden the sphere of public debate and give rise to autonomous voices, the administration responded by purchasing independent websites, promoting pro-government websites, and fostering a network of government-friendly bloggers. Russia's internet surveillance law, the System for Operational-Investigative Activities, allows state security services unfettered physical access to ISPs and requires them to report statistics about users, and has been emulated, to one extent or another, by other countries in this region. In Ukraine, where the internet remains relatively free, the state-owned provider Ukrtelecom is the largest ISP in the country; even here, however, government officials have raided the offices of on-line newspapers, such as *Obkom*, on national security grounds. In 2003 the Ukrainian Parliament passed the Law on Protection of Public Morals (OpenNet Initiative 2007). Under the guise of combating terrorism, the Ukrainian state has held that censorship is necessary to secure the "national information space".

In Belarus, whose government Reporters Without Borders called one of the world's "bitterest enemies of the Internet," President Lukashenko claimed that he would "put an end to the anarchy" online and would "not allow humanity's great technical achievement to become a news sewer" (Reporters Without Borders 2008). The point was backed up by the presence of government troops at internet cafes. All Belarussian ISPs are required to connect through Belpak, a subsidiary of the state-controlled ISP Beltelecom. During the 2006 presidential elections the government launched "just-in-time" cyberattacks against opposition party websites, which often mysteriously suffered frequent disconnections.

3.2.3 South Asia

India, despite its generally democratic practice of governance, has nonetheless also engaged in moderate internet censorship. In 2000, the Indian Parliament approved the Information Technology Act to crack down on cybercrime, allowing cybercafes and internet users' homes to be searched without warrants as part of criminal investigations. It also allowed the government to block access to sites considered pornographic or that "endanger public order, the integrity and security of the nation and relations with other countries." Those setting up "anti-Indian" websites can be jailed for up to 5 years (Reporters Without Borders 2004, p. 1). In 2002, India enacted the Prevention of Terrorism Ordinance Act authorizing the government to monitor electronic communications, including personal email. The Indian cybercafé association, the Association of Public Internet Access Providers, strenuously protested against the measures, which it said would lead to the closure of most of the country's 3,000 or so cybercafés.

The Pakistan Telecommunications Authority (PTA) repeatedly filters internet content deemed to be irreligious, antimilitary, or secessionist. All international traffic to and from the country is routed through three sites owned by Pakistan Internet Exchange, with locations in Islamabad, Lahore, and Karachi. The 2006 Net Café Regulation bill requires internet cafes to monitor patrons, although its enforcement has been dubious (Reporters Without Borders 2004). The PTA has banned dozens of URLs that published Danish cartoons ridiculing the Prophet Mohammed; indeed, the Pakistani police attempt to register all websites containing "blasphemous material" (Ahmed 2002). Baluchi nationalist and human rights sites are also blacklisted. The Pakistani cybercommunity responded to these initiatives with a "Don't Block the Blog" campaign (http://dbtb.org/), which, among other things, has exposed the military's numerous civil rights violations.

3.2.4 Southeast Asia

Many countries in Southeast Asia exhibit multiple forms of internet censorship. Many governments in the region often justify such intervention on the grounds that they share "Asian values" ostensibly at odds with Western notions of democratic access (Hachigian 2002). In Thailand, the number of blocked websites jumped markedly after the military coup of January, 2006. When YouTube posted a silly video ridiculing King Bhumibol Adulyadej in 2007, the government temporarily banned the website entirely throughout the country and deported the producer, a Swiss national, back to his country.

Vietnam's Leninist state has long pursued a rigid path of internet censorship (Pierre 2000). The country's sole ISP with a license for international connections, Vietnam Data Communications, is a subsidiary of the government telecommunications monopoly. Domestic content providers must obtain special licenses from the Ministry of the Interior and lease connections from the state-owned Vietnam Post and Telecommunications Corporation. The state uses a complex system of firewalls, access controls, and strenuously encouraged self-censorship. E-mail is regularly monitored by searches for key words. Vietnam has imprisoned those who dare to use the internet to speak out against the government, such as Pham Hong, a doctor who posted an online article calling for democracy (International Censorship Explorer 2006). Owners of cybercafés who permit searches of unauthorized websites by their clients face fines of 5 million dong, roughly US$330 (Kalathil and Boas 2003). Despite the liberalization efforts known as *doi moi*, the Vietnamese Communist Party keeps a firm grip on cybertraffic, particularly internet sites considered to be "offensive to Vietnamese culture" (Human Rights Watch 2002). In 2003, the government lashed out at Reporters Without Borders after the organization listed the country as one of the world's 15 worst censors of the internet.

The government of Burma/Myanmar, according to the OpenNet Initiative (2005, p. 4), "implements one of the world's most restrictive regimes of Internet control." The ruling junta, the State Peace and Development Council, bars 84 % of sites "with content known to be sensitive to the Burmese state." It also excludes email sites such as Hotmail and Yahoo because they cannot be monitored for political criticism, and pornography. The 1996 Computer Science Development Law requires that all network-ready computers be registered with the Ministry of

Communications, Posts and Telegraphs. Burma/Myanmar has only two internet service providers, and both outlets charge high prices for email accounts. To implement its censorship, the government purchases software from the U.S. company Fortinet to block access to selected websites and servers. At times, the state has resorted to blunter instruments: when it sought to silence demonstrators in 2007, it switched off the country's internet network altogether for 6 weeks.

Seeking to encourage growth of his country's information technology sector, Malaysian Prime Minister Mahatir Mohamad declared publicly in 1996 that there would be no censorship of the internet, in part to give his country an edge over neighboring rival Singapore. As a result, "pro-reform websites have matured from a cacophony of accusatory and insulting diatribes into an alternative, independent media" (Abbott 2001, p. 105). However, in 2002, the Malaysian government signaled its intent to require website operators to obtain licenses precisely for the purpose of monitoring content, and has tried to restrict Muslim fundamentalists from publishing on the web. The country's famed Multimedia Corridor, however, designed to attract foreign investors, remains a censorship-free zone, revealing that the geographies of censorship vary not only among countries but within them as well.

The authoritarian government of Singapore, one of the world's best-connected and technologically dynamic countries, also censors the internet regularly (Rodan 2000). Its primary vehicle in this regard is the Singapore Media Development Authority (MDA), which has regulated internet content under the guise of monitoring a broadcasting service since 1996. All ISPs are automatically licensed by the Singapore Broadcasting Authority, which routes all internet connections through government proxy servers. Licensees are required to comply with the 1996 Internet Code of Practice, which includes a definition of "prohibited material," i.e., content that it deems "objectionable on the grounds of public interest, public morality, public order, public security, national harmony, or is otherwise prohibited by applicable Singapore laws" (OpenNet Initiative 2006, p. 3). Moreover, "the government has at times taken unannounced strolls through several thousand personal computers with internet connections, subsequently explaining such actions as sweeping for viruses or pornography" (Kalathil and Boas 2003, p. 78). Self-censorship is also encouraged as a means to stifle political expression. The use of lawsuits under stringent defamation laws is also common, and can reach well beyond the island's perimeter. For example, Jiahoa Chen, a Singaporean student at the University of Illinois, was forced to shut down his caustic.blog under threat from the government-run Agency for Science, Technology, and Research (OpenNet Initiative 2006). As a result of these measures, Singapore's government has achieved near-total control over its internet environment with minimal loss of political legitimacy. Zittrain and Palfrey (2008), however, argue that Singapore's censorship has been exaggerated and is largely confined to a handful of pornographic websites.

3.2.5 Central Asia

Central Asia exhibits a pronounced tendency toward heavy internet censorship. For example, the same "event-based filtering" practiced by the Belarussian government occurred in Kyrgyzstan during the 2005 parliamentary elections there. In Uzbekistan, ISP providers must operate under government control, the government's web filter, Uzpak, enjoys a monopoly over international connections, monitors all internet traffic in the country, and the government often shuts down uzbekistanerk.org and birlik.net, the Web sites belonging to the largest opposition parties (Privacy International2003). In Kazakhstan, a journalist from the news website kub.kz, Kazis Toguzbayev, was given a 2 year prison sentence in 2008 for posting an article accusing the regime of protecting the killers of opposition leader Altynbek Sarsenbayev. Invoking an older Soviet tradition, Uzbek internet journalists who publish criticisms of the government are occasionally forced into psychiatric hospitals. The dictator of Turkmenistan, Saparmurat Niyazov, another of Reporters Without Borders's ardent "enemies of the Internet," strove to keep that country hermetically sealed from the outside world via a national intranet, although his successor, Gurbanguly Berdymukhammedov, vowed to open it up to the global internet. This promise was belied, however, by the presence of government soldiers at the doors of internet cafes (Eurasianet.org 2007). Cybercafes in which customers attempt to access banned websites are routinely closed.

McGlinchey and Johnson (2007) studied the divergent censorship paths found in the region and concluded that in Central Asian countries where international aid groups and NGOs provide assistance with the internet (e.g., infrastructure funding), governments tend to be more permissive and less restrictive about internet access. They argue (p. 275) that

> where international NGOs and bilateral and multilateral donors provide capital and assistance in drafting legislation, such as in Kyrgyzstan, Tajikistan, and to a lesser extent Uzbekistan, the formal regulatory framework is more open, clearly articulated, and permissive of electronic media. ... ICT development demands ongoing negotiations with and aid from willing foreign partners. And it is the iterative nature of this relationship that provides Western donors the ability to ensure conditionality—that is substantive reform—in return for ICT aid.

The Nazarbaev regime in Kazakhstan, for example, which can use its oil and gas revenues to purchase ICT equipment, has received less assistance from foreign organizations and has thus been relatively free to curtail internet access. Nonetheless, since 2009 Kazakhstan has enacted draconian censorship laws to the internet and traditional media alike (Lambroschini 2011) under the Kazakh Agency for Information Technology and Communications. ISPs in the country must retain electronic records of the internet activities of clients. A Kazakh journalist from the news website kub.kz, Kazis Toguzbayev, was given a 2-year prison sentence in 2008 for posting an article accusing the regime of protecting the killers of opposition leader Altynbek Sarsenbayev.

Central Asian internet censorship takes a variety of forms, and is typically justified through the excuses of protecting public morality from decadent or anti-Islamic ideas or combating terrorism and Islamist extremism. In Afghanistan, internet usage only began in 2001 following the ouster of the Taliban, which held that the web allowed foreign and anti-Islamic obscenities to enter the country. During the 2005 parliamentary elections, the government of Kyrgyzstan launched "just-in-time" distributed denial of service cyberattacks against opposition party websites, and the government closed internet connections to neighboring countries (Schwartz 2005). The Kyrgyz government's botnet used to launch the attacks also affected servers in the U.S., whose protests then forced the attacks to cease. Despite its severe control over non-digital media, Kyrgyz cyberspace is relatively deregulated and the government has relatively straightforward rules governing internet access, which may reflect its reliance on foreign aid organizations (McGlinchey and Johnson 2007; Srinivasan and Fish 2009).

A growing community of Central Asian cyberactivists resists these attempts (see EurasiaNet.org). Across Central Asia, netizens have struggled to protect internet freedoms, including Uzbekistan (Machleder 2002), where the Uzbek "For a Free Internet!" campaign has monitored bills in the lower house of parliament, the Mazhlis, which attempted to extend the government's censorship. In Kyrgyzstan, the internet and other media played an instrumental role in the Tulip Revolution of 2005 that led to the ousting of President Askar Akayev. The Tajik government's attempts to criminalize some forms of cyber-speech as libel against the state were met with heated opposition led by Nuriddin Qarshiboev, head of the National Association for Independent Media in Tajikistan. Moreover, Tajik cyber-journalists petitioned the government to abolish the requirement that the president be called "worthy" and "reliable" every time he was mentioned. More recently, those seeking to avoid government censorship can download software designed to help them do so, such as the Canadian "censorship circumvention" program Psiphon.

While Azeri internet provision is highly centralized via two state-owned ISPs, the Azeri web remains relatively free from government filtering. Nonetheless, when two Azeri bloggers posted a video ridiculing the government's purchase of high-priced donkeys, they were arrested (Barry 2009).

The internet has also been used against the state in several such countries. Between 2003 and 2005, Ukraine, Georgia, and Kyrgyzstan all experienced "color revolutions," in which opposition parties utilized the web as an integral part of their strategy and suffered just-in-time blocking by their governments (Warf 2009). A growing community of Eurasian cyberactivists resists internet censorship (see Eurasianet.org). The Uzbek "For a Free Internet!" campaign, for example, has monitored bills in the lower house of parliament, the Mazhlis, which attempt to extend the government's censorship. The Tajik government's attempts to criminalize some forms of cyber-speech as libel against the state were met with heated opposition led by Nuriddin Qarshiboev, head of the National Association for Independent Media in Tajikistan. Moreover, Tajik cyber-journalists petitioned the government to abolish the requirement that the president be called "worthy" and "reliable" every time he was mentioned. More recently, those seeking to avoid government censorship can download software designed to help them do so, such as the Canadian "censorship circumvention" program Psiphon.

3.2.6 Middle East

In most of the Arab world, the media are closely monitored and controlled by governments, either through laws and regulations or via direct ownership in state monopolies (Warf and Vincent 2007). Cyber-journalists, editors, and bloggers may face penalties for "slighting the Islamic faith," blaspheming government officials, promoting political change, or advocating "immoral behavior". Arab governments typically excuse their censorship on the grounds that they are protecting Islamic values and morality. Sometimes this justification is linked to an alleged onslaught of Western decadence against Islamic values (Fandy 1999). Offensive sites generally are held to include pornography, homosexuality, drugs, gambling, and atheism. However, like autocratic regimes the world over, many Arab governments are afraid of their citizens having access to *any* substantive political information about the outside world. Censorship may also generate profits for the government, including limited potential access of customers to rivals of state-owned telecommunications companies. Nonetheless, despite these restrictions, the internet has opened myriad spaces of Arab political debate that transcend national boundaries (Ghareeb 2000).

Censorship in the Arab world is most acute in Saudi Arabia. Public access to the internet in the kingdom was made possible only when the state deemed that it could effectively control it; the entire internet backbone network is state-owned. Thus, while the kingdom has sought to garner the economic benefits of the web, it has also strenuously tried to prevent it from challenging the highly conservative basis of its rule (Teitelbaum 2002). The Saudi state has erected extensive firewalls to control the flow of digital information. Saudi internet cafes are required to record the names of the customers and the times they arrive and depart, information that must be delivered to state security upon request; persons under 18 are forbidden unless accompanied by an adult. By royal decree, the King Abdul Aziz City for Science and Technology (KACST), a government-owned research center, is the only portal through which ISPs can make international connections (www.unesco.org/webworld). This mechanism operates using commercial software produced in the United States, Secure Computing's SmartFilter (Lee 2001), which has also been sold to and utilized by the governments of Iran, Yemen, Tunisia, the U.A.E., and Sudan (Villeneuve 2006). Requests from Saudi ISPs to access the outside world must pass through state-controlled servers. According to the OpenNet Initiative (2004), in 2004 more than 400,000 web pages were banned by the Saudi regime (about 2.2 % of all sites tested in a sample), the vast bulk of which pertained to adult material but also including some games, recreational sites, on-line shopping, Yahoo, America On-Line, and even medical websites that use words like "breast," if only in a medical context. Access attempts to banned sites are logged by the state, which understandably encourages widespread self-censorship.

Many Arab states follow the Saudi model to different degrees. In 2006, Bahrain and Jordan blocked access to Google Earth and Skype, respectively, citing national security concerns. In Syria, the government blocks access to Kurdish-language news websites overseas and any domain ending in ".il," i.e., Israel. In Tunisia, the government forbids access to services such as Hotmail and human rights websites; in addition, every ISP must submit a monthly list of subscribers to the state censorship agency. In 2002, a Tunisian court sentenced cyber-activist Zohair Ben Said al Yehiawy to 2½ years in jail for criticizing the judiciary and corrupt police practices (www.hrinfo.net/en/reports/net2004/tunis.shtml). Tunisia's suppression of freedom of speech led Reporters without Borders to criticize the United Nations' 2005 World Summit on the Information Society in Tunis as a joke. In Iraq under the regime of Saddam Hussein, internet access was strictly limited (Ghattas 2002). In 1997, the Iraq government newspaper al-Jamhuriyya denounced the internet as "an American means to enter every house in the world" (Anderson 1997).

The growth of a new generation of tech-savvy Arabs—in contrast to their frequently illiterate elders—may well portend significant changes in the future as they rise to positions of prominence and influence within the state and the private sector. As Kalathil and Boas (2003, p. 116) note, "the current generation of Saudi youth (which is large and growing rapidly) is better educated, more literate, and more aware of the outside world than ever before and is likely to want increased access to information on the Internet." Arab use of Facebook and Youtube was widely evident during the Arab Spring of 2010, which brought down the governments of Tunisia, Egypt, and Libya, although it is simplistic to attribute these revolts solely to the diffusion of digital technologies.

The United Arab Emirates (UAE) is often heralded as the internet star of the Middle East, with relatively a high penetration rate and a government eager to diversify the economy. However, here too censorship is the norm. All telecommunications passes through the government monopoly, Etisalat, which operates the country's only ISP. Filtering of internet content at cybercafes blocks sites that are blacklisted by the state, although leased lines in businesses and homes are exempt. The UAE Minister of Transportation, Ahmed Hameed Al-Taier, claimed that his government's filtering system "was the main reason behind the spread of the internet in the country. Many people allowed access to the internet inside their homes upon the condition that there be some sort of censorship to protect their families from websites offensive to their morality" (Arabic Network for Human Rights Information 2004).

Some Arab countries, such as Egypt, Jordan, and Lebanon, are relatively lenient with regards to internet regulation. Typically such states are oriented toward the West and at least grudgingly accept the need for democratic access to the internet, such as in Jordan (Cunningham 2002). Morocco is often included in this category, although it assiduously blocks access to web sites promoting independence for the

Western Sahara. Egypt is often celebrated for its relative lack of overt censorship, reflective of a regime eager to encourage tourism and court foreign investors. Even so, the Egyptian state created an agency in 2004, the Department to Combat Crimes of Computers and Internet, to censor "subversive" internet sites, and has arrested programmers, journalists and human rights activists for violating censorship standards. In 2001, Shuhdi Surour, the webmaster for *al-Ahram Weekly* newspaper was arrested for posting a poem online critical of the state (Bahgat 2004). Despite the government's attempts to halt the publication of several books, many authors found alternative outlets on the Web (Gauch 2001). The Muslim Brotherhood's cyberactivities were closely monitored by the Mubarak regime, which closed the country's internet for several days during the Arab Spring, but to no avail.

Oman and Yemen offer contrasting models of internet censorship. In Oman, the government-owned OmanTel is the monopoly provider of fixed and mobile telephony services, and facilitated the purchase of PCs through installment payments. In contrast, Yemen's government ordered all internet cafes to remove physical barriers between computers to ensure users lacked privacy when on-line (OpenNet Initiative 2006), leading to a decline in the number of such establishments. Almost all Yemen's efforts, implemented through a product called Websense, are directed against pornography, although some anti-Islamic sites are also blocked.

Israel's enduring confrontation with the Palestinians has also taken the form of internet censorship. Before the Oslo Accord of 1995, the Israeli military's Order 1279 forbid Palestinians from using electronic transmissions for political purposes, including leased telephone lines (Parry 1997). In response, Palestinians in the West Bank created a wireless network, PalNet, using microwave transmitters, which has been subject to occasional disruptions by the Israeli army. In 2000, the Israeli government attempted to shut down several Hezbollah websites, leading to retaliation by Palestinian hackers against the Israeli Foreign Ministry's website, flooding it with spam messages. The Palestinian Authority launched a Hebrew-language version of its Wafa news agency website to circumvent what it called Israel censorship of cyberinformation. The Israeli government has also actively recruited bloggers to combat anti-Zionist websites, including those that deny the Holocaust. Finally, it should be noted that the ultraorthodox community within Israel has attempted to impose internet censorship as well, efforts directed primarily at preventing access to adult material on-line.

One of the world's more repressive governments in terms of internet regulation, Iran maintains strict control over cyberspace through its state-owned telecommunications monopoly, Telecommunication Company of Iran, run through the Ministry of Information and Communication Technology, to which all Iranian ISPs are connected. Like many countries, Iran manages its censorship at the level of ISPs, which must agree to prohibit access to "non-Islamic" web sites. As the internet has emerged as prominent domain in which political dissent, the government's restrictions have grown proportionately. In 2001, the government assumed control over all international traffic entering or leaving the country, and claims to have blocked access to five million websites. Roughly 20 official categories of prohibited websites exist, including those that insult Islam, promote national discord, pornography, and immoral behavior. In 2006, all websites and blogs were required to obtain licenses from the Ministry of Islamic Culture and Guidance or risked being declared illegal. Also in 2006, the government outlawed internet connections faster than 128 kbps, entailing stiff resistance from business leaders. The government's surveillance of dissidents was abetted by purchases of European spy technology from Siemens and Nokia (Rhoads and Chao 2009), particularly a technique called deep packet inspection, which allows authorities not only to block email and Internet telephony but to identify users' names. Foreign spyware have now been complemented by domestically produced versions (OpenNet Initiative 2009a). In 2009, in the face of massive anti-government protests—themselves organized through social networking channels—the Iranian regime cracked down yet again, imprisoning dozens of dissenting bloggers under the aegis of Tehran Prosecutor Saeed Mortazavi.

However, Iran has found internet censorship increasingly difficult to administer. During the 2009 crackdown, for example, amateur videos of government attacks on demonstrations circulated virally on the Web. In response, the government slowed down the maximum transmission rates on its internet backbones, making traffic in videos slow and difficult. Using free, downloadable software to circumvent government filters called Freegate and Ultrasurf, which were developed by China's Falun Gong (Lake 2009), Iranian protestors repeatedly resisted government controls over cyberspace at critical political moments. Some observers argue that the internet has "certainly broken 30 years of state control over what is seen and is unseen, what is visible versus invisible" (Stelter and stone 2009).

Turkey briefly blocked a YouTube site that insulted the founder of the modern Turkish state, Kemal Ataturk. In 2000, the Ministry of the Interior barred internet cafes from allowing access to websites that espoused anti-secularist (i.e., Islamicist) or Kurdish nationalist views. In 2007, after the Turkish parliament passed legislation regulating internet access there in less than one hour of debate, the number of websites blocked in the country immediately jumped from zero to 2,600 (Anderson 2009).

3.2.7 Subsaharan Africa

In Subsaharan Africa, minuscule internet penetration rates and an enfeebled civil opposition have done little to curtail censorship efforts. Resisting the global tide of neoliberal deregulation and privatization that has washed over telecommunications markets worldwide, many African governments have retained state monopolies over information services. Levels of censorship vary widely across the continent, of course. At one extreme is Sudan, where internet usage is almost entirely concentrated in Khartoum, the government openly boasts of censorship; the government's telecommunications monopoly, Sudatel, was blacklisted by the United States as part of a broader strategy to resolve the violence in Darfur (OpenNet

Initiative 2009b). The other end of this censorship spectrum is South Africa, which has negligible government interference in cyberspace. Most African states fall in between these poles. In Kenya, the administration used several censorship strategies, such as restricting bandwidth offered to ISPs through the state-owned internet backbone and demanding that ISPs turn over their subscriber lists (Africa ICT Policy Monitor 2006). In 2000, the Communications Commission of Kenya ordered the closure of the month-old Kenya Internet Exchange Point, ostensibly on the grounds of preventing its use by 'terrorists' but more likely because it infringed upon Telkom Kenya's monopoly. Zimbabwe's government issued numerous laws to limit freedom of expression of the media, including the Broadcasting Services Act, the Zimbabwe Broadcasting Corporation Commercialisation Act, and the Public Order and Security Act (POSA). Its Monitoring and Interception of Communications Centre may compel ISPs to install software to intercept information deemed necessary by the state (Burnett 2005). The government also blocks certain websites using legislation such as POSA: For example, the website of the Movement for Democratic Change (www.mdczimbabwe.com) has been shut down a number of times (http://www.privacyinternational.org).

3.2.8 Latin America

Latin American Internet censorship is typically less egregious than that found in other parts of the world. The region's most restrictive policies by far are found in Cuba, where internet and e-mail access is jealously guarded by the government, which controls the country's only internet gateway and four national ISPs (Kalathil and Boas 2001). In 1996, the Cuban Executive Council of Ministers initiated Decree Law 209, which governed internet access in that country. With six competing ministries vying for control, however, it proved to be bureaucratically unfeasible, and in 2000 censorship authority was passed to the Ministry of Computing and Communications. Faced with high prices of computer equipment, partly due to the long standing U.S. trade embargo, Cuba has rejected a market-led model of internet development in favor of a collective, government-led one that emphasizes institutions, not individuals. As a result, "individual access to the Internet has been essentially prohibited" (Kalathil and Boas 2003, p. 55). Commercial ISPs are allowed to provide individual accounts only to people who have obtained sponsorship from government agencies. Until recently, all internet accounts had to be registered through the National Center for Automated Data Exchange at the cost of $260 a month (the average Cuban makes $240 per year). Relaxation of this restriction in 2006 helped to fuel the boom in Cuban internet access, which now includes about 14 % of the population. Nonetheless, differential pricing ensures that access to the nation's intranet remains considerably cheaper than international networks. Access to internet cafes with international connections must be paid for in U.S. dollars, which are scarce among Cubans.

Nonetheless, a growing network of *informáticos*, or technologically savvy individuals, has contested these restrictions, and in the U.S., conservative groups such as the Cuban American National Foundation maintain web sites criticizing the regime. World famous blogger Yoani Sanchez, for example, has a blog "Generation Y" that has become the unofficial voice of the Cuban domestic opposition. Diplomatic cables sent from the U.S. Interest Section in Havana released by Wikileaks in 2010 suggest that Cuban government officials view the island's bloggers as a "most serious challenge" to the country's political stability. In 2009 Cuban newspapers called on journalists to "man the cyber-trenches" to defend the revolution by setting up their own blogs and criticizing anti-government blogs. However, Cuba's hard line attitude may be softening. In his 2007 keynote address at the Informatica Conference in Havana, then-Minister of Informatics and Communications Ramiro Valdés Menéndez embraced "the wild stallion of the new technologies." Finally, the Cuban government has built an Intranet known as Red Cubana, which Cubans can use at universities, youth computing clubs, and post offices, but it is not connected globally. Reporters Without Borders found almost no filtering in Cuban cafes with international connections. On the other hand, in cafes with domestic-only connections, RWB found that:

> Users have to give their name and address at the door. If they write something containing suspect key-words, such as the name of a known dissident, a pop-up message appears saying the document has been blocked for "state security" reasons. The application—word processor or browser—that was used to write the text is automatically closed. So it seems that a programme installed on all internet cafes automatically detects banned content.

After Cuba, Venezuela's Hugo Chavez's Venezuela is Latin America's second worst internet censor. Venezuelan Attorney General Luisa Ortega argued that "the internet can't be a space free from the law, all activities that occur in this national territory must be subject to legal regulation." In December 2010, the government announced controls over ISPs requiring them to report violent material posted on websites they host. Venezuela's major provider, CANTV, was renationalized in 2007 and controls 90 % of its internet market and 100 % of high-speed connections in the country. The Venezuelan government has periodically blocked access to websites such as Wordpress.com and blogger.com, and has repeatedly shut down Noticiero Digital, which has been especially critical and often insulting of Chavez, who accused it of promoting a coup d'etat. However, opportunism is at work in Venezuelan politics as everywhere else: Chavez originally attacked the internet as a "current of conspiracy," and Twitter users as terrorists and traitors. However, in 2010, in a classic case of "if you cannot beat 'em, join 'em," he started using Twitter himself, and today has 500,000 followers.

Many Latin American governments with unsavory human rights records in the past, such as Brazil, now are remarkably open with regard to the internet, although Brazilian courts have ordered ISPs to block access to certain blogs and YouTube videos that carry material "defamatory" to the state. In September 2010, the satirical website *Falha de São Paulo* was removed from the web by an injunction imposed by the Brazilian courts. Brazilian national and regional governments (e.g., Paraná and Mato Grosso) have occasionally forced online magazines to remove unfavorable articles, prevented publication of polls, and forced Twitter to delete posts. Similarly, Argentina passed an anti-censorship decree for the internet. In some countries, including Costa Rica, which is known for its democratic governance, journalists have been harassed by the state when exposing corruption in ruling circles on the internet (Privacy International 2003). Argentina's National Telecommunications Commission blocked 2 websites—leakymails.com and leakymails.blogspot.com—that leaked government emails.

Less draconian is the attempt of the Chilean Chamber of Deputies, which passed a bill allowing judges to punish internet users who are "offensive to morals" or the "public order" (Cortes 2000). The order was aimed at websites located within Chile, i.e., with the.cl domain name, and was utterly ineffective against sites located outside the country. An attempt to prohibit access to Alejandra Matus's *The Black Book of Chilean Justice*, an expose of the ineffectiveness of the judiciary, led to its publication on the web and even wider readership. In contrast with Chile, the Peruvian government passed the Transparency and Access to the Public Information Act, which created public access internet terminals, and established the Telecommunications Investment Fund, which is responsible for promoting universal internet access. Peru's Transparency and Access to the Public Information Act includes the creation of public information portals and considers governmental information as accessible to citizens. In Mexico, the government does not engage in internet censorship, but the drug cartels do, including disemboweling a young couple and hanging their bodies from a bridge with a sign reading "This is going to happen to all those posting funny things on the internet, You better (expletive) pay attention. I'm about to get you."

3.2.9 Europe

Southern European countries generally exhibit less tolerance for internet dissent than do their northern counterparts. In Italy, the Vatican called for restrictions on the internet's "radical libertarianism," and the Italian government has shut down websites critical of Catholicism. The government has also attempted to force ISPs from allowing websites that defend or instigate crimes or portray the Mafia in a positive light. Following the assassination of a town councilor in northern Spain, a website for the Basque separatist electronic journal *Euskal Herria*, based in San Francisco, was shut down by email bombs believed to be initiated by the Spanish government (Conway 2007).

In Eastern Europe, with a long history of censorship under Soviet occupation, attempts to control the internet have been more explicit and widespread. In Bulgaria, for example, the government's attempt to license ISPs that included the collection of user names and passwords was defeated by the internet Society of Bulgaria on the grounds that it served political rather than economic purposes. Moldovan Internet café owners formed the Internet Club Association to lobby against restrictions to access. In the former Yugoslavia, internet censorship was widespread under the government of Slobodan Milosovic in the 1990s. Cyber-repression included: the arrest and persecution of the journalist Miroslav Filipovic, who wrote about military human rights abuses; politically motivated tampering with websites during the 2000 presidential elections; filtering of academic networks; and ordering some ISPs to close politically "unsuitable" websites. The overthrow of the Milosovic regime in 2000 greatly improved that country's affairs in this regard.

While European countries are generally relatively open in terms of internet access, there too several governments attempt to restrict what is said in cyber-space. Generally, however, censorship in economically developed countries focuses more on social concerns such as pornography or intellectual property than overt attempts to stifle political dissent. Often moves to restrict access are strenuously opposed by privacy advocates and some ISPs. Indeed, most attempts to censor the government in Europe have backfired. In addition to large, mobilized constituencies that advocate internet liberties, economic integration has reduced European states' room to maneuver on this issue: for example, in 2008, the European Parliament passed a proposal that treats internet censorship as a free trade barrier. While aimed at EU trade relations with countries such as China, the measure also limits domestic censorship.

Despite these obstacles to censorship, some European countries do engage in mild forms of internet censorship, to widely varying degrees. Northern Europe tends to be especially mild, with Reporters Without Borders reporting zero interference in Scandinavia. However, in Finland, a nation widely celebrated as a bastion of high tech democracy, when hacker Matti Nikki's website criticized government efforts to regulate the internet, the government added it to its list of proscribed child pornography sites, blocking access by ISPs. A Finnish government attempt to censor internet message boards in 2003 was met with stiff resistance from telecommunications and media companies. In the United Kingdom, it is illegal to look at any of a list of websites kept by the internet Watch Foundation (Anderson 2009). Starting in the mid-1990s, the German government attempted to shut down foreign sites that promoted racial hatred; more recent efforts, led by the Minister of Family Affairs, have focused on child pornography. Similarly, in France, the government in 2000 banned Yahoo! from allowing access to websites that promote racial hatred or sell Nazi memorabilia or those portraying child sexual abuse. In both France and Germany it is impossible to search for Nazi materials on-line using Google (Conway 2007). More recently, government officials have tracked down bloggers who insulted them and filed intimidating legal challenges (Sayare 2009). With some of the world's toughest antipiracy laws, the government now fines persons who repeatedly download illegal material.

3.2.10 United States

Although it often trumpets itself as a paragon of democracy, and although internet censorship in the U.S. is minimal, there too the state has intervened occasionally in attempts to shape internet access. Whereas the first attempts to regulate cyberspace were caught up in culture wars between liberals and conservatives, more recent attempts have been more explicitly corporatist in nature.

The most egregious case of American internet censorship involved the Communications Decency Act (CDA), passed by Congress in 1996 in an attempt to limit children's access to pornography (however loosely defined) on the internet by facilitating government censorship, particularly the distribution of "patently offensive" materials to minors, essentially catering to the political agenda of the Christian Right. Resistance to the CDA was ferocious, including lawsuits by a coalition of ISPs, leading the Supreme Court to overturn the law in 1997.

More recent government internet censorship efforts in the U.S. involve private sector proxy actors (Kreimer 2006). Thus, Congress has mandated that public schools and libraries install filtering software, and holds ISPs responsible for providing access to child pornography. In this reading, censorship is a means of controlling "negative externalities" such as internet crime and pornography that the market, left to its own devices, would fail to control. Congress has also initiated incentives for ISPs to block access to websites that infringe on intellectual property rights. Under the Patriot Act, the Federal Bureau of Investigation has a "good corporate citizen" program that encourages ISPs to censor websites that are not consonant with the public interest and to turn over information about users whose email reveals suspicious intent (Gellman 2005). The administration of George W. Bush enacted legislation encouraging telecommunications companies to engage in data mining on anti-terrorist grounds; indeed, "with respect to online surveillance, the United States may be among the most aggressive states in the world in terms of monitoring online conversations" (Deibert et al. 2008, p. 232). Whereas issues of copyright infringement or child pornography constitute legitimate concerns in this regard, other applications, particularly restrictions on political information, lie at the end of the slippery slope that such measures entail.

The Wikileaks phenomenon—particularly Bradley Manning's appropriation of a quarter million secret U.S. State Department diplomatic cables in 2010 and passing them to the NGO that specializes in disseminating classified documents—offers a useful opportunity to assess the politics of cyberspace. Wikileaks reveals several important aspects of internet geopolitics: the internet as contested political space; the advantages, limitations, and disadvantages of cyberactivism; the geographies of empathy and caring that cyberactivism is capable of fostering; and the limits of internet speech. Clearly, given resistance to censorship, the internet is a contested domain of politics, an arena of conflict in which different discourses jockey for influence (Kreimer 2001). In this light, Wikileaks is part of a much broader constellation of progressive uses of cyberspace (Warf 2011), a vast array of causes that harnesses the internet for purposes broadly oriented to social justice and protection of the politically and economically marginalized, such as promoting human rights; preventing war; attacking poverty; environmental protection; women's, gay, handicapped peoples', animal, and minority rights; and opposition to economic and political exploitation, including neoliberal globalization. By allowing alliances to be forged and synergies to be fostered, the internet greatly enhances the power of social movements, making them into relatively coherent forces that accomplish far more together than they could by acting alone. In short, Manning and Wikileaks fall squarely within the tradition of progressive hacktivism (Ludlow 2010). Cyberspace is an ideal mechanism for groups to jump spatial scales (Adams 1996), allowing them to leverage public opinion at the global scale in local struggles for justice. Wikileaks represents scale jumping at its finest: in releasing vast quantities of state secrets, Bradley Manning and Julian Assange revealed that the porosity of national borders can be utilized for emancipatory purposes. As a result, even the most powerful and best financed institution in the world—the U.S. military—was revealed as having weak points, moments and spaces of vulnerability.

3.3 Discussion: A Habermasian Critique

Many groups in closed societies can view digital information in a manner unavailable in censored print or broadcast media, undermining state monopolies over the media, and enhancing, if slowly and contingently, moves toward democratic governance (Slane 2007). Precisely because cyberspace facilitates relatively easy, unfettered access to information, it has been viewed with alarm by numerous governments. In and of itself, of course, the internet does not simply produce positive or negative effects, for its information is always filtered through national and local cultures, biases, and predispositions. However, as ever larger numbers of people are brought into contact with one another on-line, cyberspace may expand opportunities for engaging in political activity, some of which challenges or delegitimizes prevailing models of authority by undermining the monopoly of traditional elites over the means of communication. The internet is relatively low in cost and easy to use, and thus reduces a major obstacle to the participation in public debate by the poor. Because it allows access to multiple sources of information, including films and images, the internet has facilitated a generalized growth in awareness of foreign ideas, products, and political norms. Indeed, as Yang (2003) suggests, given how widespread digital communications have become, the internet and civil society have increasingly come to co-evolve, energizing and shaping one another in time and space.

In this way, cyberspace deeply resembles Jürgen Habermas's (1979) famous "ideal speech situation" in which unfettered discourse is central to the "public sphere" and in which discursive truth is constructed in the absence of barriers to communication (Poster 1997). One of the twentieth century's leading social philosophers, Habermas has long maintained that unconstrained communications are mandatory to broader processes of consensus construction, in which people of all backgrounds partake in public, positive and normative interpretations of their worlds. In what is essentially a pragmatist defense of Enlightenment ideals, his notion of communicative rationality, which is central to his critical theory, refers to the procedures of open debate and criticism, which he holds became increasingly widespread with the growth of modern bourgeois society. The "ideal speech situation" is vital to the operation of civil society in which social life is successfully reproduced and transformed. The ideal speech situation never exists in reality, but functions as a Weberian ideal type, a counterfactual yardstick by which to judge real-life contexts and the obstacles that generate distorted communication. In a situation in which all power relations constraining debate have been removed, all participants are free to provide input into the norms of truth production. As Luhmann (1996, p. 885) notes,

> Habermas does not locate the problem at the level of actually occurring communications. … Instead, he employs a theory of how the reasonable coordination of actions can take place if assured of the freely rendered agreement of all involved.

Thus, in this conception, reason, truth, logic, and self-reflexivity are not located in some abstract transcendental realm but are grounded in praxis. The only criterion that remains for resolving contesting claims is their truth-value, which rests on the "force of a better argument," leading to a consensus theory of truth that rejects absolute foundations for knowledge in favor of procedural ones. Importantly, "the participants in an ideal speech situation [must] be motivated solely by the desire to reach a consensus about the truth of statements and the validity of norms" (Bernstein 1995, p. 50). Later, in *The Structural Transformation of the Public Sphere* (Habermas 1989), he argued that civil society, located between the state and everyday life, which arose with the growth of industrial capitalism and the Enlightenment, had become thoroughly dominated by large corporations, reducing citizens to spectators and consumers of goods (see Kellner 1979, 1990).

Habermas's critics have argued that his view exaggerates the power of reason to obtain consensus and that he obfuscates inequalities in access to public discourse such as class, gender, and ethnicity. Thus, Habermas holds up an ideal that can never be realized in practice (Hohendahl 1979; Calhoun 1992). Despite these objections, it is worth noting that the ideal free speech situation remains the prevailing normative standard against most contemporary conceptions of the political economy of unfettered access to and production of knowledge are compared, particularly with regard to the legitimacy of legal institutions (Froomkin 2003).

Cyberspace in all its diverse forms—chat rooms, blogs, and email, as well as neogeographic practices such as wiki-webs—arguably exemplifies the Habermasian vision of diverse groups engaging in practical discourse more than any other realm today. Enhanced access to information empowers citizens, facilitates debate, and may alter political outcomes. In particular, the internet allows communities of shared interests to form around common discourses that express identities and foment mutual understandings within a broader, heterogeneous, differentiated civil society. Of course, the reality of unequal digital access is never a perfect reflection of the idealized norm: the digital divide, at multiple spatial scales, signifies that social and spatial inequalities are reproduced inside of cyberspace. That said, at minimal cost and easy to use, the internet allows for the construction of a negotiated consensus that lies at the heart of legitimate political rule. As Froomkin (2003, p. 856) puts it, "In Habermasian terms, the Internet draws power back into the public sphere, away from other systems." More generally, by shifting the production of meaning from the few to the many, unfettered electronic communication allows truth to be uncoupled from power.

Given this ideal, internet censorship represents a particularly egregious infringement not only upon democratic norms of liberty, equality, and informed dissent, but upon the discursive capacity of citizens to construct their worlds. Far from challenging existing power relations, censorship of cyberspace thus amplifies them. At risk, when and where censorship succeeds, is the production of reason itself: if, following Habermas, truth is the consensual outcome of reasoned debate, then government limitations on internet access and attempts to shape the contents of cyberspace fly in the face of peaceful resolutions of differences. Ever since Foucault, social science has concerned itself greatly with the ways in which power and knowledge are hopelessly entwined with one another. Censorship of whatever type is thus an affirmation that rational consensus, and thus truth, is impossible in the face of force.

3.4 Conclusions

Many groups in closed societies can view digital information in a manner unavailable in censored print or broadcast media, undermining state monopolies over the media, and enhancing, if slowly and contingently, moves toward democratic governance (Slane 2007). Precisely because cyberspace facilitates relatively easy, unfettered access to information, it has been viewed with alarm by numerous governments. In and of itself, of course, the internet does not simply produce positive or negative effects, for its information is always filtered through national and local cultures, biases, and predispositions. However, as ever larger numbers of people are brought into contact with one another on-line, cyberspace may expand opportunities for engaging in political activity, some of which challenges or delegitimizes prevailing models of authority by undermining the monopoly of traditional elites over the means of communication. The internet is relatively low in cost and easy to use, and thus reduces a major obstacle to the participation in public debate by the poor. Because it allows access to multiple sources of information, including films and images, the internet has facilitated a generalized growth in awareness of foreign ideas, products, and political norms. Indeed, as Yang (2003) suggests, given how widespread digital communications have become, the internet and civil society have increasingly come to co-evolve, energizing and shaping one another in time and space.

Despite the hyperbole exaggerating the internet's capacity to effect social change, the global diffusion of the internet has created a growing challenge for many authoritarian regimes and greatly enabled the growth and effectiveness of global civil society. Email petitions, cyberprotests, calls for action, advocacy of various marginalized political causes, and the blogosphere have become an integral part of political action, allowing local social movements to "jump scale" by reaching national and global audiences (Adams 1996). In response, government censorship, ranging from relatively mild steps such as anti-pornography measures to the arrest and execution of cyberdissidents, has become an inescapable dimension of the geographies of cyberspace. One-quarter of the world's netizens live under the harshest forms of censorship, and in most countries self-censorship accomplishes what governments have not.

The information technology revolution, however, has also brought with it promise of economic growth and improved productivity. Many governments, therefore, are caught in a conundrum, wishing to encourage the growth of information technology sectors on the one hand but fearful of its political repercussions on the other. In attempting to manage internet access and content, states must take care not to alienate investors, tourists, entrepreneurs, and software developers. For some states, such as Myanmar or North Korea, such concerns are irrelevant. But most governments seek to appropriate the economic benefits of information technology without paying the political costs of enhanced democracy. The strategies used to negotiate this predicament are contingent and reflective of a wide constellation of political, economic, and cultural circumstances; thus, censorship and its resistance are geographically specific. Contrary to early utopian predictions, the growth of the much vaulted global "information society" will not necessarily lead to greater democracy worldwide, but, in a more sober view, to enhanced avenues for civil discourse.

References

Abbott, J. (2001). Democracy@Internet.asia? The challenges to the emancipatory potential of the net: Lessons from China and Malaysia. *Third World Quarterly, 22*(1), 99–114.

Adams, P. (1996). Protest and the scale politics of telecommunications. *Political Geography, 15*, 419–441.

Africa ICT Policy Monitor (2006).Retrieved from http://africa.rights.apc.org

Ahmed, A. (2002). Pakistan's blasphemy laws: Words fail me. *The Washington Post,* May 19.

Anderson, J. (1997). Globalizing politics and religion in the muslim world. Retrieved from *Journal of Electronic Publishing.* www.press.umich.edu/jep/archive/Anderson.html

Anderson, K. (2009). Net surveillance and filters are a reality for Europe, too. Retrieved from *The Guardian,* June 24. http://www.guardian.co.uk/technology/2009/jun/24/kevin-anderson-internet-filtering

Arabic Network for Human Rights Information (2004). The Internet in the Arab world: A new space of repression? Retrieved from http://www.hrinfo.net/en/reports/net2004/

Bahgat, H. (2004). Egypt's virtual protection of morality. *Middle East Report, 230*, 22–25.

72   3 Global Internet Censorship

Bernstein, J. (1995). *Recovering ethical life: Jürgen Habermas and the future of critical theory.* New York: Routledge.
Barry, E. (2009). In Azerbaijan, a donkey suit leads to laughs, questions and possibly arrests. *New York Times*, July 15, p. A49.
Bi, J. (2001). The internet revolution in China: The significance for traditional forms of communist control. *International Journal, 56*(3), 421–441.
Burnett, P. (2005). Internet censorship on the rise in Africa? Retrieved from http://www.worldhunger.org/articles/06/africa/burnett.htm
Calhoun, C. (1992). *Habermas and the public sphere.* Cambridge: MIT Press.
Crampton, J. (2003). *The political mapping of cyberspace.* Edinburgh: Edinburgh University Press.
Crampton, J. (2007). The biopolitical justification for geosurveillance. *Geographical Review, 97*(3), 389–493.
Crovitz, G. (2010). China's web crackdown continues. *Wall Street Journal*, Jan 11. Retrieved fromhttp://online.wsj.com/article/SB10001424052748703948504574649021577882240.html
Conway, M. (2007). Terrorism and internet governance: Core issues. Retrieved from http://www.unidir.ch/pdf/articles/pdf-art2644.pdf
Cortés, M. (2000). Internet censorship around the world.Retrieved from http://www.isoc.org/inet2000/cdproceedings/8k/8k_4.htm
Cunningham, K. (2002). Factors influencing Jordan's information revolution: Implications for democracy. *Middle East Journal, 56*(2), 240–256.
Dann, D., & Haddow, N. (2008). Just doing business or doing just business? Google, Microsoft, Yahoo! and the business of censoring China's internet. *Journal of Business Ethics, 79*(3), 219–234.
Deibert, R., & Rohozinski, R. (2008). Good for liberty, bad for security? Global civil society and the securitization of the internet. In R. Deibert, J. Palfrey, R. Rohozinksi, & J. Zittrain (Eds.), *Access denied: The practice and policy of global internet filtering* (pp. 123–150). Cambridge, MA: MIT Press.
Dobson, J., & Fisher, P. (2007). The panopticon's changing geography. *Geographical Review, 97*(3), 307–323.
Dunn, M. (2000). The information revolution and the middle East: An overview of the early literature. *Middle East Journal, 54*(3), 465–476.
Eriksson, J., & Giacomello, G. (2009). Who controls what, and under what conditions? *International Studies Review, 11*, 206–210.
Eurasianet.org. (2007). In Turkemenistan, Internet access comes with soldiers Retrieved from http://www.eurasianet.org/departments/insight/articles/eav030807.shtml
Fandy, M. (1999). Cyberresistance: Saudi opposition between globalization and localization. *Comparative Studies in Society and History, 41*, 124–147.
Froomkin, A. (2003). Habermas@Discourse.net. Toward a critical theory of cyberspace. *Harvard Law Review, 116*(3), 740–873.
Gauch, S. (2001). Effects of Arab censorship blunted by the internet. *Christian Science Monitor* Jan 29, 1.
Gellman, B. (2005). The FBI's secret scrutiny: In hunt for terrorists, bureau examines records of ordinary Americans. *Washington Post* November 6 A1.
Ghareeb, E. (2000). New media and the information revolution in the Arab world: An assessment. *Middle East Journal, 54*(3), 395–418.
Ghattas, K. (2002). Surfing the net in Iraq. Retrieved from *BBC News*, May 1. http://news.bbc.co.uk/1/hi/world/middle_east/1959481.stm
Goldsmith, J. (1998). Against cyberanarchy. *University of Chicago Law Review, 1199*, 1217–1222.
Goldsmith, J., & Wu, T. (2006). *Who controls the internet? illusion of a borderless world.* New York: Oxford University Press.
Habermas, J. (1979). *Communication and the evolution of society.* Boston: Beacon Press.
Habermas, J. (1989). *The structural transformation of the public sphere: An inquiry into a category of bourgeois society.* Oxford: Blackwell.

Hachigian, N. (2001). China's cyber-strategy. *Foreign Affairs, 80*(2), 118–133.

Hachigian, N. (2002). The internet and power in one-party East Asian states. *Washington Quarterly, 25*(3), 41–58.

Harwit, E., & Clark, D. (2001). Shaping the internet in China: Evolution of political control over network infrastructure and political content. *Asian Survey, 41*(3), 377–408.

Hohendahl, P. (1979). Critical theory, public sphere and culture: Habermas and his critics. *New German Critique, 16*(winter), 89–118.

Human Rights Watch (2002). Human rights watch: World report 2001, Vietnam. Retrieved from www.hrw.org/wr2k/asia/Vietnam.html

International Censorship Explorer (2006). Vietnam strikes back Retrieved from http://ice.citizenlab.org/?p=150

James, R. (2009). A brief history of Chinese internet censorship. *Time,* March 18. Retrieved from http://www.time.com/time/world/article/0,8599,1885961,00.html

Kahn, J. (2002). China has world's tightest internet censorship, study finds. *New York Times, 4,* 1.

Kalathil, S., & Boas T. (2001). The internet and state control in authoritarian regimes: China, Cuba, and the counterrevolution. *Carnegie Endowment Global Policy Program Work*, Paper No. 21. Washington: Carnegie Endowment for International Peace.

Kalathil, S., & Boas, T. (2003). *Open networks, closed regimes: The impact of the internet on authoritarian rule*. Washington, DC: Carnegie Endowment for International Peace.

Katyal, N. (2001). Criminal law in cyberspace. *University of Pennsylvania Law Review, 1003,* 1100.

Kellner, D. (1979). TV, ideology, and emancipatory popular culture. *Socialist Review, 45,* May–June 13–53.

Kellner, D. (1990). *Television and the crisis of democracy*. Boulder: Westview Press.

Kreimer, S. (2001). Technologies of protest: Insurgent social movements and the first amendment in the era of the internet. *University of Pennsylvania Law Review, 150*(1), 119–171.

Kreimer, S. (2006). Censorship by proxy: The First amendment, internet intermediaries, and the problem of the weakest link. *University of Pennsylvania Law Review, 155,* 11–101.

Lake, E. (2009). Hacking the regime. *The New Republic,* September 3. Retrieved from http://www.tnr.com/article/politics/hacking-the-regime

Lambroschini, A. (2011). No Twitter revolt for Central Asia's closed regimes. Physorg.com (February 24). http://www.physorg.com/news/2011-02-twitter-revolt-central-asiaregimes.html

Luhmann, N. (1996). *Quod omnes tangit*: Remarks on Jurgen Habermas's legal theory. *Cardoso Law Review, 17*(4–5), 883–900.

LaFraniere, S. (2009). Censors put tighter grip on internet in China. *New York Times, 18,* A14.

Ludlow, P. (2010). Wikileaks and hacktivist culture. *The Nation* October *4,* 25–26.

Lee, J. (2001). Companies compete to provide Saudi internet veil. *New York Times* Nov., *19,* A1.

Machleder, J. 2002. Struggle over internet access developing in Uzbekistan. *Eurasia Insight.* March 12, http://www.eurasianet.org/departments/rights/articles/eav031202.shtml.

MacKinnon, R. (2008). Flatter world and thicker walls? Blogs, censorship and civic discourse in China. *Public Choice, 134,* 31–46.

MacKinnon, R. (2009). China's censorship 2.0: How companies censor bloggers. *First Monday* 14 (2). Retrieved fromhttp://firstmonday.org/htbin/cgiwrap/bin/ojs/index.php/fm/article/view/2378/2089

McGlinchey, E., & Johnson, E. (2007). Aiding the internet in Central Asia. *Democratization, 14*(2), 277–288.

Murdoch, S., & Anderson, R. (2008). Tools and technology of internet filtering. In R. Deibert, J. Palfrey, R. Rohozinksi, & J. Zittrain (Eds.), *Access denied: The practice and policy of global internet filtering* (pp. 57–72). Cambridge: MIT Press.

OpenNet Initiative. (2004). Internet filtering in Saudi Arabia in 2004. Retrieved from http://opennet.net/studies/saudi

OpenNet Initiative. (2005). Internet filtering in China 2004-2005. Retrieved from http://opennetinitiative.net/studies/china

OpenNet Initiative. (2006). Singapore. http://opennet.net/sites/opennet.net/files/singapore.pdf

OpenNet Initiative. (2007). Commonwealth of independent states. Retrieved from http://opennet.net/research/regions/cis
OpenNet Initiative. (2009a). Internet filtering in Iran. Retrieved from http://opennet.net/sites/opennet.net/files/ONI_Iran_2009.pdf
OpenNet Initiative. (2009b). Internet filtering in Sudan. Retrieved from http://opennet.net/sites/opennet.net/files/ONI_Sudan_2009.pdf
Privacy International. (2003). Silenced—Costa Rica Retrieved from http://www.privacy-international.org/article.shtml?cmd[347]=x-347-103752
Paltemaa, V., & Vuori, J. (2009). Regime transition and the Chinese politics of technology: From mass science to the controlled internet. *Asian Journal of Political Science, 17*(1), 1–23.
Parry, N. (1997). The past and future of information technology in Palestine. Retrieved from www.nigelparry.com/mideastInternet/unitednationspaper.html
Poster, M. (1997). Cyberdemocracy: Internet and the public sphere. In D. Porter (Ed.), *Internet Culture*. 202–214. London, Routledge.
Pierre, A. (2000). Vietnam's contradictions. *Foreign Affairs, 79*(6), 69–86.
Quirk, M. (2006). The web police. *Atlantic Monthly,* May. Retrieved from http://www.theatlantic.com/magazine/archive/2006/05/the-web-police/4818
Rodan, G. (2000). Singapore information lockdown: Business as usual. In L. Williams & R. Rich (Eds.), *Losing control: Freedom of the press in Asia* (pp. 66–81). Canberra: Asia Pacific Press.
Rhoads, C., Chao, L. (2009). Iran's web spying aided by Western technology. Retrieved from *Wall Street Journal,* June 22, http://online.wsj.com/article/SB124562668777335653.html
Reporters Without Borders. (2004). Retrieved from *Pakistan annual report 2004.* http://www.rsf.org/article.php3?id_article=10794
Reporters Without Borders. (2008). Belarus Retrieved from http://www.rsf.org/article.php3?id_article=25496.2008
Schwartz, S. (2005). The Kyrgyz take their stan: A democratic revolution in Central Asia? *The Weekly Standard,* April 11, *10*(28):12.
Srinivasan, R., & Fish, A. (2009). Internet authorship: Social and political implications within Kyrgyzstan. *Journal of Computer-Mediated Communication, 14*(3), 559–580.
Stelter, B., & Stone, B. (2009). Web pries lid of iranian censorship. Retrieved from *New York Times* June 22:A1 http://www.nytimes.com/2009/06/23/world/middleeast/23censor.html
Stone, B., & Barboza, D. (2010). Scaling the digital wall in china. *New York Times, 16,* B1.
Sayare, S. (2009). As web challenges French leaders, they push back. *New York Times* December *13,* 26.
Slane, A. (2007). Democracy, social space, and the internet. *University of Toronto Law Journal, 57,* 81–104.
Troianovski, A.,& Finn, P. (2007). Kremlin seeks to extend its reach in cyberspace. *Washington Post,* Oct. 28:1. Retrieved from http://www.washingtonpost.com/wp-dyn/content/article/2007/10/27/AR2007102701384_pf.html
Teitelbaum, J. (2002). Dueling for 'Da'Wa': state vs. society on the Saudi internet. *Middle East Journal, 56*(2), 222–239.
Villeneuve, N. (2006). The filtering matrix: Integrated mechanisms of information control and the demarcation of borders in cyberspace. *First Monday* 11(1–2) .Retrieved from http://firstmonday.org/htbin/cgiwrap/bin/ojs/index.php/fm/article/view/1307
Warf, B. (2009). The rapidly evolving geographies of the Eurasian internet. *Eurasian Geography and Economics, 50*(5), 564–580.
Warf, B. (2011). Google bombs, warblogs, and hacktivism: The internet as agent of progressive social change. In J. Tyner & J. Inwood (Eds.), *Nonkilling Geography* (pp. 127–148). Honolulu: University of Hawai'i Center for Global Nonkilling.
Warf, B., & Grimes, J. (1997). Counterhegemonic discourses and the internet. *Geographical Review, 87,* 259–274.
Warf, B., & Vincent, P. (2007). Multiple geographies of the Arab internet. *Area, 39,* 83–96.

Wines, M. (2010). China's censors tackle and trip over the Internet. *New York Times,* April 8, 1, 4.

Wines, M. (2012). Crackdown on Chinese bloggers who fight the censors with puns. *New York Times,* May 29, A5.

Wriston, W. (1997). Bits, bytes, and diplomacy. *Foreign Affairs*, *76*(5), 172–182.

Yang, G. (2003). The co-evolution of the internet and civil society in China. *Asian Survey, 43*(3), 405–422.

Zittrain, J., & Palfrey, J. (2008). Internet filtering: The politics and mechanisms of control. In R. Deibert, J. Palfrey, R. Rohozinksi, & J. Zittrain (Eds.), *Access denied: The practice and policy of global internet filtering* (pp. 29–56). Cambridge: MIT Press.

Chapter 4
Global E-Commerce

The impacts of telecommunications on businesses include a varieties of activities often lumped together under the term e-commerce, which includes both business-to-business (B2B) transactions as well as those linking firms to their customers (B2C) and customers-to-businesses (C2B) (Brunn and Leinbach 2001). E-commerce takes a variety of forms, including electronic data interchange (e.g., inventory data, digital invoices and contracts, purchase orders, and product updates), Internet recruiting and advertising, web-based banking and stock trading, electronic retail shopping and digital gambling. For the most part, this activity is restricted to large commercial actors, although many observers hope that the Internet will open opportunities for small and medium sized establishments to reach out to national and global markets. Digital convergence of hitherto distinct media has opened new possibilities in Internet video and telephony. Advocates maintain that the internet will open opportunities for undercapitalized small and medium sized establishments (SMEs) to access national and global markets.

This chapter explores the geography of e-commerce in several ways. It begins by pointing to the continued role of global cities in the face of the space of flows. Next it sketches the contours of electronic funds transfer systems, the means by which enormous volumes of money circulate through the world's fiber optics networks. Third, it summarizes the state of offshore banking. Fourth, it turns to the question of international back office and call center relocations, in which corporations use the internet to relocate clerical and data entry functions to developing countries. Fifth, it explores the world of internet telephony, or Voice Over Internet Protocol (VOIP). Sixth, it examines some ways in which the internet has affected retailing and distance learning. Finally, it offers a regional survey of global e-commerce to highlight the geographically uneven and contextualized nature of e-commerce, which is shaped by a multitude of regional and local policies, cultures, and economic dynamics.

B. Warf, *Global Geographies of the Internet*, SpringerBriefs in Geography, DOI: 10.1007/978-94-007-1245-4_4, © The Author(s) 2013

4.1 Global Cities and the Limits to the Internet Economy

A long-standing myth about telecommunications is that they render cities obsolete. While this fantasy can be traced to the post-industrial technocrats of the 1960s such as Alvin Toffler, if not earlier, it persists tenaciously in the age of the internet. Yet just as the internet was unfolding across the world stage, the recent round of globalization has witnessed a resurgence of "global cities" (Sassen 1991). Such places are by definition tied through vast tentacles of investment, trade, migration, and telecommunications to clients and markets, suppliers and competitors, consumers and producers around the world. Global cities serve as the home to massive complexes of financial firms, producer services, and corporate headquarters, or "command and control" centers in the world system. Typically, the trio of London, New York, and Tokyo is positioned at the top, with cascading layers demarcated by successively smaller roles in the world economy, including cities such as Paris, Frankfurt, Toronto, Los Angeles, Osaka, Hong Kong, and Singapore (Beaverstock et al. 2000). Because there exists a vast literature on this topic, it is not necessary to recite all of their characteristics here. Rather, it is their role in the internet-based economy, and the limits of the internet, which most concerns us. Not surprisingly, global cities, and indeed, most large metropolitan areas, are well-connected hubs with extensive fiber optic linkages, and often form constellations of internet-related businesses within them.

The core of such conglomerations—Manhattan or the City of London—allow for dense networks of interaction necessary to the performance of headquarters functions, including: monitoring frequent changes in niche product markets; negotiating with labor unions; keeping abreast of new technologies and government regulations; keeping an eye on the competition; staying attuned to an increasingly complex financial environment; initiating or resisting leveraged buy-outs and hostile takeovers; seeking new investment opportunities, and so forth. Because their *raison d'etre* cannot immediately be classified as "economic," but includes a vast variety of formal and informal cultural and political interactions such as tourism, the media, and fashion industries, global cities are more than simply poles for the production of corporate knowledge. The crux of global cities' role in the post-Fordist world economy is to serve as arenas of interaction, allowing face-to-face contact, political connections, artistic and cultural activities, and elites to rub shoulders easily. At their core, global cities allow the generation of specialized expertise upon which so much of the current producer services economy depends (Howells 2000). The creation of expertise is no simple task, involving the transformation of information into useful knowledge.

Analysis of the functionality of global cities can draw much from the work of Polanyi (1967), who offered a well-known and highly influential distinction between explicit (or standardized) and tacit knowledge. Explicit knowledge refers to standardized forms of information that are easily transmitted from one person to another, including quantitative data, publicly known rules and standards, and orderly records. Explicit knowledge is designed to be as free as possible from its context and easy to transmit over time and space, and involves operating rules to make it applicable to a wide array of environments, such as blueprints and operating manuals. As such, explicit knowledge is relatively easy to obtain and generates comparatively little in terms of value-added. Tacit knowledge, on the other hand, includes information that is unstandardized, changes rapidly, and is often not written down. Tacit knowledge is heavily context-dependent and subject to informal rules of organization that make it difficult to transmit from one situation to another, including gossip, oral histories, and invisible corporate cultures. Much of tacit knowledge involves the symbolic manipulation of information in ways that lead to corporate learning and innovation, a feature that makes it of great value to firms. It tends to circulate only within narrow social and geographical channels with a limited spatial range, and have a small degree of fungibility, i.e., substitutability in different contexts. Expertise of this type takes years to develop and involves the acquisition of highly specialized knowledge from diverse sources. Often such information is collected informally, over lunches, drinks and dinners, in the locker rooms of sports clubs, on golf courses, and through a variety of social and cultural events.

Face-to-face contact is essential to the performance of actors in non-routine functions. The early literature on office contact patterns (Kutay 1986), for example, revealed how difficult it is to substitute electronic contacts for personal meetings. Despite the enormous ability of telecommunications to transmit information instantaneously over vast distances, face-to-face contact remains the most efficient and effective means of obtaining and conveying irregular forms of information, particularly when it is highly sensitive (or even illegal, as the current wave of corporate malfeasance and insider trading demonstrates). Thus, in the context of face-to-face meetings, actors monitor one another's intentions and behavior through observations of body language, include handshakes and eye contact, which are essential to establishing relations of trust and mutual understanding. Such interactions are simply not substitutable to the digital form required by telecommunications.

Trading among markets and firms is largely managed, for example, by teams of traders rather than individuals, groups of people, computers and buildings that together constitute the interrelated formations that lie at the heart of actor-network theory. Such a line of thought does not collapse the importance of regional production systems to the socio-psychology of individuals; on the other hand, as the literatures on flexible production and actor-network theory demonstrate, neither can the functionality of large agglomerative complexes exist without precisely those types of interactions. The stability of such networks allows them to become "structural" in the sense that they endure over time and space, reproducing the role of these cities in the world economy.

As a sizable body of literature concerned with New York and London has demonstrated (Fainstein 1994; Longcore and Rees 1996; Mollenkopf and Castells 1991), the elites of global cities rely heavily on interpersonal contacts saturated with trust and reciprocity to "get things done." Such assets are very difficult to reproduce in other contexts, an observation that goes far to explain why the primacy of global cities such as Amsterdam, London, and New York has changed little over the last 500 years. While Polanyi's distinction has been mapped onto the global economy (Maskell and Malmberg 1999), such works typically focus on industry and have paid scant attention to the globalization of services.

The continued importance of global cities in the face of a networked space of flows is worth emphasizing. Repeated proclamations that telecommunications would allow everyone to engage in telecommuting, dispersing all functions and spelling the obsolescence of cities (O'Brien 1992; Cairncross 1997) and leading to a "borderless world" (Ohmae 1990), have fallen flat in the face of the persistence of growth in dense urbanized places. In fact, telecommunications are a rather poor substitute for face-to-face meetings, the medium through which sensitive corporate interactions occur, particularly when the information involved is irregular, proprietary, and unstandardized in nature. Most managers spend the bulk of their working time engaged in face-to-face contact, such as in meetings, and no electronic technology can yet allow for the subtlety and nuances critical to such encounters. Indeed, financial and business services firms not only pay high rents to be near city centers, and endure the congestion such locations entail, but spend lavishly to fly their executives around the world to meet with their counterparts in person. Even electronic conferencing, such as that offered by Skype, has been unable to substitute entirely for direct personal contact. For this reason, a century of technological change, from the telephone to fiber optics, has left most high-wage, white collar, administrative command and control functions clustered in downtown areas. In contrast, telecommunications are ideally suited for the transmission of routinized, standardized forms of data, facilitating the dispersal of functions involved with their processing (i.e., back offices) to low-wage regions.

Jones (2002) offers an insightful critique of the global cities thesis, noting that it tends to oversimplify the nature of corporate command and control functions by privileging physical location over networks, i.e., by focusing on the concentration of head offices. Rather, he argues, corporate power is wielded throughout the networks of international firms. He argues (p. 343) that "to use physical locations as an epistemological framework for theorizing command and control is to a large extent arbitrary and obfuscates the socially constituted complexity of managerial power within the transnational firm." The corporate decision making process is deeply embedded in various layers of the firm, including localized forms of knowledge not available at headquarters, and is often a negotiated outcome of groups involved in constant interaction with one another. Thus, by refocusing attention on the social practices that constitute multinational firms, actor-network theory has led the global cities literature to become more sensitive to issues of power and scale. In this light, *all* cities are global cities in that they are all enveloped in worldwide networks of goods, people, capital, and information.

In short, despite the near ubiquity of the internet in economically advanced countries, global cities retain their importance, and continue to exert hegemony, precisely because they facilitate the sorts of interactions that cannot be conducted easily over the web.

4.2 Electronic Funds Transfer Systems

Few industries have been more profoundly reshaped by the global fiber optic network than finance. Electronic funds transfer systems (EFTS) comprise the architecture of global capital markets, foreign exchange markets, and transactions payments, and form part of the profoundly important shift into digital money that began in the late 20th century (Schiller 1999). Aided by a massive worldwide network of fiber optics, international banks and speculators can shift significant sums around the world at a moment's notice, wreaking havoc with national monetary controls. As a result, the mounting velocity of global capital has accelerated to unprecedented speeds: freed from many technological and political barriers to movement, capital has become not merely mobile, but *hypermobile*. EFTS, therefore, are not simply economic in nature, but have important public policy ramifications (Solomon 1997b).

Since their first signs of existence in the 1970s, EFTS have spawned a copious literature, often utopian and technologically determinist in nature. By fomenting a "paperless economy," EFTS, which include business-to-consumer and business-to-business transactions, were assured to provide relief from growing mountains of paper transactions, reduce transactions costs, increase the velocity of money, improve capital market efficiency, and generate economies of scale in finance (Gallagher 1987; Kirkman 1987). The reality has been more complex.

Prior to the rise of EFTS, global finance was a relatively placid world. Under the Bretton-Woods system from 1947 to 1973, there were few exchange rate fluctuations; most currencies were pegged to the U.S. dollar, which was, in turn, was pegged to gold, at $35/ounce. Currency appreciations or depreciations reflected government fiscal and monetary policies within relatively nationally contained financial markets in which central bank intervention was effective. Trade balances and foreign exchange markets were strongly connected: rising imports caused a currency to decline in value as domestic buyers needed more foreign currency to finance purchases. Rising exports had the opposite effect, raising the price of domestic currencies on the international market. Currency fluctuations figured prominently in rectifying trade imbalances. The largely unregulated Euro market was also important to this system. The system ended abruptly with the U.S. abandonment of the gold standard in 1971 and the collapse of the Bretton-Woods system in 1973. Hereafter, supply and demand dictated the value of a state's currency. Soon currency exchange became the world's largest industry by volume: roughly $4 trillion in electronic funds crossed national borders each day in 2010, orders of magnitude more than the total value of international trade in goods.

Capital markets worldwide were profoundly affected by the digital revolution, which eliminated transactions and transmissions costs for the movement of capital much in the same way that deregulation and the abolition of capital controls decreased regulatory barriers (Batiz and Woods 2002; Solomon 1997a). Banks, insurance companies, and securities firms were at the forefront of the construction of an extensive network of telecommunications networks, particularly a seamlessly integrated worldwide skein of fiber optics lines, much of which forms the backbone of today's Internet. This infrastructure was decisive in enabling the birth of EFTS, which comprise the nervous system of the international financial economy and allow banks to move capital around a moment's notice, arbitrage interest rate differentials, take advantage of favorable exchange rates, and avoid political unrest.

One of the primary forms that EFTS take is Real Time Gross Settlement (RTGS) systems (O'Mahony et al. 2001), which handle money flows among financial institutions and governments. The largest of these is the U.S. Federal Reserve Bank's Fedwire system, which allows any depository institution with a Federal Reserve account to transfer funds to the Federal Reserve account of any other depository institution. In 2005, total Fedwire traffic amounted to $2.1 trillion per day (Federal Reserve 2009). The other major U.S. payments mechanism is the privately-owned Clearing House Interbank Payments System (CHIPS) in New York, operated by the New York Clearing House Association, a consortium run by private firms that clears about $1 trillion in daily transactions, half of which is in foreign exchange. In Europe, the Belgian-based Society for Worldwide Interbank Financial Telecommunications (SWIFT), formed in 1973, plays a comparable role; SWIFT extends into 208 countries and handles €2.6 billion daily in transactions. In the United Kingdom, settlements are made through the Clearing House Association Payments System (CHAPS) run by the Bank of England since 1984, while in the European Union, a system linking the banks of member states known as Trans-European Automated Real-time Gross settlement Express Transfer (TARGET), which began in 1999, is used to settle transactions involving the euro. In Japan, starting in 1988, the Bank of Japan Financial Network System (BOJNET) fills a comparable function.

Private firms have similar systems. Citicorp, for example, has a Global Information Network that allows it to trade $200 billion daily in foreign exchange markets around the world. MasterCard has its Banknet, which links all its users to a centralized database and payments clearing system. Reuters, with 200,000 interconnected terminals worldwide linked through systems such as Instinet and Globex, alone accounts for 40 % of the world's financial trades each day. Other systems include the London Stock Exchange Automated Quotation System (SEAQ), the Swiss Options and Financial Futures Exchange (SOFFEX), and the Computer Assisted Order Routing and Execution System at the Tokyo stock exchange. Such networks provide the ability to move money around the globe at stupendous rates (the average currency trade takes less than 25 s); supercomputers used for that purpose operate at teraflop speeds, or one trillion computations per second.

Similarly, in the securities markets, electronic funds transfer systems facilitated the emergence of 24 h/day trading, linking stock markets through computerized trading programs. Electronic trading frees stock analysts from the need for face-to-face interaction to gain information. On-line trading also allows small investors to trawl the Internet for information, including real-time prices, eroding the advantage once held by specialists, and execute trades by pushing a few buttons (e.g., via e-trade). Trade on many exchanges rose exponentially as a result. The National Association of Security Dealers Automated Quotation system (NASDAQ), the first fully automated electronic marketplace, is now the world's largest stock market; lacking a trading floor, NASDAQ connects millions of traders worldwide through the over-the-counter market, processing 2,000 transactions per second. EASDAQ, the European version of NASDAQ launched in 1996, operates similarly, albeit on a smaller scale. Facing the challenge of on-line trading head-on, Paris, Belgium, Spain, Vancouver and Toronto all recently abolished their trading floors. The volatility of trading, particularly in stocks, also increased as hair–trigger computer trading programs allow fortunes to be made (and lost) by staying microseconds ahead of (or behind) other markets.

Liberated from gold, travelling at the speed of light, as nothing but assemblages of zeros and ones, global money performs a syncopated electronic dance around the world's neural networks in astonishing volumes. The world's currency markets, for example, trade roughly four trillion U.S. dollars every day in 2007, dwarfing the funds that changes hands daily to cover global trade in goods and services. The ascendancy of electronic money shifted the function of finance from investing to speculation, institutionalizing volatility in the process. Foreign investments have increasingly shifted from foreign direct investment (FDI) to intangible portfolio investments such as stocks and bonds, a process that reflects the securitization of global finance. Unlike FDI, which generates predictable levels of employment, facilitates technology transfer, and alters the material landscape over the long run, financial investments tend to create few jobs and are invisible to all but a few agents, acting in the short run with unpredictable consequences. Further, such funds are often provided by non-traditional suppliers: a large and rapidly rising share of private capital flows worldwide is no longer intermediated by banks but by non-bank institutions such as securities firms and corporate financial operations. Thus, not only has the volume of capital flows increased, but the composition and institutions involved have changed.

Globalization and electronic money had particularly important impacts on currency markets. Since the shift to floating exchange rates, trading in currencies has become a big business, driven by the need for foreign currency associated with rising levels of international trade, the abolition of exchange controls, and the growth of pension and mutual funds, insurance companies, and institutional investors. The vast bulk (85 %) of foreign exchange transactions involves the U.S. dollar. Typically, the moneys involved in these markets follow the sun. For example, the foreign exchange (FOREX) market opens each day in East Asia while it is still evening in North America; funds then travel west, bouncing from city to city over fiber optic lines, e.g., from Tokyo to Hong Kong to Singapore to Bahrain to Frankfurt, Paris, or London, then to New York, Los Angeles, and back across the Pacific Ocean. (Given the continuous circularity of this movement, funds can originate anywhere and circle the globe within 24 h).

The neoclassical economic case for capital mobility holds that such fluidity allows countries with limited savings to attract financing for domestic investments, that it enables investors to diversify their portfolios, that it spreads risk more broadly, and that it promotes intertemporal trade. Capital mobility implies that firms can smooth consumption by borrowing money from abroad when domestic resources are limited and dampen business cycles. Conversely, by investing abroad, firms can reduce their vulnerability to domestic disturbances and achieve higher risk-adjusted rates of return. Advocates of unfettered capital flows hold that such mobility creates opportunities for portfolio diversification, risk sharing, and intertemporal trade, all important criteria for the IMF. The major problems concerning capital mobility in this view center upon the asymmetry of information in financial markets and "moral hazard," reliance upon the state (or IMF) to bail them out during crises. Yet neoclassical theory is flawed in several respects, not the least of which is an inadequate appreciation of politics and space, the ways in which national, class, gender, and other non-market relations shape and constrain flows of money, even electronic money, and information, and how the intersections of capital and nation-states play out unevenly across the globe. Capital flight, for example, can generate financial chaos as much as it harmonizes investments. Central to this issue is the relative degrees of influence and power that global capital and individual nation-states exhibit at varying historical conjunctures.

The rise of EFTS has fundamentally undermined the traditional role of national monetary policy. National borders mean little in the context of massive movements of money around the globe: it is far easier to move $1 billion from New York to Tokyo than a truckload of grapes from California to Arizona. Under Bretton-Woods, national monetary controls over exchange, interest, and inflation rates were essential to financial and trade stability; today, however, those same national regulations appear as a drag on competitiveness and have lost much of their effectiveness. In the U.S., for example, the Federal Reserve changed the reserve ratio of banks as well as the prime inter-bank loan rate multiple times in the 1990s and the 2000s, only to find that its control over the national money supply had diminished to the point of near irrelevance. The New York Federal Reserve's Foreign Exchange Office, the operational arm of the Treasury Department's Exchange Stabilization Fund, likewise attempted repeatedly to stabilize the U.S. dollar against other currencies, with mounting difficulty.

Thus, EFTS not only changed the configuration and behavior of financial markets but also their relations to the nation-state. Raymond Vernon's (1971) classic work *Sovereignty at Bay* argued convincingly that the nation-state (as classically conceived), sovereignty and the national economy were on their death-bed, victims of multinational corporations and international capital. Advocates of this perspective, of course, have long exaggerated claims that the nation-state was dying to the point of asserting that a seamlessly integrated "borderless" world was in the making. The brave new world of digital finance, however, lends credence to Vernon's predictions in ways he or his advocates may not have anticipated. Classic interpretations of the national state rested heavily upon a clear distinction between the domestic and international spheres, a world carved into mutually exclusive geographic jurisdictions. State control in this context implies control over territory. In contrast, the rise of electronic money has generated a fundamental asymmetry between the world's economic and political systems. World-systems theorists have long maintained that the fundamental political geography of capitalism is not the nation-state but the interstate system, which offers capital great leverage by flowing across borders in ways that the reach of regulatory authorities cannot.

EFTS present the global system of states with unprecedented difficulties in attempting to reap the benefits of international finance while simultaneously attempting to avoid its risks. For example, Kobrin (1997, p. 75) notes

> E-cash is one manifestation of a global economy that is constructed in cyberspace rather than geographic space. The fundamental problems that e-cash poses for governance result from this disconnect between electronic markets and political geography. The very idea of controlling the money supply, for example, assumes that geography provides a relevant means of defining the scope of the market. It assumes that economic borders are effective, that the flow of money across them can be monitored and controlled, and that the volume of money within a fixed geographic area is important. All of those assumptions are increasingly questionable in a digital world economy.

Changes in the structure of institutional investing have had profound impacts on this market: rapid movement of funds worldwide has meant that under- or over-valued currencies are likely to be subjected to speculative attacks from large hedge funds or financial institutions. The power of electronic money is evident when currency speculators mount an attack on a given national currency, such as those launched against the Thai baht in 1997, which initiated the disastrous Asian financial crisis. Under such circumstances, political authorities can attempt to manipulate exchange rates where the currency remains shackled by a "managed float" or "crawling peg" system, typically harnessed to the U.S. dollar, but often creating internal and external price distortions. Capital controls offer short-term benefits but discourage long-run investments such as infrastructure development, and often get mired in corruption. More drastically, they can raise interest rates. The goal in such situations is to convince speculators that the national bank will stay the course and commit whatever reserves are necessary to shore up its currency by using the same leveraging tools as their private adversaries, but few states possess the resources to maintain such a defense for long.

In short, Vernon's predictions, however premature, may have considerably more validity at present than they did when his book first appeared. This is not to say that the nation-state is obsolete, or event that it will be in the near future, but rather that electronic money has markedly shifted the nature of international finance and investment, undermining the effectiveness of national monetary controls.

4.3 Offshore Banking

As Wechsler (2001, p. 43) notes, "Thanks to globalization and advances in banking technologies, distant countries are now just a mouse-click away." Thus, another instance in which the peripheralization of relatively capital-intensive, routinized services is offshore banking (Gorostriaga 1984; Bowe 1998; Cobb 1998; Warf 2002). Roberts (1994) identified five major world clusters of offshore finance, including the Caribbean (e.g., the Cayman Islands, Bahamas, Panama); Europe (the Isle of Man, Jersey, and microstates on the Continent); the Middle East (Cyprus, Lebanon, and particularly Bahrain); Southeast Asia (Hong Kong, Singapore); and the south Pacific (Vanuatu, Nauru). Such places provide commercial investment services (i.e., loans and advice), foreign currency trades, asset protection (insurance), investment consulting, international tax planning, and trade finance (e.g., letters of credit). Employment in offshore banking is relatively capital-intensive when compared to the labor-intensive headquarters in global cities: for example, in the Cayman Islands, the world's largest center of offshore finance, Roberts (1995) notes that 1,000 foreign banks employ only 538 people; most are "brass plate" or shell banks. The high degree of capital intensity in this case speaks to the hybrid nature of offshore banks, which combine computers, software, buildings and an occasional worker to form actor-networks that vary from place to place.

Conventional geographic preoccupations with proximity mean little in this case, for the topologies of global finance are formed and deformed in ways that the language of location theory cannot capture. Rather, it is the political economy of actor-networks in question that are central to the evolving spatial distribution of this segment of the global service economy. Offshore centers are the "black holes" in the global topography of financial regulation, a status that emanates directly from the enhanced ability of large financial institutions to shift funds electronically to take advantage of lax regulations, freedom from taxes and currency controls, and other restrictions to be found on the periphery of the global financial system. As the technological barriers to moving money have fallen, allowing digital money to circulate at will, legal and regulatory ones have increased in importance. Globalization does not eliminate local differences, it accentuates them. Even relatively minor differences in regulations concerning corporate taxes or repatriated profits may attract or repel large quantities of capital to enter, or exit, particular places. Thus, Hudson (2000) argues that the phenomenon of offshore banking is redefining national sovereignty, uncoupling political and financial control from the territories that long held sway over financial institutions.

Offshore banking centers have long suffered from the cloud of suspicion that they constitute little more than havens for tax evasion and money laundering of illicitly obtained funds (Hampton and Christensen 1999). As electronic money has come to dominate global finance, the use of offshore banking centers for illegitimate purposes has grown apace. Indeed, just as large corporations can use the Internet and fiber optics to move funds from place to place, so can actors in the "dark side" of the global economy, including tax evaders, drug cartels, arms traffickers, terrorists, and corrupt government officials. Given that they often occupy the boundary between "legitimate" and "illegitimate" financial activity, a key issue in the success or failure of offshore banking centers is the degree of confidentiality that investors feel they can obtain. Indeed, the quality of offshore banking centers is often judged by the quality of laws protecting the privacy of investors. The use of shell companies, including holding corporations and increasingly, foundations, blurs legal lines of liability, keeping insurance rates low, and protecting assets (both legal and otherwise) from public scrutiny through deliberately impenetrable webs of cross-ownership that typically deflect even the most dogged of auditors. Thus, despite the putatively aspatial nature of electronic money and the extreme fungibility of electronic financial capital, place still matters in the geography of offshore banking in the forms of locally embedded local policies.

4.4 Back Office and Call Center Relocations

Few domains of economic activity have been as heavily affected by telecommunications as low level, routinized back office functions, which currently employ about 250,000 people in the U.S. Back offices perform clerical functions such as data entry of office records, telephone books, or library catalogues, stock transfers, payroll or billing information, bank checks, insurance claims, and magazine subscriptions. These tasks involve unskilled or semi-skilled labor, primarily women, and frequently operate on a 24-hour-per-day basis. Back offices have few of the interfirm linkages associated with headquarters activities and require extensive data processing facilities, reliable sources of electricity, and sophisticated telecommunications networks.

Historically, back offices have located adjacent to headquarters activities in downtown areas to insure close management supervision and rapid turnaround of information. However, under the impetus of rising central city rents and shortages of sufficiently qualified (i.e., computer literate) labor, many service firms began to uncouple their headquarters and back office functions, moving the latter out of the downtown to cheaper locations on the urban periphery. Most back office relocations, therefore, have been to suburbs; 95 % of all relocations of data entry jobs are within metropolitan areas.

Recently, given the increasing locational flexibility afforded by satellites and inter-urban fiber optics systems, back offices have begun to relocate on a much broader, continental scale. Under the impetus of new telecommunications systems, many clerical tasks have become increasingly footloose and susceptible to spatial variations in production costs. Digital call distribution systems have made possible the relocation of phone services that were once confined to centralized locations. Many financial and insurance firms and airlines moved their back offices from New York, San Francisco, and Los Angeles to low wage communities in the Midwest and South. Phoenix, Atlanta, and Kansas City are examples of particularly significant beneficiaries of this growth. Omaha, Nebraska, claims to have created 100,000 tele-generated jobs in the last decade, in part because of its location at the crossroads of the national fiber optic infrastructure (Richardson and Belt 2002). Similarly, with abundant cheap labor, San Antonio and Wilmington, Delaware have become well-known centers of telemarketing. Boulder, Colorado and Columbus, Ohio have moved in much the same direction, in part because their centralized geographic location gave them advantages during the era of banded WATS service.

Internationally, this trend has taken the form of the offshore office. The primary motivation for offshore relocation is low labor costs, although other considerations include worker productivity, skills, turnover, and benefits. Offshore offices are established not to serve foreign markets, but to generate cost savings for U.S. firms by tapping Third World labor pools where wages are as low as one-fifth of those in the U.S. Notably, many firms with offshore back offices are in industries facing strong competitive pressures to enhance productivity, including insurance, publishing, and airlines. Offshore back office operations remained insignificant until transoceanic fiber optics lines made possible locational flexibility on an international scale. Such functions may be either subsidiaries of multinational firms or they may operate under contract with U.S.-based businesses. Inputs, usually documents or magnetic tapes, are sent by air to offshore processing facilities (e.g., via Federal Express). After processing, generally a few days at most, the results are returned via satellite or dedicated telephone or fiber optic line. Thus, the capital investments in such operations are minimal and they possess great flexibility, maximizing their ability to choose among locations based on slight variations in cost or profitability.

Several New York-based life insurance companies have erected back office facilities in Ireland, with the active encouragement of the Irish Development Authority (McGahey et al. 1990). Often situated near Shannon Airport, they move documents in by Federal Express and the final product back via satellite or one of the numerous fiber optic lines that connects New York and London. Likewise, the Caribbean, particularly Anglophone countries such as Jamaica and Barbados, has become a particularly important locus for American back offices. American Airlines paved the way in the Caribbean when it moved its data processing center from Tulsa to Barbados in 1981; through its subsidiary Caribbean Data Services (CDS), it expanded operations to Montego Bay, Jamaica and Santo Domingo, Dominican Republic in 1987. Mullings (1999) explored how women employed in Jamaican back offices deployed a variety of tactics to cope and resist simultaneously the low wages, oppressive working conditions, and lack of occupational mobility they offer. In Asia, Manila has emerged as a back office center for British firms, with wages 20 % of those in the U.K.

Data entry functions have been supplemented by the diffusion of other types of jobs to the global periphery. The animation of cartoons such as the Simpsons, for example, has migrated to India. American high school kids can email Indian tutors for help with their homework (Lohr 2007). Some U.S. video game players, seeking to skip the easy and boring early stages of online role-playing video games, outsource this stage to hired, often impoverished, Chinese players known as 'gold farmers', allowing them to advance rapidly to the later, more challenging, stages (Barboza 2005). More serious is the out-migration of higher skilled jobs. Radiological skills such as reading X-rays and PET scans can be done by Indians at a fraction of the cost of American physicians, as firms such as Cyberteleradiology attest. So too can tax preparation, which Indian accountants handle cheaply and competently. Increasingly chip design and software debugging have moved to India as well, as have editing and proof reading functions. Such trends indicate that telecommunications may accelerate the offshoring of many low wage, low value-added jobs from the U.S., with dire consequences for unskilled workers.

A related form of low wage, low value added services involves centers of telework, often labeled call centers. Bodin and Dawson (2002, p. 39) define call centers as "places where calls are placed, or received, in high volume for the purpose of sales, marketing, customer service, telemarketing, technical support or other specialized business activity" (cf. Richardson and Belt 2002). Call centers functions include telemarketing, customer assistance, and phone-orders with designated 1–800 numbers. They range greatly in size, from as few as five to as many as several thousand employees. Despite their prevalence, call centers have remained in the shadow of other well-known information-dependent industries such as financial services. Like back offices, call centers are primarily screen-based and do not require proximity to clients. The major cost consideration is labor, although the workforce consists primarily of low skilled women, and high turnover rates are common. They are thus the epitome of a footloose industry, disembedded from their local milieu and highly mobile. There are an estimated 80,000–100,000 call centers within the U.S., which employ between 3 and 5 % of the national labor force (Uchitelle 2002), the majority of which are located in urban or suburban locations. Cities that have recently established competitive niches in this domain include Omaha, Nebraska; San Antonio, Texas; Wilmington, Delaware; Albuquerque, New Mexico; and Columbus, Ohio.

Also like back offices, call centers have become increasingly globalized. India, for example, has attracted a significant number of customer service centers near its software capital of Bangalore, where workers are trained to speak with the U.S. dialect of English and are able to gossip with customers about pop culture (Waldman 2003). Wages there, which average $2,000 per year, are higher than average Indian salaries but are only 10 % of what equivalent jobs pay in the U.S.

Call centers form nodes in networks that include First World firms, Third World workers, the internet, clients, and massive, if invisible, information flows, without which the systems would not exist and could not function. The Indian example illustrates how blurry the boundaries between the local and global is: a Bangalore operator speaking to a British customer calling for help with American software program all comprise parts of one integrated topology that erases the convenient closures afforded by conventional geography. Such observations give us a hint at the complexities of the geographies being ushered in by the internet and digital capitalism in general.

4.5 VOIPocalypse Now

One increasingly important repercussion of the internet is Voice Over Internet Protocol (VOIP), i.e., telephone traffic conducted entirely through cyberspace, allowing users to bypass the toll charges ubiquitous among public switched networks. VOIP is generally held to have begun in 1995 with a small Israeli firm,

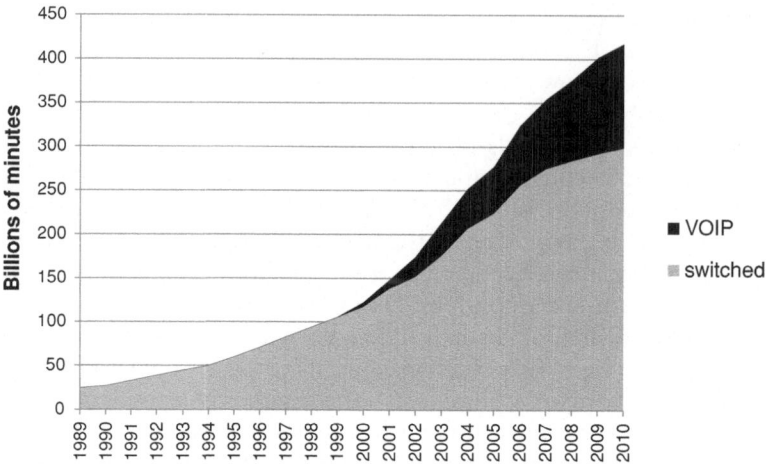

Fig. 4.1 Global telephony minutes in switched and VOIP mode, 1989–2010. *Source* redrawn from Telegeography.com

VocalTec, which introduced software allowing voice traffic among personal computers. Soon thereafter, it and other companies extended this process over the internet. Essentially, this mode allows voice traffic to ride over a system designed originally only for data by "packetizing" voices in a form amenable to TCP/IP formats, leading to a convergence of voice and data traffic. Three versions of VOIP exist: computer-to-computer, computer-to-phone, and phone-to-phone, each of which involves different technical challenges in switching data packets. The extremely low price of VOIP results from its ability to bypass expensive dedicated circuits between callers by encoding calls as two-way streams of data packets sent over broadband internet connections. Thus, VOIP is not a new product per se, but a means of utilizing the existing internet infrastructure more efficiently, an in the process, uncoupling internet access from internet services. As Werbach (2005, p. 140) puts it, "What makes it so potent is that it turns speech into digital data packets that can be stored, searched, manipulated, copied, combined with other data, and distributed to virtually any device that connects to the Internet. Think of it, basically, as the World Wide Web for the voice."

VOIP rapidly mushroomed into a multibillion dollar industry. Early concerns over poor quality of transmission were eased as the technology adapted to the growing broadband market; indeed, the growth of VOIP and broadband internet have gone hand-in-hand. As internet telephony rose in popularity, it attracted investments in routing and switching equipment from large network producers such as Lucent and Cisco. VOIP has grown rapidly at the expense of its alternative, public switched telephone network (PSTN) telephone traffic; from a minuscule 4 % of the world's telephony traffic in 2000, VOIP has expanded to roughly 27 % in 2010 (Fig. 4.1). Indeed, while traffic growth rates for PSTN systems have dropped to rates of 8–10 % annually, VOIP traffic is rising at rates twice or three times as high.

Several factors drive this phenomenon. Constantiou and Kautz (2008), in a study of Danish VOIP adopters from a technology diffusion perspective, highlighted the role of economic factors such as its low price, network effects (i.e., compatibility with fixed line systems), and switching costs (e.g., hardware and investments in learning the new system). The promise of wireless VOIP, still in its infancy, threatens to elevate its popularity yet further.

Once the province of relatively small telecommunications startups, the VOIP market has recently attracted interest from almost all telecommunications giants such as MCI-WorldCom and Deutsche Telekom, hardware and software firms such as Nokia and Microsoft, and cable television companies such as TimeWarner Cable and Comcast. As VOIP has shifted from the consumer market to include business applications, many large corporations (e.g., Boeing, Bank of America, and Cisco Systems) use VOIP to minimize their telecommunications costs, often simply by using the spare capacity of their intranets, generating considerable savings in the process. Others, such as Bank of America, deploy the technology to relocate back offices and data entry functions to India. Even some telecommunications carriers, such as Telecom Italia, France Telecom, Deutsche Telekom, Japan's NTT, Telefónica, and the Dutch firm KPN, have begun to offer VOIP services.

VOIP has also surged in the developing world in an uneven series of path-dependent trajectories (Cecere 2009). In the case of VOIP, the drivers and obstacles to adoption include the sunk costs of existing telecommunications companies and their ability to shape national regulatory structures; the legal and economic barriers faced by new entrants to the market; internet penetration rates; and the capacity of local providers and consumers (including their accumulated experiences and technological sophistication) to exploit new technological and social opportunities that internet telephony generates (Cecere 2009).

The world's most popular VOIP application by far is Skype, founded in 2003 by two Scandinavian entrepreneurs, Niklas Zennström and Janus Friis (the creators of KaZaa) using software developed by Estonian engineers. Skype essentially fused VOIP with peer-to-peer computing, a departure from traditional client–server models, and its SkypeOut application pioneered the shift from computer-to-computer VOIP to include PSTN networks. What started as a set of free services broadened to include fee-based ones, including voice mail and conference calls. In 2005, eBay paid $2.6 billion to acquire Skype, and then sold it to investors in 2009; Microsoft, attracted by the potential future growth and "click to call" advertising, acquired it in 2011 for $8.5 billion. Headquartered in Luxembourg, it relies heavily on software engineers located in Tallinn. Today, it supports 29 languages and allows users to make free calls to other Skype account holders or calls to other phones for nominal fees. In 2009, more than 560 million Skype users (Fig. 4.2)[1] accounted for 12 % of the world's international telephony minutes

---

[1] Some challenge this estimate on the grounds that it includes users with multiple accounts or unused accounts, and argue that the "real" number of users is more likely around 170 million. Most analyses of Skype traffic focus on the average simultaneous number of users, typically held to be roughly 30 million in January 2012.

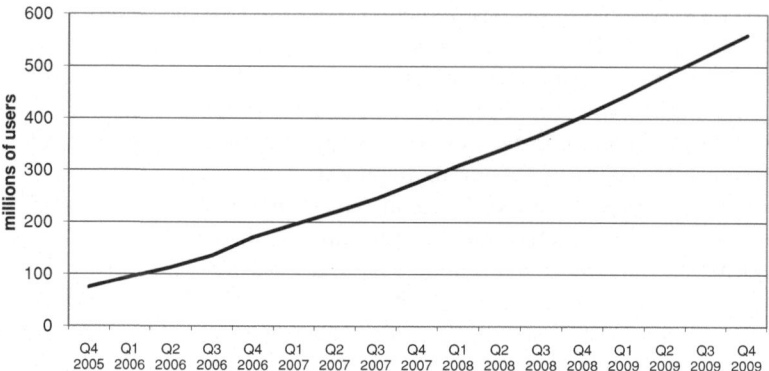

Fig. 4.2 Growth in Skype users worldwide. *Source* Schonfeld 2009

Table 4.1 Distribution of Skype users in 20 largest countries of usage, 2004

Country	% Global Skype users	No. of users (millions)
United States	9.13	6.8
Poland	7.87	5.9
Taiwan	7.80	5.8
China	6.75	5.0
Germany	6.06	4.5
Brazil	5.85	4.4
France	5.62	4.2
United Kingdom	3.50	2.6
Netherlands	3.47	2.6
Japan	3.17	2.4
Spain	2.64	2.0
Israel	2.36	1.8
Canada	2.22	1.7
Belgium	1.95	1.5
Italy	1.91	1.4
Denmark	1.73	1.3
Sweden	1.62	1.2
Turkey	1.59	1.2
Switzerland	1.42	1.1
Australia	1.41	1.0

Source http://eurotelcoblog.blogspot.com/2005/04/whose-net-is-it-anyway-stumbled-across.html

(Malik 2010), or half the global total of VOIP call minutes, overshadowing its roughly 2,000 competitors worldwide (half of which are in the U.S.). Skype is particularly important in international telephony: half of Skype calls are between countries, and account for one-fourth of all calls that cross national borders. Skype usage varies markedly among the world's countries (Table 4.1). Video calls have also surged in popularity among Skype users and now comprise 40 % of its call volume. More recent additions include file transfers and answering services.

Remarkably little has been written about the social and spatial consequences of Skype. Anecdotal evidence suggests that like mobile phones, it is popular among immigrants, who use it to stay in touch with their home countries. Migrants from Eastern Europe now living in the U.K., for example, use it extensively (Metykova 2010). In Australia, Skype has become popular among rural households, for whom it is a ready antidote to the loneliness and isolation of the outback, and has increased the volume and quality (with video) of long-distance ties (Richard 2009).

Arguably the biggest impact of internet telephony is on the telecommunications industry. VOIP is such a "disruptive technology" in the Schumpeterian sense (Rao et al. 2006) that it threatens to reduce the costs of telephone traffic to zero, in the process assassinating the pricing models based on distance and duration of calls and forcing providers to offer flat-rate billing plans. (Critics reply that because VOIP piggy-backs on existing networks, it is a parasitic, not disruptive, technology). Because voice traffic represents roughly three-quarters of telecommunications industry profits, the reduction in prices to nearly zero poses an extremely serious challenge to firms in the trillion-dollar market ("VOIPocalypse"). Telecommunications companies have responded to the VOIP challenge in different ways, including lowering prices to reduce the attractiveness of the new medium, attempting to gain market share in the VOIP market (e.g., Google Voice), fomenting fears about the security of voice traffic over unsecured internet lines, or by merging voice and data traffic and charging by the number of megabytes transmitted (Wortham 2011). Others have been forced to cannibalize their revenues from the public switched network. Some governments have banned or propose to ban VOIP in an attempt to protect their incumbent telecommunications providers, including China, India, Myanmar/Burma, Egypt, and Lebanon. However, *The Economist* concluded, "It is now no longer a question of whether VOIP will wipe out traditional telephony, but a question of how quickly it will do so."

4.6 E-tailing, Tourism, Distance Learning, and Internet Gambling

E-commerce extends far beyond banking, finance and back offices. It has restructured how firms do business. One important version of ecommerce concerns electronic data interchange (EDI) systems, which are generally used in business-to-business (B2B) contacts. Common uses of EDI include relatively cheap advertising; online product catalogues; the sharing of sales and inventory data; submissions of purchase orders, contracts, invoices, payments, and delivery schedules; product updates; and labor recruitment. E-commerce reduces delays and marketing and delivery costs, improves supply chain management, and has led to a greater emphasis on connectivity, ideas, creativity, speed, and customer service. In insurance, e-commerce has streamlined underwriting policies, and centralized database management systems. Electronic advertising is relatively cheap, and has grown in popularity as internet use has soared, although its effectiveness varies considerably among national cultures (Miller et al. 2009). Internet advertising has proven to be difficult, in part because the Internet reaches numerous specialized markets rather than mass audiences. However, cyberspace does facilitate specialized companies to reach global niche markets. Yet e-commerce should not be seen as a realm independent of the broader dynamics of capital accumulation: In many respects, it is closely bound up with the cultural logic of contemporary commodity production and consumption (Leyshon et al. 2005).

"E-tailing," or electronic retailing, reveals the growing commercialization of the Internet: in 1993, 2 % of all Web sites were commercial (i.e., "dot com") sites; by 2010, 70 % were so categorized. Shopping by the Internet requires only access, a credit card (or perhaps a service such as PayPal), and a parcel delivery service. Such a mode allows effortless price comparisons and intensifies competition among suppliers. In 2010, global e-tailing sales were estimated to exceed $680 billion. The proportion varies markedly by economic sector and region of the world. Shoppers using this mode tend to be above-average in income and relatively well educated. Web-based banking has experienced slow growth, even though it is considerably cheaper for banks than automatic teller machines, as have Internet-based bill payments, mortgages, and insurance. Of course, the use of e-tailing depends heavily on consumers' confidence that private information placed on-line will remain secure.

The internet has also had important effects on tourism (Buhalis 2003), which by employment is the largest industry in the world. Traditionally the most important role attributed to information technology in the tourism sector has been reservation services and destinations. However, the internet has greatly accelerated the spread of tourist information, leading tourists to change their behavior, and tourist companies and institutions have changed their promotion and distribution channels accordingly (Buhalis and Licata 2002). For example, it provides new opportunities and tools for tourist destinations to represent themselves and creates new opportunities in marketing channels. Internet-based tourism allows companies new ways to organize their activities, including efficiency improvements, better communications with clients and suppliers over large areas, and easier agreements with business partners, including real-time dissemination of information via the internet and electronic payments for services. For customers, the internet facilitates price transparency, better visual and graphic information, and time savings. Clearly the increasing use of the Internet for travel planning has altered the behavior among both tourists and the businesses that cater to them.

Another version of e-commerce concerns universities, many of which have invested heavily in Web-based distance learning courses. Although such programs are designed to attract nonlocal and nontraditional students, many of whom may not be able to take lecture-based courses in the traditional manner, they also reflect the mounting financial constraints and declining public subsidies that many institutions face, which may see distance learning as a means of attracting additional students, and tuition, at relatively low marginal costs. The largest example of Web-based teaching is the University of Phoenix, based in Arizona but with students located around the world; with more than 400,000 students, it is now the largest university in the world. Some universities, such as Stanford, have begun offering free on-line courses to hundreds of thousands of students at a time, and given birth to new corporations such as Coursera.org. Distance learning has provoked fears that it opens the door to the corporatization of academia and the domination of the profit motive, while others have questioned whether the chat rooms that form an important part of its delivery system are an effective substitute for the face-to-face teaching and learning that classrooms offer. It remains unclear whether Web-based learning is an effective complement or substitute for traditional forms of instruction. Others suggest that distance-learning programs may be better suited to professional programs in business or engineering than in the liberal arts.

More morally ambiguous is the growing role of Internet-based gambling systems, which include a variety of betting services, especially concerning sports events, and even online slot machines in which gamblers may use their credit cards (Wilson 2003). (Some complain that online gambling doesn't adequately substitute for the heady experience of a gaudy casino in Las Vegas or Atlantic City, New Jersey). Because the geography of legal gambling is highly uneven, the existence of such systems challenges the laws of communities in which gambling is illegal. Offshore gambling centers have grown quickly, particularly in the Caribbean, which started when Antigua licensed its first Internet casino in 1994. In 2011, an estimated 1,000 online casinos, mostly in the Caribbean, attracted roughly 12 million users. Similarly, Zook (2003) called attention to the internet's role in the "online adult industry."

4.7 Regional Geographies of E-Commerce

As with internet use more broadly, and internet censorship, there is no "one-size-fits-all" model of e-commerce. Rather, the magnitude and form it assumes is highly dependent on the contextual specifics of individual regions. As Gefen and Heart (2009) point out, e-commerce is intimately wrapped up with cultural norms of trust, reputation, familial contacts, tacit knowledge, and other related dimensions. E-commerce is also differentially enabled and constrained by national legal systems, including intellectual property rights and the degree of security of online transactions, all of which conspire to give it a very real regional geography.

4.7.1 North America

The internet is having significant effects on the Canadian economy (Janelle 2001; Michalak and Jones 2003), where numerous firms use it to raise market shares and reduce transactions costs. Online sales, which surpassed $15.1 billion in 2009

(Statistics Canada 2010), comprise roughly 11 % of the Canadian GDP and are growing quickly. The bulk of such activity occurs among businesses rather than between firms and consumers (i.e., intermediate rather than final demand). The rising popularity of e-commerce forces firms to change their business models, giving rise to new products and processes and annihilating older ones in a ceaseless process of creative destruction. For example, one-half of Canadians use the internet to make travel reservations. For some observers, e-commerce presents a danger of mounting cross-border purchases from the United States (McKeowen and Brocca 2007). In northern Canada, e-commerce is less well developed. Nonetheless, telemedicine has gained ground in Nunavut (Heaton 2011).

In early 2012, U.S. e-commerce retail sales exceeded $224 billion, and were growing at twice the rate of total retail sales. Despite predictions that "click and order" shopping would eliminate "brick and mortar" stores, e-tailing has been slow to catch on, however, comprising only 4.6 % of total U.S. retail sales, perhaps because it lacks the emotional content of shopping. e-tailing comprised the vast majority of travel reservations ($8 billion/year), 62 % of all banking trans- actions, 17 % of computer sales, and 11 % of book sales. The most successful example perhaps is Amazon.com, started by Seattle entrepreneur Jeff Bezos, which now is responsible for 60 % of all books sold online. Other examples include online auctions (e.g., eBay) and Internet music (e.g., downloading of MP3 music files), which has provoked a firestorm of opposition from music companies con- cerned about infringement of their intellectual property rights and declining over- the-counter music sales. Indeed, e-books now comprise 10 % of all book sales, and music downloads exceed purchases of CDs, sending sales of the latter crashing in a downward spiral of creative destruction. I-tunes alone comprises 10 % of all music sales. Streaming on-demand downloads of movies, through companies such as Netflix, have increased their share as well. However, internet sales have also provoked worries about tax evasion and sales of illegal goods (e.g., pharmaceu- ticals from abroad). Internet-based sales of stocks (e.g., E*Trade) now comprise 15 % of all U.S. trades. B2B e-commerce has spread from its earlier confines in large corporations to include increasing numbers of small and medium-sized enterprises (Grandon and Pearson 2004), a process that allegedly "levels the playing field" and obviates the advantages of size. E-advertising comprises only 1 % of total revenues in the United States and is overwhelmingly focused on computer and software firms. Indeed, many users are now wary of "spam" e-mail (unwanted commercial messages), which constitute an ever-larger, and increas- ingly annoying, share of e-mail traffic (by some estimates as high as 75 %).

Although the U.S. comprises one vast national market with relatively few internal cultural and political barriers, unlike Europe, e-commerce is nonetheless unevenly distributed among its cities and regions (Zook 2000, 2001, 2002). Zook (2005) offers a detailed portrait of the regional internet economy of the San Francisco Bay Area, a churning hub of dot.com entrepreneurship in the 1990s and 2000s, with companies such as Yahoo!, Google, America Online, Ebay, and Mosaic (which later gave birth to Netscape and Hotmail). Such an analysis goes far to debunk the myth of the "spaceless" internet economy, and points instead to the reality of regional clusters in which agglomeration economies, including close linkages to venture capitalists, figure prominently. As the largest single concentration of internet-based firms in the world, the San Francisco–Silicon Valley complex operates, ironically, very much through the circulation of tacit information in narrowly defined social channels. Inevitably, the attractiveness of dot.com companies attracted over-investment, leading to the dot com boom, with huge bonuses, massages and company-sponsored yoga, and early retirement, as well as overconfidence and carelessness. Given capitalism's propensity for cyclical swings, the dot.com boom turned into the dot.com crash of 2001–2003, with widespread layoffs and bankruptcies, exhibiting the Schumpeterian process of creative destruction that inevitably brings the mighty to their knees.

4.7.2 Europe

With high levels of disposable incomes, widespread credit card use, and abundant levels of technical skill among the populace, Europe is well positioned to take advantage of electronic commerce (Waesche 2003). The uneven popularity of e-commerce, as exemplified by the varying levels of e-tailing among countries (Table 4.2), testifies to enduring national differences. However, while half of all retailers in the European Union offer goods and services on-line, only 20 % of e-commerce sales extended cross national borders (Weibold 2010), reflecting the numerous cultural and linguistic barriers that fragment the continent.

As early as the 1990s, Scandinavian countries were pioneers in applications such as electronic data interchange (Damsgaard and Lyytinen 1998). With almost universal internet access, the region is well poised to take advantage of internet commerce. Unlike many countries where e-commerce is predominantly the domain of large firms, in Scandinavia the practice has become widespread among smaller enterprises as well (Eriksson and Hultman 2005; Eriksson et al. 2008). Scandinavian e-tailing takes a variety of forms. In Finland, for example, electronic banking has become very popular, and is now used regularly by 40 % of bank customers (Karjalouto 2002; Parker and Parker 2008). With aging populations, Scandinavia has become adept at electronic health care including telemedicine (Jung and Loria 2010). The internet has also allowed for a steady expansion of Scandinavian tele-work and telecommuting (Vilhelmson and Thulin 2001).

British e-commerce is booming (Dodd 2010). The internet is estimated to generate 7.2 % of British GDP, among the highest rates in the world (Robinson 2010). In 2011, on-line sales exceeded £50 billion, roughly 12 % of the total and the highest ratio in Europe. More than simply electronics, which form the most popular item bought and sold over the internet everywhere, British consumers also purchased significant amounts of groceries, home and garden products, and clothing on-line. The drivers of Britain's success in e-commerce center on aggressive strategic support from senior management of several large national retail firms (Doherty and Ellis-Chadwick 2009).

Table 4.2 European on-line retail sales as percent of total, 2011

United Kingdom	12.0
Germany	9.0
Switzerland	8.7
Denmark	8.0
Norway	8.1
France	7.3
Sweden	6.9
Benelux	5.1
Spain	3.5
Poland	3.1
Italy	1.3

Source Center for Retail Research http://www.retailresearch.org/onlineretailing.php

Germany, with Europe's largest single population of netizens, has a robust e-commerce sector, the second largest in the world. German e-commerce tends to consolidate spatially in distinct clusters, particularly in Berlin and Baden-Wurttemberg. Germany's success in this regard reflects its long tradition of adopting new technologies, its history of nonstore shopping (i.e., mail order and catalogue houses), and the politics of retail regulation, (Aoyama and Schwarz 2004). As with the U.S., a secure legal environment protects German consumers' privacy and gives them freedom from fraud. Oddly, however, a relatively small number of German consumers use credit cards compared to the U.S. E-tailing has also been greatly facilitated by online shopping clubs such as Brands4friends.de, Limango.de, and Zalando-lounge.de. The most popular items purchased online, in descending order, include travel reservations, shoes, and computer hardware. Thus, even as the number of German retail stores and their sales declines, e-commerce there grows steadily.

In France, the adoption of e-commerce was slowed by the country's reliance on Minitel, whose applicability for e-commerce was negligible; the French internet, and hence e-commerce, did not begin until 1997 (Brousseau 2003). Nonetheless, since then the French have adopted it enthusiastically. Levels of trust in France tend to be well below those in Germany, which has also affected their pattern of e-commerce adoption (Sun 2011). Nonetheless, one-half of French Internet users have purchased goods or services on-line. Segments of the European e-commerce market face limitations: French curbs on Internet gambling, for example, have faced threats from the European Union. In Italy, e-commerce supplements rather than substitutes for the highly successful model of industrial districts such as in Emilia-Romagna (Chiarvesio et al. 2004). However, e-commerce in Southern Europe is relatively undeveloped compared to their northern neighbors: less than 10 % of companies in Spain, Greece, and Portugal, for example, utilize the Internet for sales, compared to 30 % in Germany and the United Kingdom (Nicola et al. 2004), and in Italy, only 1.3 % of retail sales were conducted on-line (Table 4.2).

East European e-commerce reflects its nascent, emerging market. In Poland, on-line sales amounted to only 3.1 % of the total, but are rising rapidly, particularly as the country's internet infrastructure expands with monetary assistance from the European Union. Foreign firms, such as the French-owned Carrefour Group, have played a significant role in this respect. Major Polish e-commerce sites as Allegro.pl and Merlin.pl are benefiting from the growth. Similarly, two-thirds of Czech internet users engage in e-tailing. E-commerce in the Balkans is also underdeveloped: in Greece, for example, only 20 % of companies with ten or more employees have the capacity to take on-line orders (*Economist* 2006a). In Serbia, the cessation of hostilities in 2000 has led to an explosion of internet-related activities, including a nascent software industry in Belgrade, although collectively they remain small in comparison to economically advanced countries; tentative steps include the formation of Knjizara.com, an online bookstore emulating Amazon.com, and Balkanmedia, a Web-based music store (Travica et al. 2007). Bulgaria, despite its relatively well developed software and telecommunications sectors, has the least developed e-commerce sector of the European Union; with modest incomes and fears for consumer rights, only 6 % of the population shops on-line.

Turkey's e-commerce sector suffers from an overloaded telecommunications infrastructure and the lack of adequate legal safeguards to protect consumers and intellectual property. However, the Turkish government has supported the development of e-commerce as part of its efforts to gain entry into the European Union, including the E-Transformation Turkey Project, initiated in 2002, which aims to coordinate and standardize various EDI and business-to-business Internet activities.

4.7.3 Russia

Russian e-commerce reflects both the dynamism and pitfalls of an emerging economy (Chipaitis 2002; Decker et al. 2005). E-commerce in Russia emerged following the financial crisis of 1998, which forced many entrepreneurs to improve productivity by exploring electronic opportunities (Doern and Fey 2006). In 2007, the Russian Central Bank reported that 9.4 % of all economic transactions in the country were made over the internet (*Ecommerce Journal* 2008), a 218 % increase over the previous year. Access to such channels is highly circumscribed by wealth, power, and geography. The enactment of Federal Law 1FZ, On Electronic Digital Signatures, in 2002 accelerated the development of Russian e-commerce by applying legal contract principles to internet transactions (ECommerce Journal 2008). Digital advertising is dominated by Russia's two largest ISPs, Yandex and Rambler, which together comprise almost two-thirds of internet advertising revenues. A few stores, such as the Partia chain, introduced virtual showcases by the mid-1990s, catering primarily to the wealthy; the growth of e-commerce, however, has steadily democratized its access, and today even some supermarket chains, such as Sedmoi Kontinent, now offer online ordering (Global Technology Forum 2006). Quality Foods sells a variety of goods, including groceries, dry cleaning services, and cinema tickets online. Ozon.ru, which claims to be the most popular e-commerce site in Russia, was founded and is led by a Swiss citizen, Bernard Lukey; it sells books, software, electronic games, and digital music, and receives more than 120,000 unique hits per day (Wilsdon 2007). Likewise, Books.Ru, the Russian equivalent of Amazon.com, has done well since it began in 1996. Russian e-banking, however, is still in its infancy: in 2005, only 5 % offered on-line services (Doern and Fey 2006). However, all such transactions are geographically limited, as Moscow and St. Petersburg combined account for 60 % of the country's on-line retail exchanges.

4.7.4   East Asia

China's e-commerce sector is growing even more rapidly than its flourishing economy. China's B2B economy is still in its infancy (Zhao et al. 2008), but growing rapidly. For example, B2B ties have facilitated collaborative relationships among Chinese manufacturing firms, generating great efficiencies and cost savings in the process (Wu et al. 2011). Chinese banks have gradually upgraded to allow electronic funds transfer systems. However, as Martinsons (2008, p. 3) points out, "e-commerce in China has been stymied by inefficient telecommunications, inconvenient payment mechanisms, poor quality products, unreliable delivery, and fundamental concerns about security and trust due to a poor legal/regulatory system," all of which encourage *guanxi* and informal ties. Vague and irregularly enforced laws concerning contracts and intellectual property contribute to this dilemma. Moreover, the transparency of e-commerce challenges the monopoly over information held by corrupt, well-connected Communist Party members. The rapidly increasing number of internet users in China has also generated a large online shopping base, although limited use of credit cards (less than 5 % of the population) dampens its growth. In 2011, China had 193 million on-line shoppers, the largest such population in the world. However, Chinese shoppers tend to value the social dimensions of shopping more than do their Western counterparts (Efendioglu and Yip 2004), and e-commerce can never provide this aspect, and indeed, mitigates against it by making transactions less personal. Whereas 70 % of American netizens have used the internet for shopping, only 20 % of Chinese users have done so (Richards and Shen 2006). Lacking the right political connections, eBay closed shop in China in 2006 (Bradsher 2006). Nonetheless, a large number of netizens have even been branded as having an "online shopping addiction" as a result of the growth of online shopping; according to Sina.com, Chinese consumers with Internet access spend an average of RMB 10,000 online annually. On-line retailers such as Beijing-based 8848.net (named after the metric height of Mt. Everest) and Shanghai-based Mecox Lane began in 1999, selling books, hardware, and small appliances and more recently large online (only) retailers such as 360 buy have flourished in this environment (Powell 2011).

In Japan, e-commerce has not expanded as much as one might expect given its relative wealth and the size of its economy. As Aoyama and Schwarz (2004,

p. 511) note, "Because Japanese consumers never departed from, and are far more comfortable with, direct exchanges of cash for goods and services, the use of a credit card number against a promise of a product represents a process involving multiple layers of new and unfamiliar practice." The popularity of mobile internet access has been central to the country's e-commerce; in 2005 the total mobile internet commerce market was worth ø724 billion ($6.3 billion). However, small Japanese corner retail outlets continue to play a significant role in the country's e-commerce (Aoyama 2001).

In an economically traditionally based on cash and face-to-face interactions, South Korean internet-based financial transactions diffused relatively slowly (Cha et al. 2005). However, e-commerce flourished on the heels of the country's aggressive adoption of broadband services (Lee et al. 2006), the highest use in the world. In 2010, e-commerce sales surpassed $62 billion, of which 90 % consisted of B2B transactions. South Korea also has thousands of online shopping malls, whose success depends heavily on their website design and functionality (Kim et al. 2008).

4.7.5 Southeast Asia

Southeast Asia exhibits not only relatively well developed markets for electronic services but an institutional framework designed to maximize its growth, including the APEC Virtual E-commerce Resource Network. However, there are substantial variations among countries in the region. Southeast Asian e-commerce, with the exception of Singapore, is yet in its infancy. However, the potential of e-commerce in the region is significant: Vietnam, for example, hopes to jumpstart an IT-based software industry (Gallaugher and Stoller 2004), and e-commerce there has gradually begun to take root (Huy et al. 2012).

Given its status as an electronic communications hub, Singapore has taken the lead in this regard, developing not only the technical but also legal infrastructure that facilitates such interactions, including the Electronic Transactions Act of 1998. Singapore's advanced manufacturing clusters, with well managed supply chains, were one major impetus, as was the government's aggressive promotion of telecommunications as part of its national competitiveness strategy (Wong 2003). B2B commerce there is most common among services, government-owned firms, and those with younger managers (Teo and Ranganathan 2004; Teo et al. 2009). A densely concentrated, tech-savvy population, a highly globalized economy with numerous transnational firms, and a legal system designed to promote trust have all contributed. Internet retailing is widespread, but as in many Asian cultures, many people, especially women, continue to value the social and emotional dimensions of brick-and-mortar shopping (Hui and Wan 2007). Not surprisingly, given widespread cell phone usage there, mobile e-commerce (or m-commerce) has flourished (Yang 2005).

Malaysia, which developed a Multimedia Super Corridor (MSC) to attract high value-added producers, integrated information technology at the core of its Vision 2020 Master Plan (Mohan et al. 2004). With 934 companies in 2003, the MSC has generated 17,000 jobs, of which 80 % were knowledge-intensive. Part of this effort includes the Multimedia University in Cyberjaya, owned by the privatized Tele-kom Malaysia, which has established collaborative linkages with 37 companies and 29 universities around the world. E-banking has been offered in Malaysia since 2000 and grown rapidly in popularity (Ainin et al. 2005). B2B applications have mushroomed in the tourism sector and among electronics firms there. Barriers to use of the internet by Malaysian businesses include concerns over security, lack of legal precedence of electronic contracts, fear of hackers, insufficient skilled per-sonnel, and worries about intrusions into privacy (Abd-Mukti 2000).

Similarly, Thailand focused on e-commerce as part of its IT-2000 plan (Gray and Sanzogni 2004), including government-backed loan interest loans for start-ups and counselling and legal expertise (Sebora et al. 2009). The Thai government also initiated work on a new technology park in Chiang Mai to rival its counterpart in Malaysia. In poorer countries such as Indonesia, e-commerce is yet in its infancy, which partly reflects the monopoly position held by PT Telkom, which has exclusive rights to domestic telephone calls. Thus, despite Indonesia's vast pop-ulation, e-commerce there amounted to only $30 billion in 2009.

4.7.6 South Asia

India, currently undergoing explosive economic growth, has sought to overcome its limited telecommunications infrastructure to facilitate e-commerce, partly at the urging of the National Association of Software and Service Companies. Venture capitalists such as Himalayan IT often sponsor e-commerce start-ups. In 2009, India's e-commerce reached $39 billion in 2009, including international imports and exports of computer software. Obviously a significant share of this was gen-erated by the country's booming software industry (Patibandla and Petersen 2002; Athereye 2005; Grondeau 2007), now the world's largest, which is largely clustered in the famed center of Bangalore and to a lesser extent in Pune and Hyderabad. Indian e-banking is in its preliminary stages, but growing rapidly (Khan and Mahapatra 2009). Retail websites such as Bazaar India and IndiaMart have been highly successful. India has several examples of successful e-commerce ventures associated with rural development efforts. For example, in Madya Pradesh, the community-owned and financially self-reliant Gyandoot project, begun in 2000, provides farmers with access to the latest market quotes, while in Chennai the Foundation of Occupational Development project uses wireless radio modems to facilitate information exchange and networked solutions among nongovernmental organizations (Wagner et al. 2003). In Bangladesh, AgriNet performs a similar role.

Pakistan, the world's sixth most populous country, has minimal e-commerce. Broadband began there rather late after being introduced by Telstar, an Australian firm. With an internet penetration rate in 2011 of only 15.5 %, e-commerce is also hobbled by the lack of security for online transactions (and resulting lack of trust) and widespread corruption (Seyal et al. 2004). Pakistani internet users tend to be

Table 4.3 E-commerce revenues in selected Latin American countries and dependencies, 2007 (US$ millions)		
Brazil		4,899
Mexico		1,377
Venezuela		821
Caribbean (except Puerto Rico)		818
Argentina		739
Chile		687
Central America		499
Puerto Rico		445
Peru		218
Columbia		201

Source Pincept.com 2008

predominantly male, whereas most shopping is done by women (Sulaiman et al. 2007). In Bangladesh, with a 3.5 % penetration rate, the story is similar, although the Grameen bank is attempting to spawn a series of rural Bangladeshi dot-com firms. The export-oriented garment sector has pioneered e-commerce in the country, primarily through the Alibaba.com website.

4.7.7 Latin America

In 2009, Latin American e-commerce totalled more than US$16 billion, a market in which Brazil comprised one-quarter (Table 4.3). As in many developing countries, foreign investors often take the lead (Tigre 2003). For example, in 2000 Miami-based portal Yupi Internet launched its business-to-business portal, Amarillas, targeting entrepreneurs and small- and mid-sized enterprises in Latin America. Similarly, information-intensive sectors such as banks have played a major role, such as Bradesco, a leading private bank, which conducts e-commerce with a half million clients in Brazil. Volkswagen do Brazil used the growing Internet there to establish and extranet system of links with its suppliers (Nilles 1999). Latin American commercial use of the Internet has focused on Internet telephony (Koprowski 2005). For example, in 1998, Colombia became the first Latin American country to offer long distance VOIP service (Peña-Quiñones 2003). MercadoLibre, the Buenos Aires-based virtual company that is roughly the Latin American equivalent of eBay, had 25 million customers in 12 countries in 2008 (Chandler 2009). On-line shopping, or "e-tailing," however, has grown relatively slowly, in part due to consumers' fears about web security and identity theft. Obstacles to the growth of e-commerce include poor access to the Internet and requisite technical skills, the relatively lower use of credit cards, lack of secure on-line transactions, and the lack of a critical mass of users. In many places, concerns over copyright and intellectual property rights loom large.

Latin American e-commerce includes private, for-profit educational institutions. Several U.S.-based distance learning firms, such as the University of Phoenix, the Thunderbird School of Global Management, and Nova Southeastern University,

offer courses available to Latin Americans with sufficient funds, English profi-
ciency, and internet connections. Sylvan Learning Systems acquired an 80 % stake
in the Universidad de las Americas, one of Chile's leading private institutions of
higher education. Brazil's Klickeducacao.com.br offer numerous courses in
academic subjects as well as applied topics such as how to use spreadsheets.
Escolavirtual.com.br, a company created by Tema Informática, offers web-based
courses in 29 campuses located throughout the Rio de Janeiro metropolitan area.
Whitney International, a Bermuda-based distance learning company founded in
2005, has recently made an aggressive foray into the Latin American market
(Campbell 2008); in July, 2008, it acquired the Technological University of
Mexico, a major private university with several campuses, as well as the Latin
University of Costa Rica, that country's largest private institution. Such examples
demonstrate the range and diversity of applications of e-commerce throughout the
greater Latin American region.

4.7.8 Middle East

Most Arab e-commerce is concentrated in the Gulf States and in Saudi Arabia (Pons
2003; Ewers and Malecki 2010). As the most wired nation in the Arab world, the
UAE offers access for foreign companies through Dubai Internet City, modeled after
the Singapore Science Park, opened in 2000 and has attracted 1,200 companies,
including Microsoft, Hewlett-Packard, and Oracle, making the UAE the leading
Arab commercial center of cyberspace. The UAE's al-Lootah International University features the Arab world's first online degree program (Kalathil and Boas
2003). Banks have also energetically adopted online services (Dudley 2001). In
1999, Bahrain's Batelco launched @ltijara.com, the Arab world's first real time e-
commerce service, which expanded to include electronic advertising, credit card
purchases, corporate registration, and databases. The Saudis have followed the
UAE's lead closely. The state-owned oil monopoly Aramco has initiated on-line
procurement of inputs via the ISP OgerTel. In 2001, Saudi Arabia hosted the Arab
world's first international conference on e-commerce. In addition to B2B functions,
finance, and schools, other Internet applications include job-matching sites (e.g.,
CareerEgypt.com). Obstacles to the growth of Arab e-commerce included the relatively lower use of credit cards, lack of secure on-line transactions, and the lack of a
critical mass of users. Aladwani (2003) notes that most Arab e-customers, including
business managers, rank the lack of Internet security and intellectual property rights
to be among the greatest hindrances to the rise of e-commerce.

   As one might expect in a technologically sophisticated society with a large
computer technology industry, the Israeli e-commerce sector is robust. In 2005, the
nation's e-commerce sector witnessed roughly US$350 million in sales. Starting in
1999, Israeli banks developed a well-integrated EDI system, and today almost ½
the country's population uses electronic banking. The introduction of a centralized
portal by Bezeq, the national telecommunications carrier, greatly facilitated this

process. The digital convergence of the Internet, telephony, and broadband cable has allowed cable companies to bundle all three services, greatly expanding e-commerce in the domain of household (final) demand. Five major retail chains dominate the Israeli e-tail market (most of which centers on electronics and computer products), with a combined share of 60 %.

4.7.9 Sub-Saharan Africa

In Africa, as with much of the developing world, e-commerce is in its infancy, hobbled by low disposable incomes, modest internet penetration rates, lack of secure on-line transactions, and relatively infrequent use of credit and debit cards (Elbeltagi 2007). Many African small and medium sized enterprises (SMEs) are not e-ready, and lack the human capital, computers, and support services to take advantage of internet-based trading and financing (Mutula and Brakel 2006). Various national legal systems that inadequately protect intellectual property rights are of little help as well (Manteaw 2002–2003). Nonetheless, there are indications that an emerging African geography of e-commerce is in the making. South Africa leads the continent in this regard (Cloete 2003). For example, furniture producers in South Africa have successfully used the internet to market their wares to a global client base (Moodley 2002a, b, 2003a), and the country's automobile parts producers have used the internet to facilitate supply chain integration (Moodley 2002a, b), although its impacts on textiles exporters have been less evident (Moodley 2003b; Moodley and Morris 2004). Similarly, small Ghanaian firms have used the internet to promote exports (Hinson and Sorensen 2006). Other possibilities are emerging, such as e-tailing (e.g., kalahari.net), tourism promotion (Maswera et al. 2008; Maswera et al. 2009; Wynne et al. 2001), and job-matching sites (e.g., CareerEgypt.com). PRIDE Africa, an East African microfinance group, packages digital loans for resale to large commercial banks (Hammond 2001). The internet has enabled distance learning, literacy training, and HIV education in remote areas, and forms the basis of entire digital universities, such as the Francophone Virtual University in Cote d'Ivoire and Guinea, the African Virtual University in Kenya and five West African countries (www.avu.org), launched in 1997 by the World Bank, and SchoolNet in South Africa (van Brakel and Chisenga 2003). Kencall, a Kenyan call center service, has demonstrated that eastern Africa can be competitive with India in this regard (Rice 2008). Recent additions to the fiber network in Tanzania have spurred hopes of similar ventures there (Kircher-Allen 2009).

4.7.10 Central Asia

As more people have gained access to the internet in Central Asia, its implications and effects have multiplied accordingly. One example is the "electronic Silk

Road" (Davison et al. 2003). Still a predominantly cash-based economy, Central Asia nonetheless has witnessed a steady growth in electronic payment systems. Wireless broadband, for example, has grown steadily in Almaty. Such a phenomenon has, perhaps inevitably, integrated Central Asian economies with neighboring states. Digital connections between merchants straddling the border of Kazakhstan and Xinjang, for example, have proliferated. A new logistics center in Urumqi is streamlining paperwork for trans-border trade by using electronic documents. Moreover, many localities have turned to the web to promote the region's flourishing tourist industry; the Novinomad website (novinomad.com), for example, a Swiss-Kyrgyz joint venture, promotes ecotourism in that part of the world. Central Asian telephony has seen the growth of Voice Over Internet Protocal (VOIP) traffic. In Kyrgyzstan, ISPs seeking to provide this service must contribute 20 million *som* ($US 517,000) to a national telecommunications development fund.

4.7.11 Oceania

Australian e-commerce was estimated at $57 billion in 2007. B2B has increasingly become a necessity for Australian firms, where it is restructuring procurement systems and buyer–supplier relations (Singh and Byrne 2005). Whereas large, internationally-oriented firms have taken the lead, e-commerce adoption has gradually come to include a variety of smaller enterprises, which haltingly have come to see the benefits of electronic transactions (Hallal et al. 2010). The Australian e-tail market, at 3 % of sales, is still undeveloped compared to other OECD countries (Access Economics 2010). Similarly, in New Zealand, B2B adoption is largely a function of CEO innovativeness, organization size, and the degree of support from technology vendors (Al-Qirim 2005).

Internet-based schooling in the Pacific Ocean is increasingly popular. For example, the University of the South Pacific, which serves 12 countries in the region, uses Internet-based courses extensively; similarly, the Fiji School of Medicine trains health professionals through telehealth programs (Toland and Purcell 2002; Gold et al. 2002).

4.8 Conclusions

E-commerce takes a wide variety of forms, which play out unevenly across the planet's surface. As this chapter has demonstrated, the ascendency of electronic money has reinforced, not negated, the strategic position of global cities in the world economy. Between and among centers of finance, digital money sloshes in astounding volumes, circulating at the speed of light and wreaking havoc with national monetary controls. While high value-added functions such as investment banking remain concentrated in a few chosen locales, where they rely heavily on tacit knowledge and face-to-face communications, the internet has simultaneously facilitated the dispersal of many low wage functions such as back offices and call centers (and, increasingly, more skilled jobs such as radiologists) to the global periphery. The telecommunications industry has not been immune to the changes it has unleashed on the rest of the economy, as witnessed by the prodigious growth of VOIP telephony. Moreover, e-tailing has become a significant domain of spending and consumption in its own right and the internet has facilitated new forms of distance education and gambling, with their own, distinctive spatialities.

The loose assemblage of practices known as e-commerce is transforming the worlds of work, production, sales, advertising, and consumption. As firms and corporations across the world have adopted the internet, it has accelerated product cycles, restructured supply chains, opened new market opportunities, increased competition, and in general deepened capitalist social relations. For customers, e-tailing allows access to an unprecedented variety of options, while for small firms located in relatively inaccessible areas, the horizons for new sales possibilities are greatly expanded. Clearly, however, the implementation and impacts of e-commerce vary widely from region to region, as well as from place to place. Different national economic structures, government policies, levels of security and trust in e-commerce transactions, varying degrees of internet access and digital divides, cultural and gender roles, and variations in consumer habits and traditions all help to explain these geographies, which strongly suggest that there is no single, unified model that can be invoked.

References

Abd-Mukti, N. (2000). Barriers to putting businesses on the internet in Malaysia. *Electronic Journal on Information Systems in Developing Countries, 2*(6), 1–6. http://www.ejisdc.org

Access Economics. (2010). Household e-commerce activity and trends in Australia. http://www.dbcde.gov.au/__data/assets/pdf_file/0020/131951/Household_e-commerce_activity_and_trends_in_Australia-25Nov2010-final.pdf

Ainin, S., Lim, C-H., & Wee, A. (2005). Prospects and challenges of e-banking in Malaysia. *Electronic Journal on Information Systems in Developing Countries, 22*(1), 1–11. http://www.ejisdc.org

Aladwani, A. (2003). Key internet characteristics and e-commerce issues in Arab countries. *Information Technology and People, 16*, 9–20.

Al-Qirim, N. (2005). An empirical investigation of an e-commerce adoption-capability model in small businesses in New Zealand. *Electronic Markets, 15*(4), 418–437.

Aoyama, Y. (2001). Information society, Japanese style: Corner stores as hubs for e-commerce access. In T. Leinbach & S. Brunn (Eds.), *Worlds of electronic commerce* (pp. 109–128). Chichester: Wiley.

Aoyama, Y., & Schwarz, G. (2004). From mail order to e-commerce: Competition, regulation, and politics of nonstore retailing in Germany. *Urban Geography, 25*(6), 503–527.

Athereye, S. (2005). The Indian software industry and its evolving service capability. *Industrial and Corporate Change, 14*(3), 393–418.

Barboza, D. (2005, December 9). Ogre to slay? Outsource it to Chinese. *New York Times*, A1, C4.

Batiz, B., & Woods, D. (2002). Information technology innovations and commercial banking: A review and appraisal from an historical perspective. *Electronic Markets—The International Journal of Electronic Commerce & Business Media, 12*(3), 192–205.

Beaverstock, J., Smith, R., & Taylor, P. (2000). World city network: A new metageography for the future? *Annals of the Association of American Geographers, 90*, 123–134.

Bodin, M., & Dawson, K. (2002). *The call center dictionary: The complete guide to call center and customer support technology solutions*. New York: CMP Books.

Bowe, M. (Ed.). (1998). *Banking and finance in islands and small states*. London and Washington: Pinter.

Bradsher, K. (2006). eBay decision shows the importance of connections in China. *International Herald Tribune*. http://www.iht.com/articles/2006/12/21/business/ebay.php

Brousseau, E. (2003). E-commerce in France: Did early adoption prevent its development? *The Information Society, 19*(1), 45–57.

Brunn, S., & Leinbach, T. (Eds.). (2001). *Wired worlds of electronic commerce*. London: John Wiley.

Buhalis, D. (2003). *eTourism: Information technology for strategic tourism management*. London: Pearson.

Buhalis, D., & Licata, C. (2002). The future of e-tourism intermediaries. *Tourism Management, 23*(3), 207–220.

Cairncross, F. (1997). *The death of distance: How the communications revolution will change our lives*. Boston: Harvard Business School Press.

Campbell, M. (2008, September 12). A Texas company sees online learning as growth industry in Latin America. *Chronicle of Higher Education International*. http://chronicle.com/free/v55/i03/03a02701.htm

Cecere, G. (2009). VoIP diffusion among new entrants: A path dependent process. *Industry and Innovation, 16*(2), 219–245.

Cha, S. K., Kim, M., & McNiel, R. (2005). Diffusion of internet-based financial transactions among customers in South Korea. *Journal of Global Marketing, 19*, 95–111.

Chandler, M. (2009). MercadoLibre is sweeping Latin America's internet sales market. *Stanford Graduate School of Business News*. http://www.gsb.stanford.edu/news/headlines/mercadolibre08.html

Chiarvesio, M., Di Mariab, E., & Micelli, S. (2004). From local networks of SMEs to virtual districts? Evidence from recent trends in Italy. *Research Policy, 33*, 1509–1528.

Chipaitis, E. (2002). E-commerce and the information environment in an emerging economy: Russia at the turn of the century. In S. Palvia, P. Palvia, & E. Roche (Eds.), *Global information technology and electronic commerce* (pp. 53–72). Boston: Ivy League Publishing.

Cloete, C. (2003). SMEs in South Africa: Acceptance and adoption of e-commerce. In S. Lubbe & J. Van Heerden (Eds.), *The economic and social impacts of e-commerce* (pp. 121–134). Hershey: IGI Global.

Cobb, S. (1998). Global finance and the growth of offshore financial centers: The Manx experience. *Geoforum, 29*, 7–21.

Constantiou, I., & Kautz, K. (2008). Economic factors and diffusion of IP telephony: Empirical evidence from an advanced market. *Telecommunications Policy, 32*, 197–211.

Damsgaard, J., & Lyytinen, K. (1998). Contours of diffusion of electronic data interchange in Finland: Overcoming technological barriers and collaborating to make it happen. *Journal of Strategic Information Systems, 7*, 275–297.

Davison, R., Vogel, D., Harris, R., Gricar, J., & Sorrentino, M. (2003). Electronic Commerce on the New Silk Road: A Cornucopia of Research Opportunities. http://is2.lse.ac.uk/asp/aspecis/20030040.pdf

Decker, R., Hermelbracht, A., & Kroll, F. (2005). The importance of e-commerce in China and Russia. In D. Baier, R. Decker, & L. Schmidt-Thieme (Eds.), *Data analysis and decision support* (pp. 212–221). Heidelberg: Springer.

Dodd, M. (2010, November 25). E-commerce–Britain. *Consumer Lifestyle News*. http://cln-online.org/index.php?option=com_content&view=article&id=1304:e-commerce-uk&catid=38:research&Itemid=100

Doern, R., & Fey, C. (2006). E-commerce developments and strategies for value creation: The case of Russia. *Journal of World Business, 41*, 315–327.

Doherty, N., & Ellis-Chadwick, F. (2009). Exploring the drivers, scope and perceived success of e-commerce strategies in the UK retail sector. *European Journal of Marketing, 43*(9/10), 1246–1262.

Dudley, N. (2001, May). Arab banking—Arab banks begin to modernize. *Euromoney*, 52–61.

Ecommerce Journal, (2008). All the truth about Russian e-commerce. http://www.ecommerce-journal.com/news/all_the_truth_about_russian_e_commerce

Economist. (2006a) (Dec. 5). Greece: Overview of e-commerce. http://www.ebusinessforum.com/index.asp?layout=rich_story&doc_id=9777&title=Greece%3A+Overview+of+e-commerce&categoryid=29&channelid=4.

Efendioglu, A., & Yip, V. (2004). Chinese culture and e-commerce: an exploratory study. *Interacting with Computers, 16*, 45–62.

Elbeltagi, I. (2007). E-commerce and globalization: An exploratory study of Egypt. *Cross Cultural Management, 14*(3), 196–201.

Eriksson, L., & Hultman, J. (2005). One digital leap or a step-by-step approach? An empirical study of e-commerce development among Swedish SMEs. *International Journal of Electronic Business, 3*(5), 447–460.

Eriksson, L., Hultman, J., & Naldi, L. (2008). Small business e-commerce development in Sweden: An empirical survey. *Journal of Small Business and Enterprise Development, 15*(3), 555–570.

Ewers, M., & Malecki, E. (2010). Leapfrogging into the knowledge economy: Assessing the economic development strategies of the Arab Gulf states. *Tijdschrift voor Economische en Sociale Geografie, 101*(5), 494–508.

Fainstein, S. (1994). *The city builders: Property, politics, and planning in London and New York.* Oxford: Blackwell.

Gallagher, M. (1987). *Electronic funds transfer systems: The revolution in cashless banking and payment methods.* Oxford: Blackwell.

Gallaugher, J., & Stoller, G. (2004). Software outsourcing in Vietnam: A case study of a locally operating pioneer. *Electronic Journal on Information Systems in Developing Countries, 17*(1), 1–18. http://www.ejisdc.org

Gefen, D., & Heart, H. (2009). On the need to include national culture as a central issue in e-commerce trust beliefs. In W. Hu (Ed.), *Selected Readings on Electronic Commerce Technologies: Contemporary Applications* (pp. 384–406). Hershey: IGI Global.

Global Technology Forum. (2006). Russia: Overview of e-commerce. http://globaltechforum.eiu.com/index.asp?layout_rich_story&doc_id_9778&title_Russia%3A_Overview_of_e-commerce&channelid_4&categoryid_29

Gold, M., Swann, J., & Chief, I. (2002). Keeping it flexible: Integrating technology into distance education in the South Pacific. *Educational Technology and Society, 5*(1), 55–59.

Gorostriaga, X. (1984). *The role of the international financial centers in underdeveloped countries.* New York: St. Martin's Press.

Grandon, E., & Pearson, J. (2004). Electronic commerce adoption: an empirical study of small and medium US businesses. *Information & Management, 42*, 197–216.

Gray, H., & Sanzogni, I. (2004). Technology leapfrogging in Thailand: Issues for the support of e-commerce infrastructure. *Electronic Journal on Information Systems in Developing Countries, 16*(3), 1–26. http://www.ejisdc.org

Grondeau, A. (2007). Formation and emergence of ICT clusters in India: The case of Bangalore and Hyderabad. *GeoJournal, 68*, 31–40.

Hallal, J., Xu, J., & Quaddus, M. (2010). E-commerce adoption in small enterprises: An Australian study. In J. Xu & M. Quaddus (Eds.), *E-Business in the 21st century: Realities, challenges and outlook* (pp. 365–393). Hackensack: World Scientific Publishing.

Hammond, A. (2001). Digitally empowered development. *Foreign Affairs, 80*(2), 96–106.

Hampton, M., & Christensen, J. (1999). Treasure island revisited: Jersey's offshore finance centre crisis: Implications for other small island economies. *Environment and Planning A, 31*, 1619–1637.

Heaton, L. (2011). Internet and health communication. In M. Consalvo & C. Ess (Eds.), *The handbook of internet studies* (pp. 212–231). New York: Wiley-Blackwell.

Hinson, R., & Sorensen, O. (2006). E-business and small Ghanaian exporters: Preliminary micro firm explorations in light of a digital divide. *Online Information Review, 30*(2), 116–138.

Howells, J. (2000). Knowledge, innovation and location. In J. Bryson, P. Daniels, N. Henry, & J. Pollard (Eds.), *Knowledge, space, economy* (pp. 50–62). London: Routledge.

Hudson, A. (2000). Offshoreness, globalization and sovereignty: A postmodern geo-political economy? *Transactions of the Institute of British Geographers, 25*, 269–283.

Hui, T., & Wan, D. (2007). Factors affecting Internet shopping behaviour in Singapore: Gender and educational issues. *International Journal of Consumer Studies, 31*(3), 310–316.

Huy, L., Rowe, F., Truex, D., & Huynh, M. (2012). An empirical study of determinants of e-commerce adoption in SMEs in Vietnam: An economy in transition. *Global Information Management, 20*(3), 23–54.

Janelle, D. (2001). Globalization, the internet economy, and Canada. *Canadian Geographer, 45*(1), 48–53.

Jones, A. (2002). The 'global city' misconceived: The myth of 'global management' in transnational service firms. *Geoforum, 33*, 335–350.

Jung, M., & Loria, K. (2010). Acceptance of Swedish e-health services. *Journal of Multidisciplinary Health Care, 3*, 55–63.

Kalathil, S., & Boas, T. (2003). *Open networks, closed regimes: The impact of the internet on authoritarian rule*. Washington, DC: Carnegie Endowment for International Peace.

Karjalouto, H. (2002). Electronic banking in Finland: Consumer beliefs and reactions to a new delivery channel. *Journal of Financial Services Marketing, 6*(4), 346–361.

Khan, M., & Mahapatra, S. (2009). Service quality evaluation in internet banking: An empirical study in India. *International Journal of Indian Culture and Business Management, 2*(1), 30–46. http://dspace.nitrkl.ac.in:8080/dspace/bitstream/2080/746/1

Kim, M., Oh, H., & McNiel, R. (2008). Determinants of online shoppers' satisfaction in Korea. *Applied Economics Letters, 15*, 805–808.

Kircher-Allen, E. (2009). Broadband in Tanzania opens East Africa to outsourcing possibilities. *Huffington Post.* http://www.huffingtonpost.com/2009/08/19/broadband-in-tanzania-ope_n_262928.html

Kirkman, P. (1987). *Electronic funds transfer systems: The revolution in cashless banking and payment methods*. Oxford: Blackwell.

Kobrin, S. (1997). Electronic cash and the end of national markets. *Foreign Policy*, summer: 65–77.

Koprowski, G. (2005, September 10). VoIP providers say 'si' to Latin, South America. *E-commerce Times.* http://www.e-commercetimes.com/story/45850.html

Kutay, A. (1986). Effects of telecommunications technology on office locations. *Urban Geography, 7*, 243–257.

Lee, H., O'Keefe, R., & Yun, K. (2006). The growth of broadband and electronic commerce in South Korea: Contributing factors. *Information Society, 19*(1), 81–93.

Leyshon, A., French, S., Thrift, N., & Webb, P. (2005). Accounting for e-ecommerce: Abstractions, virtualism, and the cultural circuit of capital. *Economy and Society, 34*(3), 428–450.

Lohr, S. (2007, October 31). Hello, India? I need help with my math. *New York Times.* http://www.nytimes.com/2007/10/31/business/worldbusiness/31butler.html?pagewanted=all

Longcore, T., & Rees, P. (1996). Information technology and downtown restructuring: The case of New York City's financial district. *Urban Geography, 17*, 354–372.

Malik, O. (2010). Skype by the numbers: It's really big. *Gigaom.* http://gigaom.com/2010/04/20/skype-q4-2009-number

Manteaw, S. (2002–2003). Entering the digital marketplace: E-commerce and jurisdiction in Ghana. *Transnational Law, 345*, 346–379.

Martinsons, M. (2008). Relationship-based e-commerce: Theory and evidence from China. *Information Systems Journal, 18*, 331–356.

Maskell, P., & Malmberg, A. (1999). The competitiveness of firms and regions: Ubiquitification and the importance of localized learning. *European Urban and Regional Studies, 6*(1), 9–25.

Maswera, T., Dawson, R., & Edwards, J. (2008). E-commerce adoption of travel and tourism organisations in South Africa, Kenya, Zimbabwe and Uganda. *Telematics and Informatics, 25*(3), 187–200.

Maswera, T., Edwards, J., & Dawson, R. (2009). Recommendations for e-commerce systems in the tourism industry of sub-Saharan Africa. *Telematics and Informatics, 26*(1), 12–19.

McGahey, R., Malloy, M., Kazanas, K., & Jacobs, M. (1990). *Financial services, financial centers: Public policy and the competition for markets, firms and jobs*. Boulder: Westview Press.

McKeowen, L., & Brocca, J. (2007). Internet shopping in Canada: An examination of data, trends and patterns. Ottawa: Statistics Canada. http://www.statcan.gc.ca/pub/88f0006x/88f0006x 2009005-eng.pdf

Metykova, M. (2010). Only a mouse click away from home: Transnational practices of Eastern European migrants in the United Kingdom. *Journal for the Study of Race, Nation and Culture, 16*(3), 325–338.

Michalak, W., & Jones, K. (2003). Canadian e-commerce. *International Journal of Retail & Distribution Management, 31*(1), 5–15.

Miller, E., Griffin, T., De Paolo, P., & Sherbert, E. (2009). The impact of cultural differences on the effectiveness of advertisements on the Internet: A comparison among the United States, China, and Germany. *International Business & Economics Research Journal, 8*(4), 1–12.

Mohan, A., Omar, A., & Aziz, A. (2004). ICT clusters as a way to materialize a national system of innovation: Malaysia's multimedia super corridor flagships. *Journal on Information Systems in Developing Countries, 16*(5), 1–8. http://www.ejisdc.org

Mollenkopf, J., & Castells, M. (1991). *Dual city: Restructuring New York*. New York: Russell Sage Foundation.

Moodley, S. (2002a). Connecting to global markets in the internet age: The case of South African wooden furniture producers. *Development Southern Africa, 19*(5), 641–658.

Moodley, S. (2002b). Internet-enabled supply chain integration: Prospects and challenges for the South African automotive industry. *Development Southern Africa, 19*(5), 659–679.

Moodley, S. (2003a). E-commerce and export markets: Small furniture producers in South Africa. *Journal of Small Business Management, 41*, 317–324.

Moodley, S. (2003b). The potential of internet-based business-to-business electronic commerce for a 'technology follower': The case of the South African apparel sector. *International Journal of Internet and Enterprise Management, 1*(1), 75–95.

Moodley, S., & Morris, M. (2004). Does e-commerce fulfill its promise for developing country (South African) garment export producers?". *Oxford Development Studies, 32*(2), 155–178.

Mullings, B. (1999). Sides of the same coin? Coping and resistance among Jamaican data-entry operators. *Annals of the Association of American Geographers, 89*, 290–311.

Mutula, S., & Brakel, P. (2006). E-readiness of SMEs in the ICT sector in Botswana with respect to information access. *Electronic Library, 24*(3), 402–417.

Nicola, P., Mingo, I., La Roca, G., & Talucci, V. (2004). *Business enterprise in the information society: The regional dimension*. http://www.bisereu.com/10%20Domains%20Report/BISER_ Business_fnl_r.pdf

Nilles, J. (1999). Electronic commerce and new ways of working in Brazil. http://www.ecatt.com (see Country Reports).

O'Brien, R. (1992). *Global financial integration: The end of geography*. New York: Council on Foreign Relations Press.

O'Mahony, D., Peirce, M., & Tewari, H. (2001). *Electronic payment systems for e-commerce*. London: Artech.

Ohmae, K. (1990). *The borderless world*. London: Harper Collins.

Parker, T., & Parker, M. (2008). Electronic banking in Finland and the effect on money velocity. *Journal of Money, Investment and Banking, 4*, 20–25.

Patibandla, M., & Petersen, B. (2002). Role of transnational corporations in the evolution of a high-tech industry: The case of India's software industry. *World Development, 30*(9), 1561–1577.

Peña-Quiñones, G. (2003). Colombia: IP telephony and the Internet. http://www.itu.int/osg/spu/ni/iptel/countries/colombia/colombia-iptel.pdf

Polanyi, M. (1967). *The tacit dimension.* London: Routledge and Kegan Paul.

Pons, A. (2003). E-commerce and Arab intra-trade. *Information Technology and People, 16*, 34–48.

Powell, B. (2011, October 17). China's new e-commerce star. *Fortune, 164*(6), 66–68.

Rao, B., Angelov, B., & Nov, O. (2006). Fusion of disruptive technologies: Lessons from the Skype case. *European Management Journal, 24*(2–3), 174–188.

Rice, X. (2008, August 18). Internet: Last piece of fibre-optic jigsaw falls into place as cable links East Africa to grid. *The Guardian.* http://www.guardian.co.uk/technology/2008/aug/18/east.africa.internet

Richard, S. (2009). Are you there? Encouraging users to move from peer-to-peer to voice over broadband. *Telecommunications Journal of Australia, 59*(3), 421–427.

Richards, J., & Shen, D. (2006). E-commerce adoption among Chinese consumers: An exploratory study. *Journal of International Consumer Marketing, 18*(3), 33–55.

Richardson, R., & Belt, V. (2002). Saved by the bell? Call centres and economic development in less favoured regions. *Economic and Industrial Democracy, 22*, 67–98.

Roberts, S. (1994). Fictitious capital, fictitious spaces: The geography of offshore financial flows. In R. Martin & N. Thrift (Eds.), *Money, power and space.* Oxford: Blackwell.

Roberts, S. (1995). Small place, big money: The Cayman Islands and the international financial system. *Economic Geography, 71*, 237–256.

Robinson, J. (2010, October 27). Britain's £100 bn internet economy leads the world in online shopping. *The Guardian.* http://www.guardian.co.uk/technology/2010/oct/28/britain-internet-economy-online-shopping

Sassen, S. (1991). *The global city: New York, London, Tokyo.* Princeton, NJ: Princeton University Press.

Schiller, D. (1999). *Digital capitalism: Networking the global market system.* Cambridge: MIT Press.

Sebora, T. C., Lee, S. M., & Sukasame, N. (2009). Critical success factors for e-commerce entrepreneurship: An empirical study of Thailand. *Small Business Economics, 32*, 303–316.

Seyal, A., Awais, M., Shamail, S., & Abbas, A. (2004). Determinants of electronic commerce in Pakistan: Preliminary evidence from small and medium enterprises. *Electronic Markets, 14*(4), 372–387.

Singh, M., & Byrne, J. (2005). Performance evaluation of e-business in Australia. *Electronic Journal of Information Systems Evaluation, 8*(1), 71–80.

Solomon, E. (1997a). *Virtual money.* Oxford: Oxford University Press.

Solomon, E. (1997b). *Electronic funds transfers and payments: The public policy issues.* New York: Springer.

Statistics Canada. (2010). The Daily Statistics Canada. September 27. http://www.statcan.gc.ca/daily-quotidien/100927/dq100927-eng.pdf

Sulaiman, A., Mohezar, S., & Rasheed, A. (2007). A trust model for e-commerce in Pakistan: Empirical research. *Asian Journal of Information Technology, 6*(2), 192–199. http://docsdrive.com/pdfs/medwelljournals/ajit/2007/192-199.pdf

Sun, T. (2011). The roles of trust and experience in consumer confidence in conducting e-commerce: A cross-cultural comparison between France and Germany. *International Journal of Consumer Studies, 35*(3), 330–337.

Teo, T., & Ranganathan, C. (2004). Adopters and non-adopters of business-to-business electronic commerce in Singapore. *Information & Management, 42*, 89–102.

Teo, T., Lin, S., & Lai, K. H. (2009). Adopters and non-adopters of e-procurement in Singapore: An empirical study. *Omega, 37*, 972–987.

Tigre, P. (2003). E-commerce readiness and diffusion: The case of Brazil. http://www.crito.uci.edu/publications/pdf/gec/brazil.pdf

Toland, J., & Purcell, F. (2002). Information and communications technology in the South Pacific: Shrinking the barriers of distance. http://devnet.anu.edu.au/on-line%20versions %20pdfs/60/2460Toland.pdf

Travica, B., Kajan, E., Jošanov, B., Vidas-Bubanja, M., & Vuksanovic, E. (2007). E-commerce in Serbia: Where roads cross, electrons will flow. *Journal of Global Information Technology Management, 10*(2), 34–56.

Uchitelle, L. (2002 March 27). Answering '800' calls offers extra income but no security. *New York Times*, 1.

Van Brakel, P., & Chisenga, J. (2003). Impact of ICT-based distance learning: The African story. *Electronic Library, 21*(5), 476–486.

Vilhelmson, B., & Thulin, E. (2001). Is regular work at fixed places fading away? The development of ICT-based and travel-based modes of work in Sweden. *Environment and Planning A, 33*(6), 1015–1029.

Waesche, N. (2003). *Internet Entrepreneurship in Europe: Venture Failure and the Timing of Telecommunications Reform*. Cheltenham: Edward Elgar.

Wagner, C., Cheung, K., Lee, F., & Ip, R. (2003). Enhancing e-government in developing countries: Managing knowledge through virtual communities. *Electronic Journal on Information Systems in Developing Countries, 14*(4), 1–20. http://www.ejisdc.org

Waldman, A. (2003). More 'may I help you?' jobs migrate from U.S. to India. *New York Times*, May 26, p. A1.

Warf, B. (2002). Tailored for Panama: Offshore banking at the crossroads of the Americas. *Geografiska Annaler B, 84*, 47–61.

Wechsler, W. (2001). Follow the money. *Foreign Affairs, 80*(4), 40–57.

Weibold, U. (2010). E-commerce: Is Europe behind or just different? http://techcrunch.com/ 2010/08/26/e-commerce-is-europe-behind-or-just-different/

Werbach, K. (2005). Using VoIP to compete. *Harvard Business Review, 83*(9), 140–147.

Wilsdon, N. (2007). Index ventures invests £9.1 m in Russian Amazon. http://www.multilingual-search.com/index-ventures-invests-91m-in-russian-amazon/21/05/2007

Wilson, M. (2003). Chips, bits, and the law: An economic geography of internet gambling. *Environment and Planning A, 35*, 1245–1260.

Wong, P.-K. (2003). Global and national factors affecting e-commerce diffusion in Singapore. *Information Society, 19*, 19–32.

Wortham, J. (2011, May 15). Skype-style calls force wireless carriers to adapt. *New York Times*. http://www.nytimes.com/2011/05/16/technology/16phone.html?src=recg

Wu, J.-N., Zhong, W.-J., & Mei, S.-E. (2011). Application capability of e-business, e-business success, and organizational performance: Empirical evidence from China. *Technological Forecasting and Social Change, 78*(8), 1412–1425.

Wynne, C., Berthon, P., Pitt, L., Ewing, M., & Napoli, J. (2001). The impact of the internet on the distribution value chain: The case of the South Africa tourism industry. *International Marketing Review, 18*(4), 420–431.

Yang, K. (2005). Exploring factors affecting the adoption of mobile commerce in Singapore. *Telematics and Informatics, 22*, 257–277.

Zhao, J., Wang, S., & Huang, W. (2008). A study of B2B e-market in China: E-commerce process perspective. *Information & Management, 45*(4), 242–248.

Zook, M. (2000). The web of production: the economic geography of commercial Internet content production in the United States. *Environment and Planning A, 32*, 411–426.

Zook, M. (2001). Old hierarchies or new networks of centrality? The global geography of the internet content market. *American Behavioral Scientist, 44*, 1679–1696.

Zook, M. (2002). Hubs, nodes, and by-passed places: A typology of e-commerce regions in the United States. *Tidjschrift voor Economische en Sociale Geografie, 93*(5), 509–521.

Zook, M. (2003). Underground globalization: mapping the space of flows of the Internet adult industry. *Environment and Planning A, 35*(7), 1261–1286.

Zook, M. (2005). The geography of the internet. *Annual Review of Information Science and Technology, 40*, 53–78.

Chapter 5
Global E-Government

As the internet has spread in size and scope, its applications have included the interactions between many governments and their citizens. In addition to the growth of personal and commercial uses of the internet, electronic government, or e-government, expanded in tandem throughout the world. User-friendly graphical interfaces expedited this process enormously and opened the possibility of two-way flows of digital information between citizens and their states (and more recently, have paved the way for mobile governance, or m-government). There are many definitions of e-government (Yildiz 2007), but all essentially point to the use of information technologies (typically the internet) to facilitate the delivery of government information and services, restructure administrative procedures, and enhance citizen participation. Not surprisingly, the topic has drawn considerable scholarly attention (for a review, see Rocheleau 2007 and the *International Journal of Electronic Government Research*).

E-government takes a wide variety of forms, ranging from simple, static, one-way broadcasting of information via webpages to integration (i.e., allowing user input) that enables two-way flows and citizen feedback (Tapscott 1995). Often e-government is divided into government-to-business (G2B), government-to-government (G2G), and government-to-citizens (G2C) forms (Fountain 2001). B2B e-government includes digital submissions of bids, contracts, and bills. G2G e-government enhances communication and interaction among different government agencies. All of these variations are held to increase accessibility and efficiency; as Tapscott (1995, p. 163) notes,

> Internetworked government can overcome the barriers of time and distance to perform the business of government and give people public information and services when and where they want them. Governments can use electronic systems to deliver better quality products to the public more quickly, cost effectively and conveniently.

E-government may also encourage public bureaucracies to modernize their administrative practices, moving from classic forms based on hierarchical control to more horizontal, collaborative forms (Ho 2002; Ndou 2004). Perhaps most common is G2C e-government, which allows, for example, for the digital

B. Warf, *Global Geographies of the Internet*, SpringerBriefs in Geography,
DOI: 10.1007/978-94-007-1245-4_5, © The Author(s) 2013

collection of taxes; electronic voting; payment of utility bills, fines, and dues; applications for various types of public programs, permits and licenses; on-line registration of companies and automobiles; access to census and other public data; and reductions in waiting times in government offices. To the extent that e-government improves states' abilities to deliver services, it may increase satisfaction with existing regimes; conversely, in societies in which public sector jobs are often allocated through patronage networks, increased efficiency of e-government may minimize the growth of public employment. Cities may promote themselves on the Web as a means to entice tourists and foreign investors; interactive municipal sites give residents access to information about schools, libraries, bus schedules, and hospitals; even downloading official forms facilitates citizen participation. By making public records more open, e-government may increase responsiveness and empower citizens to challenge arbitrary government actions, enhancing transparency. Similarly, digital hotlines for submission of citizen complaints give voice to those who are typically voiceless in the circles of governance. Concerns over e-government include the potential invasions of privacy that it invites, local and national security, and the inequality of access generated by digital divides (about which more later).

Naïve views of the internet, informed from by a technologically-determinist reading, imply that the impacts are similar across the globe and that there is, or at least there can be, a generic, universal model (e.g., Grant and Chau 2005) that can be applied everywhere in cookie-cutter fashion. In contrast, more realistic appraisals focus on the institutional and political contexts in which e-government is adopted, which lead to enormous differences in effects and impacts. A central goal of this chapter is to refute such assertions by emphasizing the profound geographical variations that exist in the nature and consequences of e-government among (and within) countries. Because e-government is best developed in economically developed countries, the analysis focuses on such states, but as e-government has gradually spread to parts of the developing world, the spatial variations in its applications and impacts have multiplied correspondingly.

This chapter stresses the theme of social inclusivity and exclusivity. Its primary aim is to demonstrate the socially and geographical variable nature of e-government across the world. It proceeds in four steps. First it outlines broad arguments pertaining to the forms that e-government assumes, including different models, stages of implementation, and criteria for successful implementation and evaluation. Second, it points to the critical role of the digital divide in shaping social and spatial access to e-government. Third, it offers sketches of the contrasting experiences of e-government at the national and local scales among the world's major regions to demonstrate the plethora of types, levels, and consequences.

5.1   A Multiplicity of E-Government Models

Far from comprising some homogeneous whole, the set of ideas and practices that lie at the heart of e-government are actually quite diverse, varying over time, space, and institutional context. Recognition of this fact is essential if the geographic specificity of e-government forms is to be taken seriously.

Chadwick and May (2003) sketch three models of e-government—the managerial, consultative, and participatory—based on the experiences of the U.S., Britain, and the European Union. Managerial e-government is focused on maximizing the efficiency of delivery of government services to citizens, in which speed is the defining criterion of improved effectiveness. The consultative model centers upon citizen input into local and national governments, in which information technologies are seen as democratizing in nature: examples include internet voting, polling, referenda, and electronic town halls. Finally, the participatory model of e-government facilitates an electronic public sphere in which the state is but one of many actors, a utopian objective that falls in line with Habermas's (1979) famous vision of democracy as a negotiated consensus that lies at the heart of legitimate political rule. As Froomkin (2003, p. 856) puts it, "In Habermasian terms, the Internet draws power back into the public sphere, away from other systems." Importantly, the involvement of non-state actors, including citizens, corporations, and non-governmental organizations, broadens e-government to the wider domain of e-governance. In short, these three models lie in a continuum of social access, in which the consultative and participatory forms represent the most socially inclusive implementations.

Analogously, Layne and Lee (2001) constructed an influential sketch of developmental stages in the implementation of e-government: a simple online presence (i.e., web portal); interfaces that allow transactional access to data and services, in which citizens shift from a passive to an active role; vertically integration, in which local government portals are seamlessly meshed with those of national authorities (e.g., for license applications); and finally, horizontal integration, in which one or a few centralized sites offer "one-stop shopping" for a broad range of government functions and purposes. Empirical evaluations of e-government initiatives often include assessments of websites, including criteria such as missing links, readability, publications and data displayed, email addresses and/or telephone numbers of public officials, foreign languages access, sound and video clips, ability to use credit cards and digital signatures, security and privacy policies, and opportunities for citizen comments. Thus, those forms of e-government that exhibit the widest range of applications and ease of use may be said to be the most inclusive and useful to the largest potential pool of users.

One widely hailed application of e-government is electronic voting, or e-voting, in which votes are cast over the internet (not to be confused with electronic reading of paper ballots). Largely due to security concerns, internet voting is still in its infancy. In the United States, only Arizona has experimented with this approach as one among several (Gibson 2001; Solop 2001). In Europe, the popularity of this phenomenon varies geographically: Svensson and Leenes (2003:4) note that even in the rather homogenous context of democracies in Western Europe, different countries take very different positions with respect to e-voting. Estonia held the world's first elections that allowed internet voting, including local ones in 2005 and a national parliamentary one on March 4, 2007, but saw only 30,275 people—3.5 % of the electorate—participate on-line; in 2009 it extended this process to the local European Parliament elections there (EurActive 2009).

While there is no simple means to guarantee that e-government implementation will be successful, key ingredients to implementation include decisive leadership, cooperation by senior bureaucrats, centralized funding and control of e-government initiatives, clear lines of responsibility and accountability, explicit metrics of success or failure, involvement of all stakeholders, and effective mechanisms for feedback and change (Rose and Grant 2010). In short, e-government is every bit as much an administrative process as a technological one. Such issues demonstrate that the adoption of e-government is not some linear, teleological process with a predetermined outcome, but contingent and susceptible to a variety of cultural, legal, and political forces, including visions, competencies, and strategic agendas, within different institutional environments. The highly political and contingent nature of e-government implementation and use imply that its usage will reflect the nature of different national and institutional environments, that the degree of social inclusivity or exclusivity it exhibits will change over time and space, and that its consequences will be geographically variable.

5.2 E-Government and Digital Divides

A central concern about the adoption of e-government is the digital divide, the social and spatial inequalities in internet access that are common among and within countries around the world (Cooper and Compaine 2001; Crang et al. 2006; Norris 2001). Often discussions of e-government emphasize its egalitarian nature, a view that overlooks how social and spatial inequalities are reinscribed in cyberspace. For a significant share of the population—typically including the poor, the elderly, the undereducated, and many ethnic minorities—the digital domain is a foreign and inaccessible realm. As Fountain (2001, p. 48) notes, "An increasingly digital government favors those with access to a computer and the Internet and the skills to use these sophisticated tools competently." For countries in which many people lack the requisite technical skills, the income to acquire a personal computer at home, jobs that provide reliable internet access, large portions of the population are excluded from the benefits of e-government. In societies such as the United States, in which levels of inequality are higher than other OECD states, the digital divide tends to be markedly worse than in Europe or Japan. In many developing states, characterized by high income inequalities, it is markedly worse.

The digital divide is a major obstacle to the successful adoption and implementation of e-government (Yigitcanlar and Baum 2006). Offering convenient public services and information over the internet is useless to those without access to the technology, so e-government and the digital divide are deeply intertwined phenomena (Helbig et al. 2009). Becker et al. (2008) therefore conclude that due to social and spatial discrepancies in internet access, the adoption of e-government is primarily a demand-side rather than supply-side issue. This issue has serious implications: lack of internet access implies that those most in need of government services have the least opportunity to them in digital form. In the Australian context, for example, Dugdale et al. (2005) found that those who use government services the most are least likely to use the internet. Indeed, ironically, by facilitating access to government for those with internet access and denying it to those without, e-government may enhance the inequalities in opportunity that the digital divide represents. Kuk (2003), for example, found that in a sample of UK local government websites, those in lower income regions had considerably less information content and utility than those in higher income ones. Selwyn (2002) maintains that despite the British government's rhetoric about its commitment to social goals such as building an inclusive society with equality of access, the primary motivation behind its adoption is an economic rationale rooted in labor market restructuring, occupational change, and national competitiveness. To some extent, the diffusion of "best practices" concerning e-government among local authorities can help to ameliorate the problems generated by the digital divide, as the Italian experience indicates (Ferro and Sorrentino 2010).

5.3 Global Variations in E-Government

As Jaeger and Thompson (2004, p. 95) note, "e-government is quickly becoming 'simply the way things are done' in technologically advanced nations." E-government has become increasingly common across the OECD, propelled by efforts to modernize administrative bureaucracies, improve accountability, and raise the efficiency of public service delivery Organisation for Economic Co-operation and Development (2003). Most OECD states have initiated plans for restructuring their administrations in line with the requisites of the "information economy," typically by creating national information portals and establishing agencies to coordinate the adoption of e-government among local authorities. Such efforts should be seen within the broader context of global neoliberalism, persistent financial constraints, and associated efforts to trim the size of the public sector, reduce taxes, enhance accountability, and privatize and deregulate many government functions. Indeed, e-government in many respects reflects a new form of governmentality in the Foucauldian sense (Giritli Nygren 2009), one designed to make the state more flexible in the face of mounting international competition and mobile capital.

The degree of e-governance readiness varies considerably, reflecting both supply conditions (e.g., different levels of enthusiasm in attempts to initiate it) and demand conditions (i.e., contrasting stances towards its use and adoption). The United Nations Survey of E-governance in 2012 compared various countries on

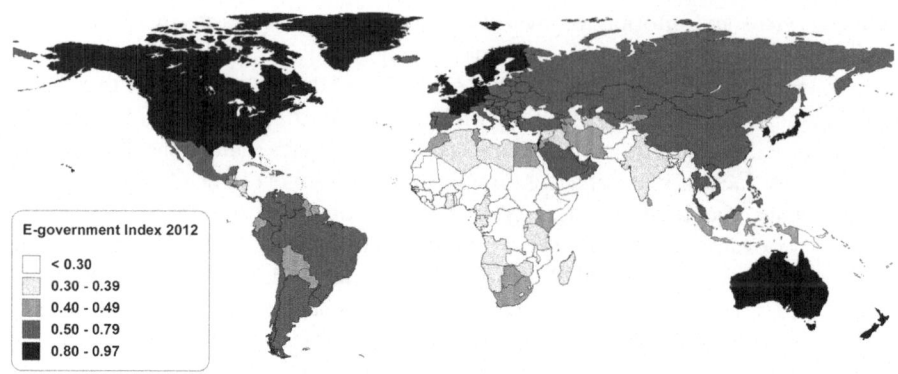

Fig. 5.1 Map of United Nations E-government Readiness Indices, 2012. *Source* http://www2.unpan.org/egovkb/global_reports/12report.htm

the basis of several measures, including the government's web presence, the country's technological infrastructure, and the human capital available to disseminate e-government service. The resulting map yields the depressingly familiar contours of global wealth and poverty (Fig. 5.1). The top 20 countries indicate a serious commitment to e-government efforts (Table 5.1). South Korea exhibits the world's best developed e-government system. Closely following are the United States and Canada. European countries dominate the list numerically, comprising 17 of the top 25 countries. Of this list, only a few countries are not OECD members, including Singapore (rank 11), Bahrain (13), Liechtenstein (23), and Luxembourg (25), all of which are prosperous but numerically small in population. Although e-government is best developed in the world's economically advanced countries (Basu 2004), where high internet penetration rates facilitate citizen access, it has also made slow but steady inroads in many countries of the developing world. To a much greater extent than in the developed world, e-government initiatives are greeted with considerable fanfare and hyperbole but disappointing results, often as the result of exaggerated expectations and resistance from bureaucrats.

5.3.1 North America

Since the first initiatives of the Clinton Administration in the 1990 s, the United States has been a major force in promoting e-government. In 1997 it started the National Partnership for Reinventing Government's Access America program, and in 2000 launched its first federal government internet portal, FirstGov.gov; similar websites include USA.gov, Data.gov, and USAspending.gov, which offer a wealth of information and links to various agencies. The E-government Act of 2002 created the Office of E-government and Information Technology (http://www.whitehouse.

Table 5.1 United Nations Top 25 E-government Readiness Rankings, 2012

Rank	Country	Score
1	South Korea	.9283
2	Netherlands	.9125
3	United Kingdom	.8960
4	Denmark	.8889
5	United States	.8687
6	France	.8635
7	Sweden	.8599
8	Norway	.8593
9	Finland	.8505
10	Singapore	.8474
11	Canada	.8430
12	Australia	.8390
13	New Zealand	.8381
14	Liechtenstein	.8264
15	Switzerland	.8134
16	Israel	.8100
17	Germany	.8079
18	Japan	.8019
19	Luxembourg	.8014
20	Estonia	.7987

Source http://www2.unpan.org/egovkb/global_reports/12report.htm

gov/omb/e-gov/), part of a series of initiatives designed to avoid redundancies in reporting efforts among agencies, with associated provisions to minimize invasions of privacy. In total, U.S. federal e-government includes tens of millions of individual webpages, which are typically seen as the most authoritative and "objective" source of information about government and have been used by two-thirds of Americans online (Jaeger and Thompson 2004), most of whom are middle class. Larsen and Rainie (2002, p. 5) note that "More Americans have visited government Web sites than have sought financial information online, made travel reservations, sent instant messages, or gotten sports scores online." More than 3.5 million Americans file their federal taxes electronically, and the federal job search website USAjobs.com has attracted tens of millions of visits. More than one-half of Americans report having used a government website at one time or another.

Adoption of e-government by the various U.S. states, often legitimized by discourses of "reinventing government," has been spatially uneven (Fig. 5.2), with Michigan and Utah exhibiting the most comprehensive systems according to the Center for Digital Government. McNeal et al. (2003) argue that it is the ideological orientation of state legislatures, not citizen demand, that drives the adoption of e-government, with Republican-leaning administrations that weigh criteria of efficiency heavily being the most likely to implement digital measures. Tolbert et al. (2008) maintain that state levels of wealth or urbanization are unrelated to uptake rates of e-government, although median level of education did exert an

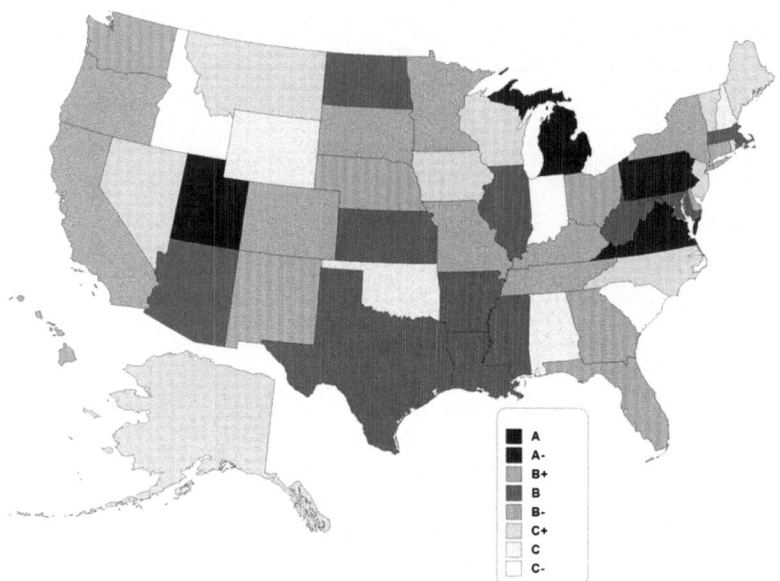

Fig. 5.2 E-government Grades for U.S. States, 2010. *Source* data from http://www. centerdigitalgov.com/survey/61

important influence, as did ethnic homogeneity and local support for policy innovation.

Similarly, municipal e-government in the U.S. exhibits enormously diverse variations ranging from non-existence to highly sophisticated digital interactions, depending on availability of financing, personnel, and leadership. Few cities offer e-government services beyond the most basic provision of digital forms and information (Reddick 2004). Moon (2002) suggests that larger cities are more likely to have e-government portals and to offer a broader array of applications. The most common forms of local e-government applications include payments of parking tickets, filing of complaints, and service requests (Lee et al. 2005). Norris and Moon (2005), however, found that while simple government websites have become almost universal among U.S. municipalities, the shift toward transactional ones has been much slower and spatially uneven. A few municipalities (e.g., Bakersfield, CA) broadcast city council meetings on the web; some (e.g., Durham, NC; Scottsdale, AZ; Fort Lauderdale, FL) offer on-line geographical information systems (GIS) that permit location-based searches and interactive mapping Kaylor et al. (2001).

Canada's first steps toward e-government began in the 1990 s with the launch of its flagship website, strategis.cn (Allen et al. 2001; Roy 2006). The Government On-line program, launched in 1999, enables electronic access to 130 federal government services, attracting 600 million visits annually. However, as elsewhere, the implementation of fully developed e-government services ran into a common conundrum: whereas most neoliberal policy initiatives attempt to promote the autonomy of local organizational units, effective e-government requires a considerable degree of centralized coordination. Thus, attempts by Revenue Canada or Canada Post to implement digital procurement processes have been repeatedly delayed. In response, traditional vertical bureaucratic structures have had to adapt, in part by entering into partnerships with one another and with private interests (e.g., outsourcing), which in turn raises thorny problems of accountability.

5.3.2 Europe

In Europe, e-government assumes a multiplicity of national and local forms. In general, Northern and Western Europe fare better than their Eastern and Southern counterparts (Fig. 5.1). In 2004, the European Union launched IDABC (Interoperable Delivery of European e-Government Services to Public Administrations, Businesses and Citizens) to stimulate e-government adoption by its member states. Despite this supranational level of encouragement, EU e-government has emerged in a nebulous legal environment that has left implementation to member states rather than a coordinated central policy (Strejcek and Theil 2003). Within countries, regions exhibit enormous differentials in e-government implementation (Lassnig and Markus 2003). Finally, the municipal scale adds further diversity: Pina et al. (2007) analyzed e-government websites of cities in 15 countries of the European Union, finding significant variations in their degree of transparency, interactivity, and utility among and within countries (see also Druke 2005; Torres et al. 2005). Despite the unevenness in access, the internet has become an important forum of European politics, greatly enhancing citizen participation in democratic governance (Norris 2005).

Britain's attempts to promote e-government can be traced to the 1996 government paper *Government Direct*, which sought to advance electronic provision of payments, tax collections, data gathering, and benefits dispersal. Subsequently, e-government goals in the U.K. were broadened to include digital job searches, appointments with government offices, dispersal of health care information, and other activities. The central point of access is ukonline.gov.uk. Under the neoliberal impulse to privatize and decentralize, the government frequently contracted the work for the creation of many e-government websites to private suppliers. In addition, the devolution of national state authority to many local governments has generated wide variations in the rate and nature of e-government adoption; thus Pratchett (2004, p. 3) argues that "despite a nationally prescribe strategy and nationally imposed targets, the reality of local e-government is one of variable practice and disparate successes." Despite its earnest efforts, e-government usage in the United Kingdom has been low compared to other OECD states. Critics of the government lampooned its efforts by creating "a parody site www.directionlessgov.com to illustrate how the by now ubiquitous search engine Google was a better tool for finding government information than the official government portal" (Margetts 2006, p. 252). Among local boroughs, e-government has been manifested at a variety of types and levels of success (Weerakkody and Choudrie 2005).

In Germany, e-government implementation started slowly and has lagged behind other countries, in part due to the lack of coordination among the various Länder (Klumpp 2002; Eifert 2004; Siegfried 2007). Based on an analysis of web pages, Wohlers (2009) concludes that e-government in Germany is more widespread than it is in the U.S., but less sophisticated. The BundOnline 2005 program aims to offer federal government services over the internet, but as yet most websites are confined to one-way provision of information rather than transactional relations. E-government has been unevenly adopted among the various German *länder* and cities (Schuppan 2009), with widely varying local effects. The Dutch government has plunged enthusiastically into e-government, only to confront a variety of responses from citizens based on the perceived usefulness, degree of risk, experience of users, and level of trust (Horst et al. 2007), all of which are central to understanding the contingent nature of this process. In the Dutch case, as elsewhere, a flexible politics of national-local collaboration is critical to successful e-government adoption (Bekkers 2009).

Scandinavian e-government strategies include a variety of attempts to place these countries at the helm of global network societies and today exhibit some of the world's most comprehensive systems for the delivery of public information and services electronically (Anderson et al. 2005). The "Digital Denmark" program, for example, sought to harness information technology to democratize access to public information Falch and Henten (2000). In Sweden, e-government implementation has been marked by the absence of substantive national administrative reforms (Löfgren 2007) and an enormous number of local applications; Giritli Nygren (2009) quotes one local development authority as saying "there are 290 local authorities in Sweden, and there've been 290 different ways forward." Similarly, in Finland, e-governance unfolded in a complex medley of national and local governments (Hyyryläinen 2004), in which municipal governments play a key role: the city of Tampere, Finland, for example, allows citizens to provide urban planners with their views and experiences (Jaeger 2003). In contrast, despite its abundant information technology network, Norwegian cities often exhibit surprisingly rudimentary e-government applications (Flak et al. 2005).

France exhibits well developed e-government, including easy access to government forms, legislation, libraries, public transportation information, and tax payments. The core of the French government's e-government strategies go back to its formation of the Government Action Programme for an Information Society (PAGSE) in 1998 (Chatillon 2004). The national one-stop e-government portal mon.service-public.fr offers easy access to government forms, legislation, libraries, public transportation information, and tax payments. Users may create personal accounts to track information and pay taxes. Almost all of the country's schools are connected to the Internet, with important implications for the nature of education. Some municipalities, such as Issy-les-Mollineaux, have experimented with cyber-voting. In the 2007 French presidential election, 1.3 million people submitted digital votes out of a total of 43 million. However, French departments, the primary unit of local authority, vary in their rate of adoption: those in the

Parisian region tend to be the most advanced, while many poorer and rural ones lag considerably.

In Spain, Portugal, and Italy, where e-government lags behind France, it has been used to reduce the size of public bureaucracies. Often with the assistance of European Union funds, governments in Southern Europe have sought to overcome the digital divide in their respective countries, facilitating access in rural and low income regions, encouraging telemedicine for those who live far from hospitals or doctors, emergency communications services, targeted information assistance for disabled persons and the elderly, and promoting "distance learning" in secondary schools and universities. In Greece, the nation's first "digital city," Trikala, was launched in 2006, giving 70% of its residents internet access and giving them an ability to participate in telework, on-line library and school programs, emergency response systems, environmental and transportation information, and demographic data that can be utilized through publicly available geographical information systems. Spain's complex political geography, with multiple, overlapping regional administrative bodies and autonomous areas and the resulting Byzantine legal environment they generate, played no small role in the slow onset of e-government there (Muñoz-Cañavate and Hípola 2011), including the number and quality of local government websites that serve local citizens (Muñoz-Cañavate and Chain-Navarro 2004).

5.3.3 East Asia

South Korea possesses an e-government system often rated the world's most comprehensive and sophisticated (Shin 2007; Taubman Center of Brown University 2007). Largely due to a series of government initiatives stretching back to the 1980s and culminating in the Electronic Government Act of 2001, the country developed a world-class telecommunications infrastructure (including the highest rate of broadband penetration in the world). It gradually implemented e-government in a series of stages by forcefully overcoming bureaucratic inertia and resistance through the erection of a well-coordinated network of agencies involved in the effort (Song 2002; Im and Seo 2005). Highlights of the Korean system include electronic delivery of social insurance payments, tax collections, and widespread electronic education services. Struggles over privacy were a significant aspect of the adoption of these processes (Jho 2005). The presidential Blue House's *shinmoongo* system allows citizens to appeal judicial decisions and report corruption directly with the president's offices. An important lesson from the Korean experience is the need for attention to stakeholders' trust and commitment and an understanding of the dynamics of organizational learning for e-government to be successful (Kim et al. 2007). The government's E-jiwon electronic records management system, for example, including vast digital archives, succeeded because of the institutional changes that accompanied it, not simply the technological advantages it offers (Lee and Lee 2009).

   Although Japan has an excellent information technology infrastructure, its steps toward e-government have lagged behind other OECD nations (Koga 2003). The Japanese government, which long exhibited a lackluster attitude toward government openness that threatened the power of its entrenched bureaucracy, developed an e-government master plan in 1997 that led to the e-Japan Strategy I in 2001 and e-Japan Strategy II in 2003 (Yonemaru 2004). However, national e-government websites are largely confined to the simple provision of forms and information, putting the country in the first stage of Layne and Lee's (2001) developmental sequence. At the core of this initiative is the e-Gov.go.jp website, designed to serve as a centralized gateway to national e-government channels. The Juki-Net resident registry network, launched in 2002, compiles personal information about residents to facilitate the dispersal of government entitlement funding and allows them to move among cities without duplicating registration efforts. However, despite the centralized nature of the Japanese state, e-government implementation has been uneven among the nation's prefectures, with well-established systems in the greater Tokyo-Yokohama region and lesser degrees of implementation in Hokkaido and Shikoku. Japanese cities have implemented e-government in a wide range of modes and levels of sophistication (Tanaka et al. 2005), ranging from almost nil involvement among some hamlets to inter-government local area networks (LANs).
   China's burgeoning ventures into e-government have also attracted considerable attention (Holliday and Yep 2005; Ma et al. 2005; Chen et al. 2009; Zhao 2010; Yang et al. 2012). Initially its efforts were aimed at purely economic goals such as tariff collection, import–export licenses, and currency exchange settlement; more recently these have given way to the wider strategy to decentralize the mechanisms of public governance, gain control over corruption, enhance responsiveness, and accelerate economic competitiveness under the National Informatization (*Guojia Xinxihua*) plan. China's Government Online Project (*Zhengfu Shangwang Gongcheng*), launched in 1999, has focused on putting government documents on the web and promote online databases. China's deeply centralized political system, however, presents obstacles to this strategy, including conflicting priorities and offices with bloated staff numbers. It should, of course, be recalled that China is among the most severe internet censors in the world Chapter 3. At the municipal level, Beijing, Shanghai, Nanjing, Nanhai, and Shenzen have taken the lead in online company registrations, tax collections, and community information services. For example, Shanghai has a digital social security smart card system in place.

5.3.4 Southeast Asia

The rapidly emerging economies of Southeast Asia reveal considerable variation in e-government readiness and implementation, ranging from Singapore, one of the world's leaders in e-government, to countries such as Myanmar, where it is non-existent.

Because it has implemented e-government so well, Singapore has been the focus of significant attention (Chan and Pan 2008; Baum et al. 2008). Singapore's e-government initiatives began as early as 1980, with the launch of the Civil Service Computerisation Programme. It has, for example, a state-of-art digital tax filing system (Tan et al. 2005), an e-citizen center (http://www.ecitizen.gov.sg), and most government services can be delivered on-line (Ke and Wei 2004). The active participation of the island's business community, which anticipated its benefits, was central to the success of these initiatives (Tung and Rieck 2005). Because multiple stakeholders were included in the design and implementation of e-government initiatives, they enjoy widespread trust among different segments of the population: as with e-commerce, trust is central to the effective adoption of e-government, and trust, like all social constructions, varies greatly over time and space.

Similarly, e-government has enjoyed modest success in Malaysia, in part because its residents trust the state to implement it (Lean et al. 2009). E-procurement of government contracts, for example, has steadily become the norm. Like Singapore, Malaysia's cultural diversity was important, as e-government is intertwined with the culture's emphasis on egalitarianism, fatalism, and individualism (Seng et al. 2010).

In Thailand, the eGovernment Interoperability Framework has guided the slow initiation of digital communications among different government agencies (Kawtrakul et al. 2011; Funilkul et al. 2011). However, star programs such as Smart ID cards (which contained the owner's demographic and economic data) failed there, largely due to its haphazard and unsystematic program of implementation. Elsewhere, such as Vietnam, where its vaulted Project 112 collapsed in failure, e-government is confined to a few websites, although even Cambodia is getting into the act (Sang et al. 2009).

Indonesia, Southeast Asia's behemoth, has had limited success with e-government, in part due to endemic corruption, lack of political will, and shortages of qualified personnel. Its efforts have rarely moved beyond simple web pages, although Surabaya, the second largest city, has initiated an e-procurement system.

5.3.5 South Asia

South Asia's e-government efforts pale in comparison with those found in East Asia, and more closely approximate the rankings of sub-Saharan Africa (Fig. 5.1). In India, e-government is having widespread effects (Haque 2002). Although the national government has been generally positive in this respect, most initiatives arise from Indian states (Monga 2008). In Tamil Nadu, for example, the Sustainable Access for Rural India project, which sponsored a series of internet kiosks, improved villagers' access to government services, including telehealth, and reduced corruption (Kumar and Best 2006). Similarly, the Gyandoot project, which began in 2000, established kiosks in rural Madhya Pradesh, helping farmers learn about prices and using Geographical Information Systems to map soil types and ground water. The Akashganga project helped 50,000 dairy farmers in rural Gujarat. Project

Bhoomi in Karnataka facilitated the digitization of 20 million land ownership records, saving farmers 1.3 million workdays in waiting time (Bertot et al. 2010), and in Andhra Pradesh the Smartgov project expedited processing times for paper, squeezing efficiency from India's notoriously hidebound public bureaucracy. In Chandigarh, Project Sampark has allowed for digital filing of taxes, filing of birth and death certificates, and payments of utility bills. Kerala launched a project called FRIENDS ('fast, reliable, instant, effective network for disbursement of services') in 2000 to provide one-stop IT-enabled payment counters (Madon 2004). More broadly, more Indians know more about their government today than ever before (Paul 2007). However, Indian e-government faces several serious problems (Faisal and Raman 2008; Gorla 2007, 2008), including widespread illiteracy, relatively low internet penetration (10 %), discriminatory caste and gender norms, and under-funded and at times mismanaged programs.

Pakistan's e-governance lags far behind that of India, and beyond a few gov-ernment websites, has been primarily manifested in a network of telecenters designed to spur rural development in its 50,000 villages (Mahmood 2005). One major obstacle is that the administrative duties for Pakistani e-government are spread over a vast array of agencies, with little centralized coordination (Shafique and Mahmood 2008). Nonetheless, the country boasts the Virtual University of Pakistan and a growing capacity in telemedicine, and the tax department was reorganized electronically to minimize chances for bribery (Bertot et al. 2010). Likewise, in Bangladesh e-government has taken a few halting steps, although it is plagued by bureaucratic inefficiencies (Hasan 2003).

5.3.6 Central Asia

Central Asian governments exhibit a variety of levels of sophistication in their pre-paredness and willingness to adopt e-government. The region as a whole lags far behind the developed world in this regard. According to the United Nations' e-government index, Kazakhstan and Mongolia are best situated in this regard, Uzbe-kistan and Kyrgyzstan exhibit somewhat less ability to adopt e-government initiatives, and Afghanistan, devastated by decades of invasion, war, and unrest, ranks at the bottom. As Bhuiyan (2010) notes, Kazakhstan's e-government initiatives include interactive government portals (www.e.gov.kz) with more than 900 information services in Kazakh, Russian, and English; interagency electronic workflows in 39 government branches; and almost all *akimats* (municipal governments) have virtual reception rooms. Most countries in the region have distance-learning programs in varying stages of development and effectiveness. Similarly, Mongolia has imple-mented government portals and explored the possibility of web-based distance learning programs in rural areas (Sukhbaatar 2005). Yet the motivations behind the implementation of e-government in this region are not necessarily benign. Morozov (2011, p. 87), in a sobering analysis of internet freedom, argues that

> Authoritarian regimes in Central Asia ... have been actively promoting a host of e-government initiatives. But the reason why they pursue such modernization is not because they want to shorten the distance between the citizen and the bureaucrat but because they see it as a way to attract funds from foreign donors (the likes of IMF and the World Bank) while also removing the unnecessary red-tape barriers to economic growth.

Seen in this light, the implementation of e-government in Central Asia acquires far more sinister overtones, one motivated by international, not domestic, priorities.

5.3.7 Middle East

Turkey's e-government efforts, which arose in tandem with its hopes of entry into the European Union, have been used, among other things, to improve public management, minimize duplication of efforts, distribute public payments, solicit corporate bids and issue contracts, collect customs duties and some types of taxes, and enable digital job hunting (Çayhan 2008). Because the government has prioritized corporate needs over those of households, however, the resources directed at schools, households, and marginalized social groups have been relatively small.

E-government in the Arab world, where it generates more hype than reality, is in its infancy. Major barriers to its successful implementation include these countries' relatively low literacy and penetration rates, lack of technical skills among civil servants, a "brain drain" from the public to the private sector, lack of government financial commitment and systematic coordination of efforts, and unstable, often corrupt, administrative hierarchies with high rates of personnel turnover. Frequently e-government is viewed as cosmetic and complementary to existing, paper-based means of administration rather than as the basis of a thorough reworking of the public administrative apparatus (Salem 2006). Several countries, including Egypt, Jordan, Lebanon, Morocco, and Tunisia, have launched government portals that offer free e-mail accounts and some electronic bills payments. For example, the Egyptian government site, alhokoma.gov.eg provides information but not interactive services. Egyptian schools that have attempted to include distance learning via the Web have encountered formidable bureaucratic obstacles and hide-bound teachers with little enthusiasm for innovation (Warschauer 2003). Tunisia offers several services through its portal, bawaba.gov.tn, including income tax payments, job searches, and building applications. By increasing the probability of discovery, e-government may lower levels of corruption, enhance accountability, circumvent dictatorial leadership, and by making government records more open, may empower citizens to challenge arbitrary government actions. Dubai pioneered an e-government portal in 2001, www.dubai.ae, which allows access to services and payment of bills Kalathil and Boas (2003). The Saudi state set up Web browsers to carry prayers from Mecca and Medina, and established a web portal to facilitate processing of paperwork for those visiting Islamic holy sites.

In Israel, by far the best-connected and most high tech society in the Middle East, the government's Merkava Project, which started in 1999, forms the core of a sustained effort to improve delivery of government services. Government offices rely heavily on the gov.net intranet. The government's gov.il web portal serves as an important conduit with its citizens, with a wide variety of online forms and payment options. Such sites attract 3.2 million visits each month, and are responsible for 21 % of all government transactions. Such sites are often the object of attacks by hackers. In contradistinction, Palestinians have begun widespread use of blogging to shore up attempts to gain national sovereignty (Martin and El-Toukhy 2012).

5.3.8 Sub-Saharan Africa

This part of the world tends to score very low on e-government readiness indices (Fig. 5.1). Numerous African countries have static, one-way web interfaces between governments and their citizens (Ngulube 2007). Others, such as Egypt, Morocco, and Tunisia, have launched interactive government portals that offer free e-mail accounts and some electronic bills payments. Yet other countries have specialized internet services dedicated to specific ends; for example, Zambia launched Zamlii, a legal information portal, Ethiopia has devinet.org to coordinate actions of non-governmental organizations, and Mozambique has SISTAFE for the electronic disbursement of government salaries. East African e-government is still relatively primitive (Kaaya 2004). Unfortunately, most African e-government initiatives have ended in partial or total failure, victims of the gap between project design and political reality (Heeks 2002); for example, an internet based municipal land licensing system in South Africa was thwarted by powerful interests who appropriated it for their own purposes. Thus, e-government adoption must be viewed in light of local institutional and administrative contexts rather than a simplistic "one-size-fits-all" strategy (Schuppan 2009).

5.3.9 Latin America

Latin American e-governance exhibits numerous manifestations. Brazil, for example, became the first country in the Americas to introduce electronic voting (Finquelievich et al. 2004). Mexico launched Mexico On-Line in 1996, which allows electronic submission of tax returns. The Brazilian government launched in 2000 an electronic procurement auction, Electronic Pregão, to expedite bids on government contracts (Joia and Zamot 2002). Some, such as Peru's InfoDes project in Cajamarca, a World Bank project, allow rural citizens to access local libraries digitally Wagner et al. (2003). In 1998, Argentina's Ministry of Communications launched the Argentina@Internet.todos program aimed at enhancing access for residents of low income rural areas. More mundanely, most cities in the region promote themselves on the Web as a means to entice tourists and foreign investors, interactive municipal sites give residents access to information about schools, libraries, and hospitals, and even downloading official forms facilitates citizen participation. Electronic payment of dues and fines, moreover, short-cuts corrupt government bureaucrats and helps to minimize corruption, and digital hotlines for submission of citizen complaints give voice to those who are typically voiceless in the circles of governance. On the other hand, the digital divide in Latin America—about which very little is known—may also enhance disparities between those who can make use of cyberspace and those who are not, reinforcing and deepening long-standing inequalities (Hawkins and Hawkins 2003).

Public internet-based schooling is also increasingly popular in Latin America. Most national and many local governments throughout Latin America have subsidized programs to install the Internet in schools, with mixed results. In Chile, for example, over 90 % of classrooms now have internet access (Arredondo 2004). Argentina launched its TELAR ("Todos en la red") program in 1994 in association with international education NGOs. Similarly, Mexico's Red Enlaces network has significantly improved access for children in the public school system. Many schools, however, are handicapped by lack of equipment, obsolete machines, slow and inefficient maintenance, and inadequately prepared teachers; moreover, often computers may be lost or stolen. Nonetheless, computer-based courses tend to be highly popular among students, often forming the highpoint of the school week. As Cabrera Paz (2004) points out in a study of Colombian school children, internet usage transforms their geographical imaginations, although not always for the better:

> The things that can be seen on the World Wide Web serve to highlight what is unavailable locally. The globalization upon which the Internet is built becomes a symbol for the limitations of one's own space. The user's gaze is expanded to embrace other territories, a wider place, desired objects that are beyond reach and available only in the 'developed world' of others. That distant and hardly imaginable space is the space of abundance, of greater pleasures, with objects that 'we never dreamed we could explore' [quoting a child at the end].

5.3.10 Oceania

Australia and New Zealand provide contrasting examples of e-government in action. The Australian government's CentreLink Agency, which offers a centralized point of access to government information, has proved to be very popular. As the national state has shifted many functions onto local governments, e-government has become important in enhancing local flexibility and productivity (Shackleton et al. 2006). However, Australian government agencies, for example, tend to be less responsive to citizen input than their counterparts in New Zealand (Gauld et al. 2009). However, local authorities in New Zealand exhibited differences in their willingness and ability to implement e-government initiatives (Deakins and Dillon 2002). Moreover, the demand for e-government services varied substantially between and within both countries, with significantly less interest exhibited by the elderly and less educated (Gauld et al. 2010). What these case studies reveal, therefore, is that in the adoption of e-government, place and location matter profoundly.

5.4 Conclusion

This chapter has emphasized the significant geographical variations in e-government that exist among states. Rather than consisting of a single, abstract model that can be applied identically everywhere, the design, implementation, and consequences of e-government reflect a wide variety of national and local political, economic, cultural, and institutional contexts. E-government has been implemented at a variety of levels of enthusiasm, ranging from grudging acceptance to energetic promulgation, and has encountered variable levels of success or failure. For example, while e-government has been implemented decisively and successfully in countries such as South Korea, the U.S., Canada, and Denmark, in contrast, Japan has exhibited a surprising reluctance. The varying forms that e-government assumes, and its levels of implementation and success, reflect national and local political structures, levels of economic development, cultural practices, and the contingent, path-dependent characteristics of individual countries and regions. Moreover, e-government impacts vary considerably. In some countries, e-government has successfully facilitated reductions in the size of the public sector and greater efficiency by limiting duplications in paperwork and streamlining bureaucracies; in others, it has reduced corruption through enhanced transparency and accountability; in yet others, it offers more empty hype than substantial impacts. Within countries, adoption of e-government exhibits considerable spatial variation, as indicated by the uneven patterns among U.S. states, British local authorities, French departments, and Japanese prefectures. In addition to national and local political environments, the matter of the digital divide, which exhibits its own, distinct, but related geography, is also critical in shaping who has access to e-government services and who does not. While the bulk of residents in the developed world can utilize the internet easily, a substantial minority, including the familiar litany of the poor, uneducated, and politically marginalized, does not. The socially and spatially uneven distribution of internet access among and within countries produces complicated spatialities of inequality that further contribute to the diversity of e-government impacts. Thus, e-government adoption must be viewed in light of local institutional and administrative contexts rather than a simplistic "one-size-fits-all" strategy.

References

Allen, B., Juillet, L., Paquet, G., & Roy, J. (2001). E-governance and government on-line in Canada: Partnerships, people and prospects. *Government Information Quarterly, 18*(2), 93–104.
Anderson, K., Grönlund, A., Moe, C., & Sein, M. (2005). E-government in Scandinavia. *Scandinavian Journal of Information Systems, 17*(2), 3–10.

Arredondo, M., Catalán, R., Montesinos, J., & Monsalve, S. (2004). Introducing new information and communication technologies in two rural schools in central Chile: An ethnographic approximation. In . M. Bonilla and G. Cliché (Eds.). *Internet and society in Latin American and the Caribbean* Toronto: Southbound. http://www.idrc.ca/en/ev-45776-201-1-DO_TOPIC.html.

Basu, S. (2004). E-government and developing countries: An overview. *International Review of Law, Computers and Technology, 18*(1), 109–132.

Baum, S., Yigitcanlar, T., Mahizhnan, A., & Andiappan. N. (2008). E-government in the knowledge society. In T. Yigitcanlar, K. Velibeyogluand, and S.Baum (Eds.). *Creative urban regions: Harnessing urban technologies to support knowledge city initiatives.* (132–147). Hershey: IGI Global.

Becker, J., Niehaves, B., Bergener, P., & Räckers, M. (2008). Digital divide in e-government: The e-inclusion gap model. *Lecture Notes in Computer Science, 5184*, 231–242.

Bekkers, V. (2009). Flexible information infrastructures in Dutch e-government collaboration arrangements: Experiences and policy implications. *Government Information Quarterly, 26*(1), 60–68.

Bertot, J., Jaeger, P., & Grimes, J. (2010). Using ICTs to create a culture of transparency: E-government and social media as openness and anti-corruption tools for societies. *Government Information Quarterly, 27*, 264–271.

Bhuiyan, S. (2010). E-government in Kazakhstan: Challenges and its role to development. *Public Organization Review, 10*(1), 31–47.

Cabrera Paz, J. (2004). Navigators and castaways in cyberspace: Psychosocial experiences and cultural practices in school children's Internet. In M. Bonilla and G. Cliché (Eds.), *Internet and society in Latin American and the Caribbean.* Toronto: Southbound. http://www.idrc.ca/en/ev-45776-201-1-DO_TOPIC.html.

Çayhan, B. (2008). Implementing e-government in Turkey: A comparison of online public service delivery in Turkey and the European Union. *Electronic Journal of Information Systems in Developing Countries, 35*(8), 1–11. http://www.ejisdc.org.

Chadwick, A., & May, C. (2003). Interaction between states and citizens in the age of the internet: "E-government" in the United States, Britain, and the European Union. *Governance, 16*(2), 271–300.

Chan, Y., Lau, M., & Pan, S. (2008). E-government implementation: A macro analysis of Singapore's e-government initiatives. *Government Information Quarterly, 25*(2), 239–255.

Chatillon, G. (2004). E-government in France. In M. Eifert & J. Püschel (Eds.), *National electronic government: Comparing governance structures in multi-layer administrations* (pp. 82–115). London and New York: Routledge.

Chen, A., Pan, S., Zhang, J., Huang, W., & Zhu, S. (2009). Managing e-government implementation in China: A process perspective. *Information and Management, 46*(4), 203–212.

Cooper, M., & Compaine, B. (Eds.). (2001). *The digital divide.* Cambridge: MIT Press.

Crang, M., Crosbie, T., & Graham, S. (2006). Variable geometries of connection: Urban digital divides and the uses of information technology. *Urban Studies, 43*(13), 2551–2570.

Deakins, E., & Dillon, S. (2002). E-government in New Zealand: The local authority perspective. *International Journal of Public Sector Management, 15*(5), 375–398.

Druke, H. (Ed.). (2005). *Local electronic government: A comparative study.* London: Routledge.

Dugdale, A., Daly, A., Papandrea, F., & Maley, M. (2005). Accessing e-government: Challenges for citizens and organizations. *International Review of Administrative Sciences, 71*(1), 109–118.

Eifert, M. (2004). Electronic government in Germany. In M. Eifert & J. Ole Püschel (Eds.), *National electronic government: Comparing governance structures in multi-layer administrations* (pp. 116–135). London and New York: Routledge.

EurActive. (2009). Internet sees Estonia vote first in EU elections. http://www.euractiv.com/en/eu-elections/internet-sees-estonia-vote-eu-elections/article-182706

Faisal, M., & Raman, Z. (2008). E-government in India: Modelling the barriers to its adoption and diffusion. *Electronic Government, 5*(2), 181–202.

Falch, M., & Henten, A. (2000). Digital Denmark: From information society to network society. *Telecommunications Policy, 24*(5), 377–394.

Ferro, E., & Sorrentino, M. (2010). Can intermunicipal collaboration help the diffusion of e-government in peripheral areas? Evidence from Italy. *Government Information Quarterly, 27*(1), 17–25.

Finquelievich, S., Martinez, S., Jara, A., Baumann, P., Casas, A., Zamalvide, M., Fressoli, M., & Turrubiates, R. (2004). The social impact of introducing ICTs in local government and public services: Case studies in Buenos Aires and Montevideo. In M. Bonilla and G. Cliché (Eds.). *Internet and society in Latin American and the Caribbean.* Toronto: Southbound. http://www.idrc.ca/en/ev-45776-201-1-DO_TOPIC.html

Flak, L., Olsen, D., & Wolcot, P. (2005). Local e-government in Norway: Current status and emerging issues. *Scandinavian Journal of Information Systems, 17*(2), 41–84.

Fountain, J. (2001). The virtual state: Transforming American government? *National Civic Review, 90*(3), 241–251.

Froomkin, A. (2003). Habermas@Discourse.net. Toward a critical theory of cyberspace. *Harvard Law Review, 116*(3), 740–873.

Funilkul, S., Chutimaskul, W., & Chongsuphajaisiddhi, V. (2011). E-government information quality: A case study of Thailand. *Lecture Notes in Computer Science, 6866,* 227–234.

Gauld, R., Goldfinch, S., & Horsburgh, S. (2010). Do they want it? Do they use it? The 'demand-side' of e-government in Australia and New Zealand. *Government Information Quarterly, 27*(2), 177–186.

Gauld, R., Gray, A., & McComb, S. (2009). How responsive is e-government? Evidence from Australia and New Zealand. *Government Information Quarterly, 26*(1), 69–74.

Gibson, R. (2001). Elections online: Assessing internet voting in light of the Arizona Democratic primary. *Political Science Quarterly, 116*(4), 561–583.

Giritli Nygren, K. (2009). E-governmentality: On electronic administration in local government. *Electronic Journal of e-Government, 7*(1), 55–64.

Gorla, N. (2007). A survey of rural e-government projects in India: Status and benefits. *Information Technology for Development, 15*(1), 52–58.

Gorla, N. (2008). Hurdles in rural e-government projects in India: Lessons for developing countries. *Electronic Government, 5*(1), 91–102.

Grant, G., & Chau, D. (2005). Developing a generic framework for e-government. *Journal of Global Information Management, 13*(1), 1–30.

Habermas, J. (1979). *Communication and the evolution of society.* Boston: Beacon Press.

Haque, M. (2002). E-governance in India: its impacts on relations among citizens, politicians and public servants. *International Review of Administrative Sciences, 68,* 231–250.

Hasan, S. (2003). Introducing e-government in Bangladesh: Problems and prospects. *International Social Science Review, 78*(3/4), 111–125.

Hawkins, E., & Hawkins, K. (2003). Bridging Latin America's digital divide: Government policies and Internet access. *Journalism and Mass Communication Quarterly, 80,* 646–665.

Heeks, R. (2002). E-government in Africa: Promise and practice. *Information Polity, 7,* 97–114.

Helbig, N., Gil-Garcia, J., & Ferro, E. (2009). Understanding the complexity of electronic government: Implications from the digital divide literature. *Government Information Quarterly, 26*(1), 89–97.

Ho, T. (2002). Reinventing local governments and the e-government initiative. *Public Administration Review, 62*(4), 434–444.

Holliday, I., & Yep, R. (2005). E-government in China. *Public Administration and Development, 25,* 239–249.

Horst, M., Kuttschreuter, M., & Gutteling, J. (2007). Perceived usefulness, personal experiences, risk perception and trust as determinants of adoption of e-government services in the Netherlands. *Computers in Human Behavior, 23*(4), 1838–1852.

Hyyryläinen, E. (2004). Electronic government in Finland. In M. Eifert & J. Ole Püschel (Eds.), *National electronic government: Comparing governance structures in multi-layer administrations* (pp. 46–81). London: Routledge.

Im, J., & Seo, J. (2005). E-government in South Korea: Planning and implementation. *Electronic Government, 2*(2), 188–204.

Jaeger, P. (2003). The endless wire: E-government as global phenomenon. *Government Information Quarterly, 20*(4), 323–331.

Jaeger, P., & Thompson, K. (2004). Social information behavior and the democratic process: Information poverty, normative behavior, and electronic government in the United States. *Library and Information Science Research, 26*(1), 94–107.

Jho, W. (2005). Challenges for e-governance. Protests from civil society on the protection of privacy in e-government in Korea. *International Review of Administrative Sciences, 71*(1), 151–166.

Joia, L., & Zamot, F. (2002). Internet-based reverse auctions by the Brazilian government. *Electronic Journal on Information Systems in Developing Countries, 9*(6),1–12. http://www.ejisdc.org

Kaaya, J. (2004). Implementing e-government services in East Africa: Assessing status through content analysis of government websites. *Electronic Journal of E-Government, 2*(2).

Kalathil, S., & Boas, T. (2003). *Open networks, closed regimes: The impact of the internet on authoritarian rule*. Washington: Carnegie Endowment for International Peace.

Kawtrakul, A., Mulasastra, I., Khampachua, T., & Ruengittinun, S. (2011). The challenges of accelerating connected government and beyond: Thailand perspectives. *Electronic Journal of e-Government, 9*(2), 183–202.

Kaylor, C., Deshazo, R., & Van Eck, D. (2001). Gauging e-government: A report on implementing services among American cities. *Government Information Quarterly, 18*(4), 293–307.

Ke, W., & Wei, K. (2004). Successful e-government in Singapore. *Communications of the ACM, 47*(6), 95–99.

Kim, H., Pan, G., & Pan, S. (2007). Managing IT-enabled transformation in the public sector: A case study on e-government in South Korea. *Government Information Quarterly, 24*(2), 338–352.

Klumpp, D. (2002). From websites to e-government in Germany. *Electronic Government, 2456*, 18–25.

Koga, T. (2003). Access to government information in Japan: A long way toward electronic government? *Government Information Quarterly, 20*(1), 47–62.

Kuk, J. (2003). The digital divide and the quality of electronic service delivery in local government in the United Kingdom. *Government Information Quarterly, 20*(4), 353–363.

Kumar, R., & Best, M. (2006). Impact and sustainability of e-government services in developing countries: Lessons learned from Tamil Nadu, India. *Information Society, 22*, 1–12. http://mikeb.inta.gatech.edu/papers/infosoc.egov.kumar.best.pdf

Larsen, E., & Rainie, L. (2002). *The rise of the e-citizen: How people use government agencies' web sites*. Washington, DC: Pew Internet and American Life Project.

Lassnig, M., & Markus, M. (2003). Usage of e-government services in European regions. *Electronic Government, 2739*, 143–146.

Layne, K., & Lee, J. (2001). Developing fully functional e-government: A four stage model. *Government Information Quarterly, 18*(2), 122–136.

Lean, O., Zailani, S., Ramayah, T., & Fernando, Y. (2009). Factors influencing intention to use e-government services among citizens in Malaysia. *International Journal of Information Management, 29*(6), 458–475.

Lee, K., & Lee, K.-S. (2009). The Korean government's electronic record management reform: The promise and perils of digital democratization. *Government Information Quarterly, 26*(3), 525–535.

Lee, S., Tan, X., & Trimi, S. (2005). Current practices of leading e-government countries. *Communications of the ACM, 48*(10), 99–104.

Löfgren, K. (2007). The governance of e-government: A governance perspective on the Swedish e-government strategy. *Public, Policy and Administration, 22*(3), 335–52.

Ma, L., Chung, J., & Thorson, S. (2005). E-government in China: Bringing economic development through administrative reform. *Government Information Quarterly, 22,* 20–37.

Madon, S. (2004). Evaluating the developmental impact of e-governance initiatives. An exploratory framework. *Electronic Journal on Information Systems in Developing Countries, 20*(5), 1–13. http://www.ejisdc.org

Mahmood, K. (2005). Multipurpose community telecenters for rural development in Pakistan. *The Electronic Library* 23(2):204-220. http://www.geocities.ws/khalidmahmood/mcts.pdf.

Margetts, H. (2006). E-government in Britain—A decade on. *Parliamentary Affairs, 59*(2), 250–265.

Martin, J., & El-Toukhy, S. (2012). Blogging for sovereignty: An analysis of Palestinian blogs. In Tatyana Dumova & Richard Fiordo (Eds.), *Blogging in the global society: Cultural, political and geographical aspects* (pp. 139–151). Hershey: IGI Global.

McNeal, R., Tolbert, C., Mossberger, K., & Dotterweich, L. (2003). Innovating in digital government in the American states. *Social Science Quarterly, 84*(1), 52–70.

Monga, A. (2008). E-government in India: Opportunities and challenges. *Journal of Administration and Governance, 3*(2), 52–61.

Moon, M. (2002). The evolution of e-government among municipalities: Rhetoric or reality? *Public Administration Review, 62*(4), 424–433.

Morozov, E. (2011). *The net delusion: The dark side of internet freedom.* New York: Public Affairs.

Muñoz-Cañavate, A., & Chain-Navarro, C. (2004). The world wide web as an information system in Spain's regional administrations (1997–2000). *Government Information Quarterly, 21*(2), 198–218.

Muñoz-Cañavate, A., & Hípola, P. (2011). Electronic administration in Spain: From its beginnings to the present. *Government Information Quarterly, 28*(1), 74–90.

Ndou, V. (2004). E-government for developing countries: opportunities and challenges. *Electronic Journal on Information Systems in Developing Countries, 18*(1), 1–24. http://www.ejisdc.org

Ngulube, P. (2007). The nature and accessibility of e-government in sub-Saharan Africa. *International Review of Information Ethics 7.*

Norris, P. (2001). *Digital divide: Civic engagement, information poverty, and the internet worldwide.* Cambridge: Cambridge University Press.

Norris, P. (2005). The impact of the internet on political activism: Evidence from Europe. *International Journal of Electronic Government Research, 1*(1), 19–39.

Norris, D., & Moon, M. (2005). Advancing e-government at the grassroots: Tortoise or hare? *Public Administration Review, 65*(1), 64–75.

Organisation for Economic Co-operation and Development. (2003). *The e-government imperative.* Paris: OECD.

Paul, S. (2007). A case study of e-governance initiatives in India. *International Information and Library Review, 39*(3–4), 176–184.

Pina, V., Torres, L., & Royo, S. (2007). Are ICTs improving transparency and accountability in the EU regional and local governments? *An empirical study. Public Administration, 85*(2), 449–472.

Pratchett, L. (2004). Electronic government in Britain. In M. Eifert & J. Ole Püschel (Eds.), *National electronic government: Comparing governance structures in multi-layer administrations* (pp. 13–45). London: Routledge.

Reddick, C. (2004). A two-stage model of e-government growth: Theories and empirical evidence for U.S. cities. *Government Information Quarterly, 21*(1), 51–64.

Rocheleau, B. (2007). Whither e-government? *Public Administration Review, 67*(3), 584–588.

Rose, W., & Grant, G. (2010). Critical issues pertaining to the planning and implementation of e-government initiatives. *Government Information Quarterly, 27*(1), 26–33.

Roy, J. (2006). *E-government in Canada: Transformation for the digital age.* Ottawa: University of Ottawa Press.

Salem, F. (2006). Exploring e-government barriers in the Arab states. Dubai School of Government. http://www.dsg.ae/LinkClick.aspx?link=DSG+Policy+Brief_e-gov_Fadi+Salem_2006.pdf &tabid=308&mid=826&language=en-US.

Sang, S., Lee, J.-D., & Lee, J. (2009). E-government adoption in ASEAN: the case of Cambodia. *Internet Research, 19*(5), 517–534.

Schuppan, T. (2009). Local level structural change and e-government in Germany. In C. Reddick (Ed.), *Handbook for research on strategies for local e-government adoption and implementation* (pp. 17–36). New York: IGI Global Press.

Selwyn, N. (2002). 'Establishing' an inclusive society? Technology, social exclusion and UK government policy making. *Journal of Social Policy, 31*(1), 1–20.

Seng, W., Jackson, S., & Philip, G. (2010). Cultural issues in developing E-Government in Malaysia. *Behaviour and Information Technology, 29*(4), 423–432.

Shackleton, P., Fisher, J., & Dawson, L. (2006). E-government services in the local government context: An Australian case study. *Business Process Management Journal, 12*(1), 88–100.

Shafique, F., & Mahmood, K. (2008). Indicators of the emerging information society in Pakistan. *Information Development, 24*(1), 66–78.

Shin, D.-H. (2007). A critique of Korean National Information Strategy: Case of national information infrastructures. *Government Information Quarterly, 24*(3), 624–645.

Siegfried, T. (2007). E-government in Germany. In P. Nixon & V. Koutrakou (Eds.), *E-government in Europe: Rebooting the state* (pp. 90–102). London: Routledge.

Solop, F. (2001). Digital democracy comes of age: Internet voting and the 2000 Arizona Democratic primary election. *PS: Political Science and Politics, 34*(2), 289–293.

Song, H. (2002). Prospects and limitation of the e-government initiative in Korea. *International Review of Public Administration, 7*(2), 45–53.

Strejcek, G., & Theil, M. (2003). Technology push, legislation pull? E-government in the European Union. *Decision Support Systems, 34*(3), 305–313.

Sukhbaatar, B. (2005). A study on e-government policies in Mongolia. *Information and Telecommunication Technologies, 10*, 254–259.

Svensson, J., & Leenes, R. (2003). E-voting in Europe: Divergent democratic practice. *Information Polity, 8*(1–2), 3–15.

Tan, C. W., Pan, S., & Lim, E. (2005). Managing stakeholder interest in e-government implementation: Lessons learned from a Singapore e-government project. *Journal of Global Information Management, 13*(1), 31–53.

Tanaka, H., Matsuura, K., & Sudoh, O. (2005). Vulnerability and information security investment: An empirical analysis of e-local government in Japan. *Journal of Accounting and Public Policy, 24*(1), 37–59.

Tapscott, D. (1995). *The digital economy. Promise and peril in the age of networked intelligence.* New York: McGraw-Hill.

Taubman Center of Brown University. 2007. South Korea climbs to top rank in global e-government. http://www.brown.edu/Administration/News_Bureau/2006-07/06-007.html.

Tolbert, C., Mossberger, K., & McNeal, R. (2008). Institutions, policy innovation, and e-government in the American states. *Public Administration Review, 68*(3), 549–563.

Torres, L., Pina, V., & Acerete, B. (2005). E-government developments on delivering public services among EU cities. *Government Information Quarterly, 22*(2), 217–238.

Tung, L., & Rieck, O. (2005). Adoption of electronic government services among business organizations in Singapore. *Journal of Strategic Information Systems, 14*, 417–440.

Wagner, C., Cheung, K., Lee, F., & Ip, R. (2003). Enhancing e-government in developing countries: Managing knowledge through virtual communities. *Electronic Journal on Information Systems in Developing Countries, 14*(4), 1–20. http://www.ejisdc.org.

Warschauer, M. (2003). Dissecting the digital divide: A case study in Egypt. *The Information Society, 19*, 297–304.

Weerakkody, V., & Choudrie, J. (2005). Exploring e-government in the UK: Challenges, issues and complexities. *Journal of Information Science and Technology, 2*(2), 25–45.

Wohlers, T. (2009). The digital world of local government: A comparative analysis of the United States and Germany. *Journal of Information Technology and Politics, 6*(2), 111–126.

Yang, K., Zhang, C., & Tang, J. . (2012). Internet use and governance in China. In Y-C. Chen and P-Y. Chu (Eds.) *Electronic governance and cross-boundary collaboration: Innovations and advancing tools.* (pp. 305–324). Hershey: IGI Global.

Yigitcanlar, T., & Baum, S. (2006). E-government and the digital divide. In M. Khosrow-Pour (Ed.), *Encyclopedia of e-commerce, e-government, and mobile commerce* (pp. 353–358). Hershey: IGI Global.

Yildiz, M. (2007). E-government research: Reviewing the literature, limitations and ways forward. *Government Information Quarterly, 24*(3), 646–665.

Yonemaru, T. (2004). Electronic government in Japan. In M. Eifert & J. Ole Püschel (Eds.), *National electronic government: Comparing governance Structures in multi-layer administrations* (pp. 136–181). London: Routledge.

Zhao, Q. (2010). E-government evaluation of delivering public services to citizens among cities in the Yangtze River Delta. *International Information and Library Review, 42*(3), 208–211.

Chapter 6
Social Media

Today, more people are better connected to one another, and the world, than at any other time in human history. For vast segments of the world's population, mobile phones, the internet and email, instant messaging, and various forms of digital social media have become deeply woven into the fabric of daily life (Kellerman 2002; Thrift and French 2002; Dodge and Kitchin 2005). All of these technologies facilitate the easy exchange of information, which is a nonrival good increasingly important to economic and social life. What are the implications of the rapid rise and enormous popularity of digital communications systems for how people view one another and themselves?

This chapter explores this issue in several ways. It begins by situating digital communications networks within the wider theorization of the networked society, and continues with a brief empirical overview of the popularity of technologies that facilitate and expedite telemediated interpersonal interactions, including mobile phones, the internet, and networking sites such as Facebook. Although access to these technologies is socially and spatially uneven, vast (and rapidly growing) numbers of people have ready access to mobile phones, texting, email, and social networking services. Second, it delves into the implications of telemediated connections for the construction of the self. Unlike the prevailing forms of socialization prior to the microelectronics revolution, it argues, the self for many people is increasingly constructed via an on-line web of interactions. In contrast to the prevailing Western model of subjectivity, the autonomous individual, digital media allow for a new type of self that is explicitly relational. In this context, "weak" ties that lack substantive emotional depth come to be more important than intimate "strong ties" (Grannovetter 1985). The argument is buttressed with discussions of on-line communities, cyborg selves, the blogosphere, and digital panopticons. Finally, it summarizes some progressive uses of cyberspace and social media.

B. Warf, *Global Geographies of the Internet*, SpringerBriefs in Geography, DOI: 10.1007/978-94-007-1245-4_6, © The Author(s) 2013

6.1 Mobile Phones, the Internet, and the Networked Society

Telecommunications, including telephony and the internet, are prime reflections, as well as producers of, the global space of flows. The hegemony of post-Fordist capitalism, which centered largely on the adoption of computers and the digitization of information, ushered in an unprecedented era of social and individual connectivity. In the context of interpersonal relations, two key innovations in this regard were mobile telephony and the internet.

One of the most impressive technological changes of the last two decades has been the mobile or cellular telephone (Dekimper et al. 1998; Goggin 2006; Campbell and Park 2008; Comer and Wikle 2008; Ling and Donner 2009). Rapid decreases in the size and cost of mobile phones, and the minimal infrastructure necessary to cultivate their networks, have made them increasingly affordable for vast numbers of people. Today, the vast majority of the world's telephones are mobile phones, which offer unprecedented convenience and ease of access. In 2011, 59.6 % of the world's inhabitants—5.2 billion people—used mobile phones, more than ten times as many as use landlines and far more than the two billion who used the internet. For example, China now has the world's largest population of mobile phone users (Dong and Li 2004; Ding et al. 2010). The extent of mobile telephony worldwide is evident in Fig. 6.1. Average penetration rates in 2010 exceeded that of landlines everywhere, and in many countries there are far more mobile phones than people. Even in much of sub-Saharan Africa, the world's least connected region, 10–50 % of the population uses mobile phones. Mobile telephony is expanding even more quickly than the internet: between 2003 and 2010, the world's number of mobile phone users jumped by 187 %. This growth was, unsurprisingly, unevenly distributed around the world: while rates of increase were relatively modest throughout the economically advanced world, in much of Africa and Central Asia they exceeded 1,000 %.

The worldwide adoption of mobile communication technologies has led to a widespread reconfiguration of identity and the contours and rhythms of everyday life, allowing users to connect and interact with one another to unprecedented degrees (Farman 2011). For example, mobile phones have engineered a mounting porosity between the private and public realms as once private conversations are held in public spaces (Townsend 2000; Hampton, and Wellman 2001; Mäenpää 2001; Fortunati 2002; Ling 2004; Pain et al. 2005; Ling and Campbell 2009). They have allowed for sharply improved coordination of mobility, improved use of time while driving or walking, and security in case of emergencies. Increasingly equipped with cameras, mobile phones allow for digital transmission of graphics as well as voice and text messages. Ling (2010) argues that the ubiquity of mobile telephony enhances social cohesion, although at times this unity is purchased at the cost of lower rates of face-to-face contact among proximate persons. Thus, Sooryamoorthy et al. (2011) found in a study of Kerala, India that mobile phone users were more likely to develop more nonlocal ties than were non-users, hinting at a generalized expansion of social relations over space.

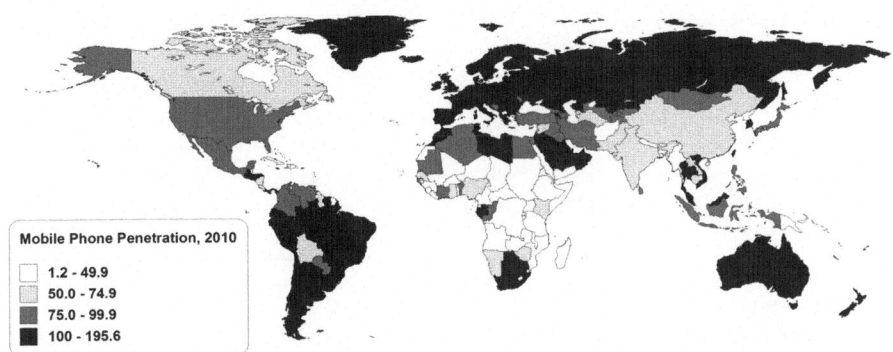

Fig. 6.1 Map of world mobile phone penetration rates, 2010. *Source* International Telecommunications Union

A critical consequence of mobile phones, and a central medium of communication for vast numbers of people, is text messaging. In 2010, 74 % of the world's mobile phone users, or 3.85 billion people, engaged in texting, sending a total of 6.1 trillion messages, or 192,000 per second (International Telecommunications Union 2010). Everywhere, teenagers took the lead in adopting texting, decisively choosing this medium far more than their elders as the core of their interpersonal interactions (Bolin and Westlund 2009; Lenhart et al. 2010). In the United States, where 93 % of the population uses a cellular phone, the average user sends 534 messages per month, and one in three teens sends more than 3,000 per month (Lenhart et al. 2010). In the developing world, texting has become a popular substitute for voice traffic because it is much lower in cost. Instant messaging services such as Twitter have also grown explosively. Starting with its foundation in 2006, Twitter had 140 million users worldwide in early 2012; the world sends more than 340 million tweets and 1.6 billion search queries per day. The Twitter website, one of the most heavily visited on Earth, hosts a service largely used by older persons, although it has become a vehicle for celebrity self-promotion as well.

The textbook example of the network society is, of course, the internet. Computers have been used for the exchange of personal information since the creation of USENET in the 1970s. In December, 2011, roughly 2.2 billion people, or 32 % of the planet's population, were logged in. A sizable body of scholarship has traced the social and spatial contours of cyberspace and need not be reiterated here (Kellerman 2002). For the purposes of this chapter, the centrality of email, which is by far the most common application of the internet, should be noted. Cheap (or free), instantaneous, and asynchronous, email allows both one-to-one and one-to-many modes of communication, but also strips information of its context and for many people induces information overload. Email is the most widely used medium of communication in the business world (the typical corporate user exchanges 110 messages per day), and has become central to both professional and personal success. Thus, in 2012 the world had more than 3.3 billion email accounts and sent 144.8 billion email messages per day (Radicati 2012).

Table 6.1 Year of origin of
selected social networking
sites

1997	Six Degrees
1999	Live Journal
2001	Cyworld
2002	Friendster
2003	LinkedIn, MySpace
2004	Flickr, Facebook
2005	YouTube
2006	Twitter

Another measure of the networked society is the use of digital social networks, which greatly expedite the creation of an online presence and facilitate the instantaneous exchange of information with friends and acquaintances. Social networking sites like Friendster, LinkedIn, MySpace, and Facebook began in the early 2000s (Table 6.1). While some services are aimed at finding romantic partners (e.g., Match.com), others such as YouTube allow sharing of digital content with everyone, including like-minded strangers. The growth in popularity of such networks is evident in Fig. 6.2: more than one-half of the U.S. population used social media sites in 2011, and roughly three-quarters of those under age 30 do so.

One particularly striking example of digital social networks is Facebook, by far the most popular networking site in the world (Kirkpatrick 2010). In February 2012, Facebook had more than 845 million users (Fig. 6.3), or 12 % of the planet's population: if Facebook were a country, it would be the third largest in the world. These users are, of course, unevenly distributed around the world (Table 6.2; Fig. 6.4). By far the largest single national group of Facebook users is found in the United States, which has more than 157 million subscribers, or half of the total population. Facebook is also popular throughout the Western hemisphere, Europe, the Indian subcontinent, most of Southeast Asia, and Australia and New Zealand. Within the U.S., the highest Facebook penetration rates are found in relatively wealthy, educated states such as Massachusetts, New Jersey, Washington State, and those with a cosmopolitan primate city, such as Illinois and Georgia (Fig. 6.5). Indeed, Facebook has decisively trounced competing networking services such as Myspace, which in the eyes of many users has become relegated to ethnic minorities and low-income users.

Facebook is only the largest of several social networking sites worldwide (Fig. 6.6). Thus, in much of the former Soviet Union, the Kontakte network is popular. China, ever suspicious that foreign systems might facilitate democratic impulses, has promoted its home-grown Qzone system, while in Brazil Zing reigns supreme. Dozens of other smaller networking sites also exist, such as Maktoob (in the Arab world), hi5.com (Mongolia), and Habbo (Finland). Regardless of the system used, however, the impacts of such networks on the social construction of the self remain similar.

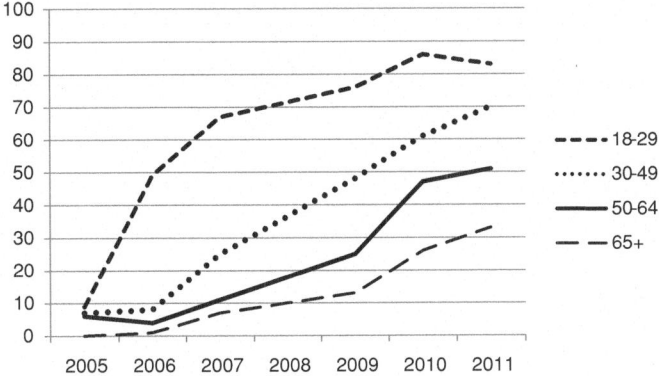

Fig. 6.2 Percent of U.S. population using digital social networks by age, 2005–2011. *Source* Redrawn from Pew Research Center.http://www.pewinternet.org/Reports/2011/Social-Networking-Sites/Report.aspx?view=all

Fig. 6.3 Facebook users worldwide, 2004–2011. *Source* Author, using data from Internetworldstats.com

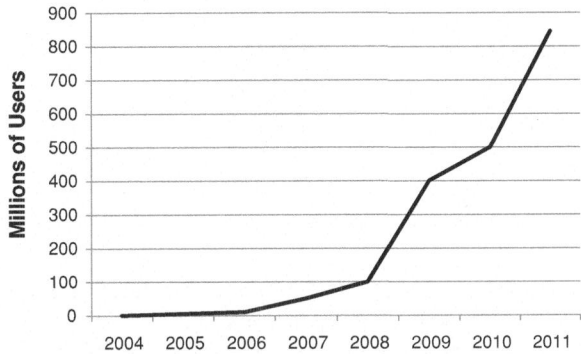

6.2 Telemediated Networks and the Relational Ontology of the Self

As the network society has grown apace, new forms of identity have risen in its wake (Giddens 1991). Much of social science, consequently, has become preoccupied with relational understandings of how people view themselves and one another, particularly as these perceptions and discourses are mediated through digital communications (Whatmore 1997). In contrast to the disembodied, autonomous individual standing apart from the world who has occupied the heart of modernist social theory since Descartes (most explicitly in that desolate creature *homo economicus*), the relational self is conscious of its embodiment, embeddedness, and social origins and consequences as they are manifested in a variety of ties to others. Relational views of identity emphasize the construction of difference and the power relations that accompany this process (Pile 2008). In light of poststructuralist theorizations,

Table 6.2 Facebook users and penetration rates by world region, December 2011

	Users (millions)	Penetration Rate
Europe	223	27.4
Asia	184	4.7
North America	175	50.3
Latin America and Caribbean	147	25.5
Africa	38	3.6
Middle East	17	8.4
Oceania	13	37.7

Source Internetworldstats.com

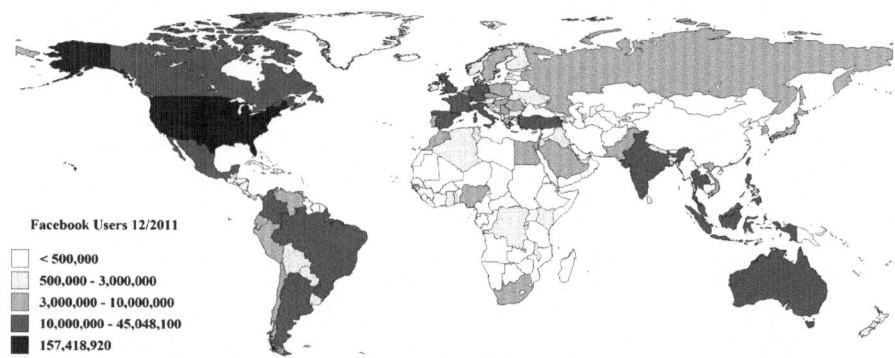

Fig. 6.4 Map of Facebook users worldwide, December 2011. *Source* internetworldstats.com

identities are never fixed or given, but fluid, multiple, contingent, context-dependent, and always under construction.

Theorizations of the number and quality of ties that individuals share owe much to the important contribution of Grannovetter (1985), who, in studying the embeddedness of the economy within culture, differentiated between strong and weak ties. Drawing on a long tradition of sociological theory, including Emile Durkheim's mechanical and organic solidarity, Ferdinand Tönnies's *Gemeinschaft* and *Gesellschaft*, as well as that of the Chicago School's Louis Wirth, Granovetter held that strong ties are characterized by high degrees of repeated interaction, trust, and emotional sustenance, such as those with family members and close friends. Weak ties, in contrast, tend to be more casual, instrumental, fleeting, and utilitarian. Generations of sociologists noted that urbanization tended to reduce the number of strong ties, enhancing alienation, and increase the number of weak ties. In highly developed socioeconomic contexts, weak ties vastly outnumber strong ones, and they are vital to the accumulation of social capital and professional success.

There can be little question that digital networks offer the opportunity for forming numerous weak ties. However, the degree to which telemediated interactions translate into powerful interpersonal connections is debatable. The literature on this issue, which has a long history, reveals two contrasting positions (Nie 2001).

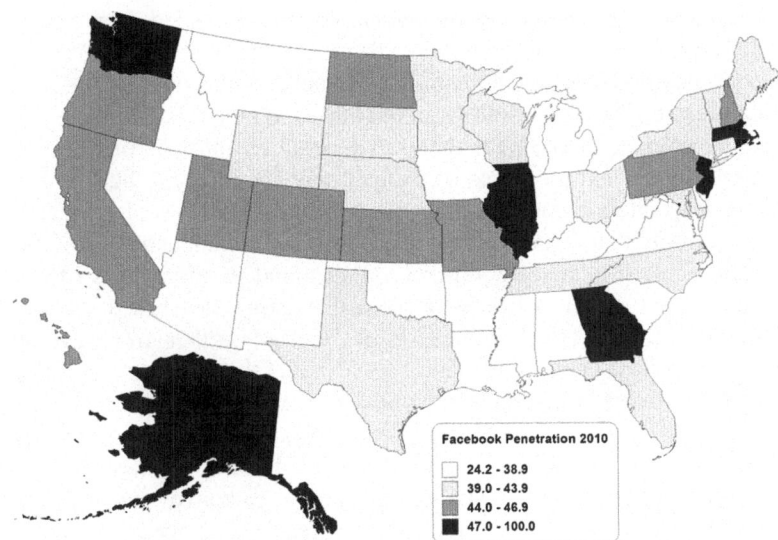

Fig. 6.5 Map of U.S. Facebook penetration rates, 2010. *Source*. author, using data from Internetworldstats.com

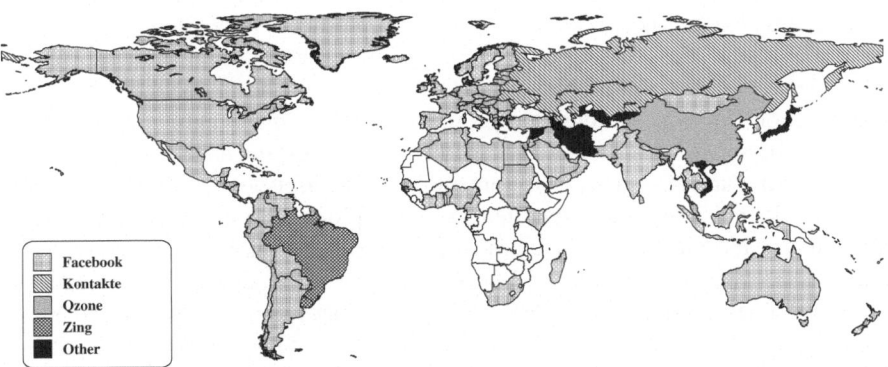

Fig. 6.6 Map of world's dominant social networking services, 2011. *Source*. author, redrawn from http://vincos.it/world-map-of-social-networks

Works on the telephone, for example, held that it allowed the rise of "communities without propinquity," or groups of people with similar interests who lack a common geographic location (Webber 1973). Some observers hold that digital networks can successfully replicate the emotional depth of face-to-face contacts (Hampton and Wellman 2001), that internet users have *more* off-line social interactions than do non-users (Castells 2001), and that digital networks are replacing spatial communities as the primary vehicles of sociability. The growth of massively multiplayer online role-playing games (MMORPGs) such as *World of Warcraft*, with eight million players worldwide, has been cited as an example of like-minded people voluntarily entering a community of choice unfettered by the need for proximity (Li et al. 2010).

The contrasting view of the potential of telemediated ties to enhance sociability holds that precisely because it allows anonymity and nonverbal cues such as body language, cyberspace discourages the growth of close, intimate ties. In this reading, mobile phones, text messages, and email may complement, but not substitute for, face-to-face interactions. For example, Fischer's (1992) social history of the telephone showed that it strengthened pre-existing social networks rather than created new ones; similarly, Wellman (2001a) found in an analysis of Canadian internet users that email typically reinforced existing ties based on family or friendship, and that a distance-decay effect existed farther from the physical location of the users. Haythornthwaite (2005) holds that substantive connections among social network users are almost always preceded or accompanied by off-line relationships. Computer-mediated communities tend to be ephemeral and lack significant levels of emotional commitment. After all, the 140 characters that limit the maximum length of a tweet hardly allow room to convey much information about oneself. Thus, telemediated interactions are ideal for weak ties, but not for strong ones. For example, Hampton et al. (2011) note that the average Facebook user has 229 "friends," although an overabundance of friends is detrimental to one's capacity to sustain close ties (Ellison et al. 2007; Tong et al. 2008). Few Facebook users, however, deploy the site to cultivate ties with people of a different cultural background (Vasalou et al. 2010). Turkle (2011) makes a powerful argument that social networks have isolated large numbers of users and deprived them of intimate ties. She argues that social media lead people to be alone even when they are together, and blames texting in particular for a decline in the art of conversation: a new skill, for example, includes being able to maintain eye contact with one person while texting another. Digital networking in this context inevitably reverberates to shape self-perceptions: she argues that the identities of teenagers increasingly are shaped not by self-exploration, but by the expectations of their on-line audiences. In confusing connectivity with conversation, social media users who are "always on" become unable to be alone, and consequently often feel lonely. Indeed, the growth of ersatz intimacy on Facebook has coincided with a surge in loneliness in the U.S. (Marche 2012). Others (Jackson 2008; Carr 2010) worry that the internet is unleashing subtle but pervasive changes in brain structure, including shortened attention spans, echoing Postman's (1985) devastating critique of television.

The creation of close ties involves the exchange of tacit knowledge and the cultivation of trust. Ettlinger (2003) helpfully differentiates between two types of trust, *emotive trust*, which includes an emotional component, and *capacity trust*, which centers on professional competence. While telemediated weak ties may be instrumental in the formation of capacity trust, their potential to forge emotive trust, which relies on tacit information that is typically communicated face-to-face, is dubious. Given the widespread use of electronic communications, interpersonal relations are increasingly, but never completely, freed from face-to-face contact (Warf 1994; Stutzman 2006). As a considerable body of work has shown, electronic communications are a poor substitute for face-to-face contact, which is necessary to transmit what Storper and Venables (2004) call "buzz," the intangible, culturally-saturated dimensions of agglomeration. Face-to-face contact allows for substantial depth in interpersonal interactions, including body language (including handshakes and eye contact), and emotional cues or affect (as stressed in nonrepresentational theory), it eliminates the possibility of anonymity that haunts digital interactions, enhances the ability of actors to engage in mutual monitoring, and it induces feelings of belonging to a community that are necessary to the creation of trust, synergies, and mutual understandings that arise from dense networks of individuals in close contact with one another. The creation and exchange of irregular, unstandardized, context-bound tacit knowledge is the key to the success of innovative clusters, global cities, and post-Fordist centers of flexible production that drive successful regional economies (Maskell and Malmberg 1999; Allen 2000). Similarly, Richard Florida's (2002) celebrated "creative class" focuses on places in which the opportunities for both formal and informal interactions abound. Thus, for all of the hyperbole surrounding the network society and digital technologies, face-to-face contact still retains a vital role in contemporary economic and social life.

The massive social changes unleashed by digital communication technologies have, not surprisingly, changed what Lanier (2010) calls "what a person can be." In enhancing human extensibility, telemediated ties allow for a far-reaching rescripting of the self: from a system of one-to-one ties to a system characterized by one-to-many connections, increasingly large numbers of people socialize today via a vast network of weak digital ties. The result has been a series of convoluted interpersonal landscapes marked by wormholes and tunnels, yielding complicated, origami-like spatialities of daily life. Social media allow multiple spaces and times to be folded into the self to an unprecedented degree: the computer screen allows "being at a distance," blurring the boundaries between self and other. Gergen (1991, p. 49) asserts that the immersion of individuals in networks of digital technologies leads to a condition of "multiphrenia," "a world in which we no longer experience a secure sense of self, and in which doubt is increasingly placed on the very assumption of a bounded identity with palpable attributes." The poststructural self, if it can be said to exist at all, is stretched across multiple locations, both synchronously and asynchronously (Adams 1995), mirroring the rhyzomic structure of the internet. Telemediated networks both reflect and produce a self with no core but consists simply of an assemblage of interactions. In contrast to the modernist self, purportedly stable and coherent, the networked subject consists of a pastiche of multiple selves, sometimes at odds with one another. As Jameson (1984:63) argued, "the alienation of the subject is displaced by the fragmentation of the subject."

If digital technologies muddle the boundaries between self and other, they also problematize the dichotomy of human and machine, or, as actor-network theorists have maintained, between human and non-human actors. Haraway (1991) famously argued that in the current age the boundaries between bodies and machines, the natural and the artificial, have become progressively blurrier, a notion manifested in her famous use (but not invention) of the term "cyborgs" (cybernetic organisms), complex articulations of tissue and technologies that seamlessly integrate humans and machine. Similarly, Graham and Marvin (1996, p. 107) note that "Humans and machines (have) become fused in ways that make the old separations between technology and society, the real and the simulated, meaningless." Such a trope problematizes dominant conceptions of "nature" as non-mechanical. In relying on telemediated networks so heavily, mobile phone and internet users become part of a cybernetic system in which humans and non-humans co-constitute one another, a theme dear to the hearts of actor-network theorists.

Deibert (1997, p. 182) holds that "the postmodern view of the self 'fits' the hypermedia environment—ways that suggest it might resonate strongly as that environment deepens and expands." He cites in particular increasingly blurry notions of authorship and intellectual property rights on the internet. Rather than being passive consumers of information, the internet has allowed many people to become active producers, or in Ritzer and Jurgenson's (2010) term, "prosumers" or what Bruns (2008) calls "produsage." Web 2.0 technologies facilitate the creation of websites that allow instantaneous user interactions, such as blogs. The interactive websites characteristic of Web 2.0 allow users upload locations into online content and apply their data in diverse ways fostered an unprecedented democratization of geographic knowledge, often with roots far removed from academic experts, users can create share and use information via "crowd sourcing," which allows large, widely distributed groups to work together toward a common goal. Web 2.0 media have enabled large numbers of people to pick and choose those sources of information that mesh conveniently with their ideological presuppositions. There are obviously both advantages and disadvantages to this approach. It is not always the case that the "wisdom of the crowd" is superior to that of a few experienced individuals; by utilizing data that only confirm their beliefs, users may never be confronted with disturbing or contradictory sources of information.

The networked self is much more public and much less private than the autonomous human subject who lies at the core of most traditional thought in the social sciences. Clearly mobile phones and social media are blurring the boundaries between public and private life. Who has not overheard a private conversation via cell phone in a public space? Increasingly, networked selves are performed in public, to borrow Butler's (1990) famous terminology. In this context, the virtual self becomes an integral part of one's public image, or, to use an older terminology, what Goffman (1959), using a dramaturgical model, called each person's "front stage." As Katz and Aakhus (2002) make clear, cell phone usage often involves public displays of performance. Similarly, given the propensity of many young people to post every detail of their private lives on the web, social media constitute a form of panopticon, facilitating self-policing of internal worlds in conformity with the aesthetics of the internet. Through constant status updates on Facebook, for example, the public self is carefully edited and micro-managed. Social networks point to a changing sense of privacy, one in which the personal is

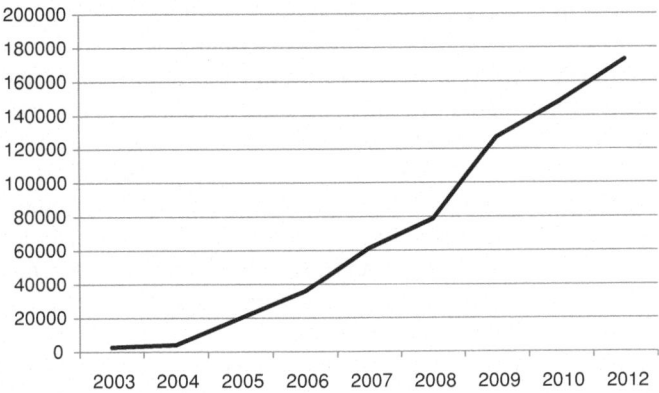

Fig. 6.7 Growth in World's Blogosphere, 2003–2011 (millions). *Source.* redrawn from Technorati 2007 and SMI 2012

often trotted out for public display and consumption (Debatin et al. 2009). In shifting the role of users from simple broadcasting of information to engagement with others, social networks facilitate a marketing of the self, as if it were a brand name, in which the public presentation of self is carefully micromanaged. Goffman's (1959) front stage, as it were, has gone virtual. Livingstone and Brake (2010, p. 76) argue that social networking satisfies "a desire to construct a valued representation of oneself which affirms and is affirmed by one's peers." However, there are costs to this strategy: for example, by allowing the posting of photos, including when poster is engaged in unsavory or illegal behavior, social networks may create problems later when prospective employers view such material as part of their assessment of job candidates (Hill 2011; Waters 2011). Increasingly, users have become self-conscious of this phenomenon: indeed, an example of auto-panopticonic behavior can be found when college students on spring break min-imize their normal rowdiness for fear that photos or videos of them posted on-line may come back to haunt them later (Alvarez 2012).

The public, networked self is also evident in the blogosphere, which for many people has emerged as an important dimension of social networking (Bruns 2008). In 2011, the internet hosted more than 173 million blogs (Fig. 6.7), with an additional 30,000 added every day. Typically blogs are interwoven with other blogs, forming complicated spatialities of hyperlinks that may be both local and global in scope and scale (Lin 2007). Free and uncensored, some blogs operate as on-line personal diaries and are aimed a variety of audiences ranging from family members to the public at large, sometimes with tags that organize posts along the lines of a given theme, and often with "comment" features that allow readers to post feedback. Others exist simply as mills for the dissemination of rumors and gossip, often with RSS ("really simple syndication") feeds that notify readers of blog updates. The majority of bloggers are women, and half are under age 35 (SMI 2012). This sort of self-publishing demonstrates the public performance of the self at its best, and worst. Geographical work on blogs has been slow to evolve (but see Gopal 2007). Jones et al. (2010) maintain that networks of blogs can duplicate the "buzz" typically generated through face-to-face contact, allowing users to deploy virtual pipelines to acquire tacit knowledge over great distances. Fuller and Askins (2010) note that blogs are central to the creation and performance of "public geographies," a series of unplanned, shifting, and often serendipitous encounters that largely fall outside the purview of academia. This trend illustrates how blogs, like other social media, are blurring the long-standing dichotomy between the ivory tower and the non-academic world, much as other digital communications have dissolved dualities such as economic/cultural, private/public, human/nonhuman, and local/global.

Finally, the visibility of the public, networked self inevitably raises serious concerns about digital privacy (Curry 1997). Numerous corporations such as Equifax Marketing use sophisticated search engines to engage in data mining, targeted digital advertising, and collect vast amounts of information about individuals on-line (Zook and Graham 2007). Information gathered from user profiles is highly useful in targeted advertising and marketing campaigns. What is the self, then, when so much of it circulates in computer networks beyond the individual's control, or even knowledge? The vulnerabilities of large commercial or government datasets have been highlighted by groups such as Anonymous or Germany's Chaos Computer Club. Google has been sued for its use of private information in services such as GoogleMaps (Gordon and de Souza e Silva 2011). Morozov (2011) gives several disturbing examples of how many governments use social media against their own citizens, and Pinkerton et al. (2011) note that many social networking sites have become securitized. Indeed, the collection of information about digital individuals is part of a broader post-Fordist panopticonic regime that also includes the widespread use of closed circuit surveillance cameras (Dobson and Fisher 2007).

6.3 Progressive Political Uses of Social Media

The internet has become a mainstay for large numbers of progressive social and political organizations operating at the local, national, and international scales, crossing borders, forging alliances, raising funds, exposing local inequalities, voicing criticisms, pressuring public officials, and mobilizing public opinion. Of course, there is also a parallel military history and set of applications of the internet (which began as a means to link military computers), ranging from electronic surveillance to cyberwarfare. Cyberspace has also been successfully utilized by numerous racist, reactionary, terrorist, and xenophobic groups for their own ends. The focus here is on uses of the internet for progressive causes of social justice and peaceful reform. "Progressive activism," of course, is a vague term, but here is taken to mean the constellation of non-profit and advocacy groups and social movements dedicated to causes such as promoting justice and human rights; preventing war;

attacking poverty; environmental protection; women's, handicapped peoples', animal, and minority rights; and opposition to economic and political exploitation, including some types of corporate globalization (Lipshutz 1992; Hawken 2007).

The internet has become indispensible to grassroots social movements advocating "globalization from below" (Della Porta et al. 2006). As neoliberalism has gutted state functions throughout the world, numerous non governmental organizations and other civil society actors have grown accordingly. Social movements are non-state actors whose intentions, behavior, and strategies cannot be reduced to market forces. The internet has become indispensible for such groups, linking like-minded people on a global scale through the day-to-day coordination of transnational organizations dedicated to nonviolent social change (Bandy and Smith 2005; Della Porta et al. 2006). Indeed, the recent, prolific growth of nongovernmental organizations, social movements, and global civil society is inconceivable without the internet. Cyberspace allows the expression of numerous subaltern voices in this regard that would otherwise remain silent, including those that circumvent government attempts at censorship and suppression internet-based "network armies" also often lobby offline (Cammaerts 2005). The internet is relatively low in cost and easy to use, and its low barriers to entry reduce a major obstacle to the participation in public debate by the poor and disenfranchised. Cyberspace provides an accessible venue for information, lessons, best practices, and expertise to be shared, moral commitments and group solidarity to be enhanced, publicity to be gained, dissent made public, sympathizers alerted, resources to be pooled, and funds to be raised. Over the internet, activists can not only organize but also publicize their actions. For groups that have little expertise in public relations, the internet allows communications to be leveraged to maximum success (Taylor et al. 2001).

The rhizomic architecture of cyberspace, without a clear core or periphery, is well suited to the decentralized, polycentric types of organizations that dominate civil society movements. It thus favors bi-directional, interactive forms of communication among geographically dispersed individuals rather than traditional, hierarchical flows within narrow social and spatial channels. Such a structure stands in marked contrast with the oligopolized, one-way nature of traditional print, radio, and television media. Moreover, the internet is well adapted to accommodating diverse views among progressives, who are often given to fractious in-fighting. Bennett (2003, p. 154) argues that internet-driven campaigns "allow different political perspectives to co-exist without the conflicts that such differences might create in more centralized coalitions." In Harvey's (1996) words, such strategies constitute a form of "militant particularism," in which local solidarities find common ground with one another. Langman (2005) goes further, holding that internetworked social movements may be a qualitatively new form of social movement. Similarly, Blood (2001, p. 160) argues that due to cyberspace, "the centre of gravity of the non-governmental organisation (NGO) movement as a whole is being shifted to a more radical and more overtly anti-capitalist position."

There is a relatively short, but rich, history of the use of the internet by protest groups. Of course, the use of communications technologies by subaltern groups generating geographies of resistance is nothing new: in their day, newspapers, the telegraph, and the telephone were used to coordinate actions among dispersed actors. For example, Featherstone (2005) illustrates how networks of correspondence among strikers in eighteenth century London were critical to coordinating their actions. Yet cyberspace has taken this process to an entirely different level of participation and activism, allowing the ready expansion to truly global networks. In the late 1980s, peace and environmental activists used the internet in Britain (GreenNet), the U.S. (PeaceNet), and Sweden (NordNet), projects that merged in 1990 to form an umbrella network under the name of the Association for Progressive Communications (Deibert and Rohozinski 2008). Various groups that coagulated around the United Nations' Earth Summit in Rio de Janeiro in 1992 used the internet to coordinate their actions.

Cyberspace famously played a significant role in the Zapatista uprising in Mexico in 1994, the world's first highly publicized case of internet activism, when subcommander Marcos became known worldwide through his email missives (Froehling 1997; Cleaver 1998; Knudsen 1998) and rebel hacktivists launched denial-of-service attacks on Mexican government websites (Johnston and Laxer 2003). The international publicity that internet activism brought to bear on the Zapatistas is widely credited with preventing the Mexican government from instigating a military crackdown on Chiapas. The "Zapatista effect," however, has also led many international donors to exaggerate the emancipatory role of information technology and foster unwarranted optimism about its potential (Mercer 2004).

Today, internet usage among social activists is so common as to be unremarkable, as demonstrated by the burgeoning literature on the topic (Hill and Hughes 1998; Palczewski 2001; van de Donk et al. 2004; Chadwick 2006). The agents who deploy cyberspace, and the purposes and means to which it is put, are as varied as the multiple causes that they take up. So widespread and diffuse is internet usage that progressive internet portals arose to help coordinate disparate sources of information, such as those offered by the Institute for Global Communications (www.igc.org), the Association for Progressive Communications (www.apc.org), and One World (www.oneworld.net). Two decades of practice and scholarship have demonstrated that cyberspace neither confirms the fantasies of early utopians nor the dystopian visions of techno pessimists.

The internet has been widely used by anti-globalization activists, such as in the coordination of protests against the World Trade Organization in the famous "Battle in Seattle" in 1999 (Smith 2001), a key moment in contemporary struggles against corporate hegemony, against the World Bank and IMF in Washington, DC in 2000 (Juris 2005), and against the G-8 meeting in Genoa in 2001 (Johnston and Laxer 2003; Porta and Mosca 2005). The Canadian-led global campaign in 1998 against the Multilateral Agreement on Investment (MAI), put forth by the Organization for Economic Cooperation and Development to facilitate the movement of capital but not labor, succeeded in pushing it off the OECD's agenda using broad alliances forged over the internet, one of series of blows against neoliberalism and the Washington Consensus (Deibert 2000; Johnston and Laxer 2003).

Similarly, corporate behavior has come under mounting cyberscrutiny. The global movement to improve working conditions in textile and footwear sweatshops, often focused on Nike, was primarily a web-based campaign (Carty 2001). Fair trade movements, such as that advocating coffee grown under environmentally beneficial conditions and purchased directly from growers for higher prices than standard coffee, have been significant users of web-based tactics (Bennett 2003). Successful internet campaigns against large multinational firms such as Monsanto, Microsoft, and De Beers have held their logos, brands and reputations hostage to the media spotlight (Bennett 2003; Clark and Themundo 2003). Other anti-corporate cybercampaigns include boycotts against companies producing genetically engineered foods, forcing the Sydney Hilton hotel in Australia to rehire employees laid off due to renovations, and forcing Samsonite suitcase manufacturer to rehire workers in Thailand who had been illegally fired (Cammaerts 2005). In other cases, corporations have been the targets of email campaigns by unhappy employees or consumers. The Corporate Watch website (corpwatch.org) enables viewers to see hundreds of instances of company malfeasance around the world. So effective has anti-corporate cyberactivism become that Juris (2005) asserts that police often specifically target independent media coordinators in crackdowns on protesters designed to protect corporate rights and property. At a minimum, such campaigns have forced companies to be more careful in their actions to protect their reputation and public image (Illia 2003).

Progressive political uses of cyberspace abound. At the local level, "insurgent campaigns" can make use of cyberspace as a low cost medium (Chadwick 2006). Rutherford (2000) describes how the International Campaign to Ban Landmines, a loose coalition of over 1,300 groups from more than 75 countries that won the Nobel Peace Prize in 1997, made extensive use of the Internet in a successful campaign to prohibit their future use. The worldwide protests against the war in Iraq that materialized on February 15, 2003, relied enormously on internet linkages. Routledge (2003, 2008) offers the example of People's Global Action, an international alliance of progressive activists in places as distant from one another as India, Brazil, and Europe, which crystallized using the internet as their primary means of communication, forming what he labels a "space of convergence." Similarly, Bosco (2007) describes how the internet was used by Argentine human rights activists deploring the disappearance of thousands of loved ones under the murderous military regime of the 1970s to organize local as well as trans-national networks of supporters, utilizing cyberspace as a complement to the deep emotional bonds they forged through face-to-face contacts. When the Turkish government arrested Kurdish rebel leader Abdullah Ocalan in 1999, the Kurdish diaspora responded with worldwide demonstrations within a matter of hours, calling upon supporters using well established internet linkages (Denning 2002). During the U.S. bombing of Serbia in 1999, Serbs deplored their status with messages seeking to generate support in an effort led by cybermonk Sava Janjic (Wasley 2007), although such email was often derided as "Yugospam" (Denning 2002); cyberspace was also a critical link to the world for anti-Milosevic forces. The first World Social Forum, launched in Porto Alegre, Brazil in 2001, was primarily organized over cyberspace (Juris 2005). Between 2003 and 2005, Ukraine, Georgia, and Kyrgyzstan all experienced democratic "color revolutions," in which opposition parties utilized the web as an integral part of their strategy (Warf 2009). The Burmese/Myanmar government's ferocious oppression of Buddhist monks and democracy activists was met with organized internet resistance (Wasley 2007), among other forms. The website Protest.net serves "to help progressive activists by providing a central place where the times and locations of protests and meetings can be posted."

Cyberspace has facilitated the resurgence of progressive grassroots politics in the U.S. (Armstrong and Moulitsas 2006) in various ways. Democratic Party fund raising over the Web, for example, which was initiated by the presidential campaign of Howard Dean in 2004, has consistently outpaced parallel attempts by conservative groups. Internet-based groups such as Moveon.org, which began in 1998 and had more than 6 million members in 2009, played important roles in supporting Barack Obama's presidential bid in 2008, primarily through large numbers of small contributions. Moveon.org's efforts have been imitated by like-minded groups such as People for the American Way, New Democratic Network, and the New Majority Fund. At the leftist edges of the political spectrum, PunkVoter.com used cyberspace effectively to mobilize hundreds of thousands of new, typically young, voters.

Feminist cyberpolitics has also grown by leaps and bounds (Wise 1997; Escobar 1999; van Zoonen 2001; Youngs 2002). This phenomenon is particularly important given that the Internet has historically been an overwhelmingly masculine phenomenon, and that even today in many countries, women are less likely to use the internet than are men, although in the economically developed world the gender dimension of the digital divide has essentially evaporated. Cyberfeminist applications include connecting women's and reproductive rights groups, exposing atrocities such as female genital mutilation and "honor killings," mobilizing against domestic abuse, struggles for sex workers' rights, advocating for women's literacy in developing countries, and supporting women-owned businesses. Feminist NGOs in Mexico, for example, use the internet to bypass state-dominated media in their reform efforts (Merithew 2004). Moreover, the internet allows for the creation of feminist subaltern "counterpublic" spaces, run by women, for women (Travers 2003). In deeply patriarchal societies such as in much of the Muslim world, the internet allows women far wider means of communication than are found traditionally (Mojab 2001). UNESCO's Women on the Net project, launched in 1997, focuses on empowering women around the world. Finally, cyberspace is both a vehicle for advancing women's rights in the non-virtual world and an arena of struggle in its own right, as with attempts to combat pornography or advertising that is degrading to women.

Internet-based activism plays a key role in numerous environmental movements (Pickerill 2003). An early example is O'Lear's (1996) observation of Russian environmentalists using email to network and share information in the early 1990s. More recently, Cammaerts (2005) describes how activists saved the Lapperfort Forest near Brugge, Belgium, in 2001 by coordinating their actions online. The group 350.org organized the International Day of Climate Action, held on October 24, 2009, which coordinated 5,200 events in 181 countries entirely using the internet. Envirolink (www.envirolink.org) lists 1,200 organizations dedicated to environmental issues and corporate social responsibility, offering them free web services. Greenpeace, the world's largest environmental activist group and one of the first to initiate e-campaigns (Wasley 2007), has encouraged civil disobedience using the web, circulated "subvertisements" that undermine Coca Cola's allegedly ecofriendly public image (www.cokespotlight.org), and empowered victims of the Bhopal chemical disaster in India. Ecological Internet, run by forest activist Glenn Barry, runs continuous cyber-campaigns on issues such as global warming, rainforest protection, and sustainable development.

Within the growing domain of animal rights activism, the internet plays a key role (Herzog et al. 1997; Swan and McCarthy 2003). This issue takes several forms. At some universities, for example, activists protesting the mistreatment of laboratory animals used the internet to publicize their cause. People for the Ethical Treatment of Animals (PETA) has deployed the internet to expose cases of animal cruelty and lobby for more human treatment, including the use of Facebook pages, streaming videos, and blogs. Others have mounted successful cybercampaigns to publicize the mistreatment of greyhounds and horses used for racing; decry the sale of fur from baby seals, reindeer, and chinchillas; illuminate the plight of stray pets; raise funds for humane societies; expose animal mistreatment in zoos and circuses; mobilize against the use of whale sharks in commercial aquaria; circulate petitions to ban whaling; bring sadists who abuse animals to justice; organize boycotts of cosmetic companies that use animal products gained under unsavory conditions; promote spay and neuter programs; advocate vegetarianism; unveil the inhumanity of factory farms; reduce the human consumption of dogs and cats in China; and raise funds for wildlife habitat protection. Militant animal rights activists can use anonymizing contacts to coordinate disparate cells and evading filters to ensure that their message gets through to target email accounts. Stop Huntingdon Animal Cruelty (SHAC), for example, is an international campaign to shut down Huntingdon Life Sciences, Europe's largest animal-testing laboratory; SHAC describes itself as "leaderless resistance" coordinated entirely over cyberspace. Similarly, the Animal Liberation Front has launched repeated internet stalking campaigns against firms engaged in animal testing and cruelty. Of course, the internet may also enable phenomena such as illegal trade in wildlife, allowing buyers and sellers to be anonymous.

The blogosphere has become an increasingly important terrain over which contemporary politics is constituted. Of course, conservative bloggers also deploy the medium aggressively (e.g., the Drudge Report), and in the early days of blogging were far more successful than leftists. However, whereas conservative blogs tend to reinforce the views of their offline constituencies, progressive ones have focused more on reaching out to new participants and building online communities of activists (Bowers and Stoller 2005). Thus, in 2005, the largest 150 U.S. conservative blogs attracted 10 million page views per week, while the largest 98 liberal blogs attracted 15 million. Progressive blogging including "warblogs" that challenged the rationale for the U.S. invasion of Iraq in 2003, exposing racist remarks by Republican Speaker of the House Trent Lott, attacking George W. Bush's scheme to privatize Social Security, and providing real time, alternative media coverage of major events such as the World Summit for Sustainable Development. Some bloggers engaged in "Google bombs," campaigns designed to catapult their target blog to the top of the behemoth search engine's rankings (Kahn and Kellner 2004). Today, Daily Kos is easily the largest blog in the world: founded by Markos Moulitsas in 2002, it averages over 600,000 hits per day, supports and raises funds for progressive political candidates and serves as a forum for a wide variety of leftist groups. Similar blogs include Democratic Underground, FireDogLake, Raw Story, Talking Points Memo, Americablog, and Metafilter.

A virtual sit-in is the cyberspace equivalent of a physical sit-in or blockade. A group calling itself Strano Network conducted one of the first such demonstrations as a protest against French government policies on nuclear and social issues. On December 21, 1995, they launched a one-hour NetStrike attack against the web sites operated by various government agencies. On September 9, 1998 the Electronic Disturbance Theater (EDT) took the concept of electronic civil disobedience a step further; they organized a series of web sit-ins, first against Mexican President Zedillo's web site, then against the Pentagon and the Frankfurt Stock Exchange, delivering 600,000 hits per minute to each (Denning 2002); they also targeted the GOP convention in New York in 2004.

Social movements' uses of the internet also include aggressive instances of hacktivism, a series of cybertactics that includes denial-of-service attacks, defacement of websites, information theft, and virtual sabotage (Jordan and Taylor 2004). For example, in 1998 the group Milworm hacked into India's Bhabha Atomic Research Center in Mumbai, posting an anti-nuclear message on its website. The 1999 meeting of the G8 in Cologne, Germany, was attacked by a group called J18, including hackers from Indonesia, Israel, Germany, and Canada who launched 10,000 denial of service attacks in a five hour period against the computers of at least 20 companies and the London Stock Exchange (Ungoed and Sheehan 1999). In 2000, a group of "electrohippies" overloaded the webpages of the World Trade Organization (Langman 2005). Tamil guerrillas swamped Sri Lankan embassies around the world with thousands of electronic mail messages that read "We are the Internet Black Tigers and we're doing this to disrupt your communications" (Denning 2002). Cult of the Dead Cow, one of the largest and most famous hacktivist groups (with spin-offs such as Ninja Strike Force and Hacktivismo), launched repeated denial-of-service attacks against the Church of Scientology, and also cooperated with Hong Kong hackers working against Chinese internet censorship. Other anonymous hackers have attacked websites of conservative commentators Bill O'Reilly and Sarah Palin. Of course, this tactic works both ways: Chinese hackers, for example, have launched attacks against CNN and film festivals deemed to be critical of the Chinese state. Still other hacktivists released open source software such as OpenOffice, a shareware version of Microsoft's Office suite, to challenge the behemoth's dominance in this sector. As Huschle (2002) points out, cyberspace transforms the nature of civil disobedience, allowing small groups or even single individuals in one country to have far larger significant impacts at a distance in other countries than is possible through conventional tactics such as demonstrations and sit-ins.

One of the most important uses of cyberspace by progressive social groups is scale jumping, the use of one scale to facilitate political action at another, allowing the local to become global (and vice versa). A fecund body of literature has recently portrayed scale as made, not given, denaturalizing it as a social construction with powerful and contested political dimensions (Marston 2000; Benner 2001; Marston et al. 2005; Moore 2008). Such a perspective avoids the common error of conceiving as scales hierarchically, i.e., like nested Russian *matroyshka* dolls; rather, it allows processes to be viewed as deeply multiscalar in nature, and foregrounds the nature of social relations as networks and flows rather than spaces, a notion essential to poststructuralist perspectives. Telecommunications are an ideal mechanism for groups to jump scale (Adams 1996), allowing them, for example, to leverage public opinion at the global scale in local struggles for justice. Prominent examples of scale jumping using cyberspace by progressive social movements include the Zapatista uprising (Cleaver 1998), linking local community networks in the U.S. (Longan 2002), farmers' opposition to transnational mining companies in Peru (Haarstad and Fløysand 2007), and the Indian Farmers' Movement resistance to foreign biotechnology (Featherstone 2003). Leveraging the global to shape local struggles is a tool long used by transnational firms; the internet offers the same strategy to groups operating in civil society. In Cox (1998) terms, the internet allows local groups to expand their spaces of engagement, i.e., the geography of their supporters and audience, well beyond their spaces of dependence, the locations of their support networks on the ground.

The internet is often used by diasporic networks to maintain contacts among persons living outside their country of origin (Cunningham 2001), keeping them in touch with one another and with their origin country, forming a globalized "imagined community" of the sort made famous by Benedict Anderson (1983). Parham (2004), for example, notes its use by the Haitian diaspora to form Haitian Global Village, a sprawling website that receives one-half million visits per month. Indian emigrants forged a Hindu cyber diaspora in the early 1990s (Lal 1999), and Tamilnet.com links Hindu Sri Lankans worldwide. Often such groups have contacts in cyberspace that cross caste, gender, or religious lines in ways that would not be possible in person. The Iranian diaspora, for example, is linked by a series of cyber channels that connect people of varying ages, degrees of religiosity, different levels of fluency in Farsi, and political outlooks (Graham and Khosravi 2002). These lines of connection serve to problematize prevailing conceptions of citizenship, as some diasporic communities may be more informed about and more involved in political affairs in their home country than their brethren in remote rural villages. Some diasporas, such as Russian Jews in the late 1980s, Kurds, Palestinians, and East Timorese, deployed the internet in struggles against oppressive governments in their respective homelands (Dahan and Shefer 2001). As Appadurai (1996, p. 10) puts it, "The transformation of everyday subjectivities through electronic mediation and the work of the imagination is not only a cultural fact. It is deeply connected to politics. The diasporic public spheres that such encounters create are no longer small, marginal, or exceptional."

More broadly, the internet may help to foster a relational ontology of space and place and corresponding alternative geographic imaginaries, in which identity is defined through lines of power and feelings of belonging and responsibility rather than simple proximity (Bennett 2003; Massey 2009). Vivid pictures and films of atrocities and injustices circulating over the internet can have powerful impacts in raising awareness about a variety of issues. Indeed, formal ideologies, political parties, and elections may be giving way to network-based identity and lifestyle politics. In facilitating rhizomatic networks of power, the internet can be an agent for the generation of geographies of compassion and empathy that stand in sharp contrast to xenophobic discourses of hate and exclusion. Such a view is in keeping with the emerging literature on geographies of care and the ethics of responsibility (Lawson 2007), particularly in the face of the neoliberal assault on state-funded interventions in the sphere of reproduction and the associated growth of discourses of individual, rather than collective, responsibility. In such a context, the moral community to which each person owes an obligation is, by definition, worldwide, generating an obligation to "care at a distance," in which the concerns of distant strangers are held to be as important as those of people nearby (Ginzburg 1994; Corbridge 1998).

Overreliance on the internet can in fact undermine other forms of political action: as Johnston and Laxer (2003, p. 64) ask, "Is Internet solidarity a lazy activism of e-mail petitions, or simply a convenient tool to facilitate grass-roots organizing?" Notably, Internet use by itself does not necessarily lead to heightened interest in political issues or greater participation. Ayres (1999) asserts that cyber-activism's "politics at a distance" has displaced traditional street-based forms of protest such as marches, which are far more telegenic and visible locally. Likewise, Morozov (2011) cautions against the easy substitution of signing email petitions for real political action. Social movements that rely exclusively on the internet to foment long-term linkages are unlikely to succeed: cyberspace is a complement, not a substitute, for "real world" contacts. In this sense, the internet is not only social groups' greatest asset, but their Achilles' heel as well. Thus, the internet spawns movements that are not quite true cohesive communities in the classic sense of the word, but more than coincidental coordinations of isolated groups. Deibert (2000, p. 264) maintains that "What the Internet has generated is indeed a new 'species'—a cross-national network of citizen activists linked by electronic mailing lists and World Wide Web home pages that vibrate with activity, monitoring the global political economy like a virtual watchdog." Moreover, politically active individuals are likely to be active with or without the internet (Van Aelst and Walgrave 2002).

6.4 Conclusions

Telemediated social media—including mobile phones, the internet, email, Facebook, and blogs—are now used by a substantial share of the planet's population. Sixty percent of the world uses mobile phones, one-third uses the internet, and one out of eight uses Facebook, indicating an historically unprecedented degree of connectivity. While Castells (1996, 1997) conceived of the networked society in terms of interconnected elites, digital social media allow substantial numbers of people to become linked with one another in ways never seen before. The implications of this change, which has unfolded within a remarkably narrow slice of historical time, have yet to be fully explicated. The digital reconstruction of the self is reflective of the massive wave of contemporary wave of time–space compression, or "distanciation," to use Giddens's (1991) term for how societies are stretched over time and space. In the same vein, Jameson (1984, p. 83) notes that postmodern hyperspace "has finally succeeded in transcending the capacities of the individual human body to locate itself, to organize its immediate surrounding perceptually, and cognitively to map its position in a mappable external world." Without doubt, telemediated social networks have led to an ongoing reconstruction of what it means to be a human subject.

In contrast to the long hegemony of the Cartesian model of the subject—atomistic and highly individualistic, a view that denies its embodiment and social origins—the networked self unleashed via digital social media is explicitly relational. For many users of the internet, the dichotomy between "off-line" and "on-line" no longer makes sense: in a world of ubiquitous connectivity, we exist in both of these domains simultaneously, all the time. Because telemediated ties are unlikely ever to be equivalent to face-to-face interactions and the possibility they allow for the creation of deep emotional ties forged through the exchange of tacit knowledge, technologies such as email, phone calls, blogs and the like forge networks of "weak" ties, to use Granovetter's (1985) terminology. The networked self is thus extensible to large numbers of people and places but its relations with others tend to be shallow, utilitarian, and transient. Digital networks constitute not only extensions of the self, but also reverberate to shape the self, as the careful maintenance of front stages on Facebook and blogs illustrates. Because technology is indispensable in enabling (and constraining) the networked self, those who construct and reproduce digital identities are necessarily cyborgs, seamless articulations of people and machines in which the role of one is inseparable from the other.

Although oceans of trivia circulate through cyberspace, the internet is also an indisputably political phenomenon. Numerous groups concerned about changing—and improving—the status quo have harnessed the technology to connect with one another. Social media thus have powerful emancipatory potential, although it is not always realized. Such an observation provides a glimmer of optimism in an age otherwise marked by triumphant neoliberalism.

Despite the hyperbole that the internet or other forms of digital communications have made geography obsolete, the stubborn fact remains that location is still important in the age of networked social media (Wellman 2001b; Papacharissi 2009; Gordon and de Souza e Silva 2011). The location of users' physical bodies, their non-virtual, face-to-face ties, family and local context, the digital divide, and the spatiality of institutions and processes that shape the form, content, and nature of digital networks and the flows of information across them all testify to the enduring significance of place. Not surprisingly, the emergence of the relational ontology of the self and identity has been accompanied by relational ontologies of place and space, in which space as formed by contingent, rapidly changing, interconnected sets of networks in which relational connections among locales rather than their absolute positionality is the dominant characteristic (Massey 2005; Murdoch 2006; Jones 2009). Cheap, instantaneous, and ubiquitous digital communications have made the notion of place as a discreet, bounded entity increasingly problematic by allowing people to be in several places simultaneously. As a result, Cosgrove (2008, p. 47) notes that today, "Places and landscapes are no longer thought of by geographers simply as bounded containers, but as constellations of connections that form, reform and disperse in space and over time." In contrast to the frozen geometries of positivism, relational space thus portrays geographies as fluid, mutable, and ever-changing. Digital media are central to these new geographies of networks (Abrams and Hall 2006). This view is compatible with the DeleuzeGuattarian "flat ontology," or in geographic terms, spatialities unmired by the obfuscating effects of scale (Marston et al. 2005). Relational space has also been injected into discourses of globalization, which exhibits a "fibrous, thread-like, wiry, stringy, ropy, capillary character that is never captured by the notions of levels, layers, territories, spheres, categories, structures, or systems" (Paasi 2004, p. 541).

References

Abrams, J., & Hall, P. (2006). *Else/where: Mapping—New cartographies of networks and territories*. Minneapolis: University of Minnesota Press.

Adams, P. (1995). A reconsideration of personal boundaries in space-time. *Annals of the Association of American Geographers, 85*, 267–285.

Adams, P. (1996). Protest and the scale politics of telecommunications. *Political Geography, 15*, 419–441.

Allen, J. (2000). Power/economic knowledge: Symbolic and spatial formations. In J. Bryson, P. Daniels, N. Henry, & J. Pollard (Eds.), *Knowledge, space, economy* (pp. 15–33). London: Routledge.

Alvarez, L. (2012). Spring break gets tamer with world watching online. *New York Times*, March 16, 1.

Anderson, B. (1983). *Imagined communities: Reflections on the origin and spread of nationalism*. London: Verso.

Appadurai, A. (1996). *Modernity at large*. Minneapolis: University of Minnesota Press.

Armstrong, J., & Moulitsas, M. (2006). *Crashing the gate: Netroots, grassroots, and the rise of people-powered politics*. White River Junction: Chelsea Green Publishing.

Ayres, J. (1999). From the streets to the internet: The cyber-diffusion of contention. *Annals of the American Academy of Political and Social Science, 566*, 132–143.

Bandy, J., & Smith, T. (Eds.). (2005). *Coalitions across borders: Transnational protests and the neoliberal order*. Oxford: Rowman and Littlefield.

Bennett, W. (2003). Communicating local activism: Strengths and vulnerabilities of networked politics. *Information, Communication and Society, 6*(2), 143–168.

Blood, R. (2001). Activism and the internet: From e-mail to new political movement. *Journal of Communication Management, 5*(2), 160–169.

Bolin, G., & Westlund, O. (2009). Mobile generations: The role of mobile technology in the shaping of Swedish media generations. *International Journal of Communication, 3*, 108–124.

Bosco, F. (2007). Emotions that build networks: Geographies of human rights movements in Argentina and beyond. *Tijdschrift voor Economische en Sociale Geografie, 98*(5), 545–563.

Bowers, C., & Stoller, M. (2005). Emergence of the progressive blogosphere: A new force in American politics. http://newpolitics.net/sites/ndn-newpol.civicactions.net/files/The-Emergence-of-the-Progressive-Blogosphere.pdf

Bruns, A. (2008). *Blogs, Wikipedia, Second Life, and beyond: From production to produsage.* New York: Peter Lang.

Butler, J. (1990). *Gender trouble.* London and New York: Routledge.

Cammaerts, B. (2005). ICT-usage among transnational social movements in the networked society—to organise, to mobilise, and to debate. In R. Silverstone (Ed.), *Media, technology, and everyday life in Europe: From information to communication* (pp. 53–72). Aldershot: Ashgate.

Campbell, S., & Park, Y. (2008). Social implications of mobile telephony: The rise of personal communication society. *Sociology Compass, 2*(2), 371–387.

Carr, N. (2010). *The shallows: What the internet is doing to our brains.* New York: W.W. Norton.

Carty, V. (2001). The internet and grassroots politics: Nike, the athletic apparel industry, and the anti-sweatshop campaign. *Tamara: Journal of Critical Postmodern Organization Science, 1*(2), 34–48.

Castells, M. (1996). *The information age, volume I: The rise of the network society.* Oxford: Blackwell.

Castells, M. (1997). *The information age, volume II: The power of identity.* Cambridge: Blackwell.

Castells, M. (2001). *The internet galaxy.* Oxford: Oxford University Press.

Chadwick, A. (2006). *Internet politics: States, citizens, and new communication technologies.* Oxford: Oxford University Press.

Clark, J., & Themundo, N. (2003). The age of protest: Internet-based 'dot causes' and the anti-globalization movement. In J. Clark (Ed.), *Globalizing civic engagement: Civil society and transnational action* (pp. 109–126). London: Earthscan.

Cleaver, H. (1998). The Zapatista effect: The internet and the rise of an alternative political fabric. *Journal of International Affairs, 51*(2), 621–640.

Comer, J., & Wikle, T. (2008). Worldwide diffusion of the cellular phone, 1995–2005. *Professional Geographer, 60*(2), 252–269.

Corbridge, S. (1998). Development ethics: Distance, difference, plausibility. *Ethics, Place and Environment, 1*, 35–53.

Cosgrove, D. (2008). *Geography and vision.* London: I.B. Taurus.

Cox, K. (1998). Spaces of dependence, spaces of engagement and the politics of scale, or: Looking for local politics. *Political Geography, 17*(1), 1–23.

Cunningham, S. (2001). Popular media as public 'spericules' for diasporic communities. *International Journal of Cultural Studies, 4*, 131–147.

Curry, M. (1997). The digital individual and the private realm. *Annals of the Association of American Geographers, 87*, 681–699.

Dahan, M., & Shefer, G. (2001). Ethnic groups and distance shrinking communications technologies. *Nationalism and Ethnic Politics, 7*, 85–107.

Debatin, B., Lovejoy, J., Horn, A., & Hughes, B. (2009). Facebook and online privacy: Attitudes, behaviors, and unintended consequences. *Journal of Computer-Mediated Communication, 15*(1), 83–108.

Deibert, R. (1997). *Parchment, printing, and hypermedia.* New York: Columbia University Press.

Deibert, R. (2000). International plug 'n play? Citizen activism the internet, and global public policy. *International Studies Perspectives, 1*(3), 255–272.

Deibert, R., & Rohozinski, R. (2008). Good for liberty, bad for security? Global civil society and the securitization of the internet. In R. Deibert, J. Palfrey, R. Rohozinksi, & J. Zittrain (Eds.), *Access denied: The practice and policy of global internet filtering* (pp. 123–150). Cambridge: MIT Press.

Dekimper, M., Parker, P., & Sarvary, M. (1998). Staged estimation of international diffusion models: An application to global cellular telephone adoption. *Technological Forecasting and Social Change, 57*, 105–132.

Della Porta, D., Andretta, M., Mosca, L., & Reiter, H. (2006). *Globalization from below: Transnational activists and protest networks*. Minneapolis: University of Minnesota Press.

Denning, D. (2002). Activism, hacktivism, and cyberterrorism: The internet as a tool for influencing foreign policy. In J. Arquilla & D. Ronfeldt (Eds.), *Networks and netwars: The future of terror, crime, and militancy* (pp. 239–288). Santa Monica: Rand Corporation.

Ding, L., Haynes, K., & Li, H. (2010). Modeling the spatial diffusion of mobile telephones in China. *Professional Geographer, 62*(2), 248–263.

Dobson, J., & Fisher, P. (2007). The panopticon's changing geography. *Geographical Review, 97*(3), 307–323.

Dodge, M., & Kitchin, R. (2005). Code and the transduction of space. *Annals of the Association of American Geographers, 95*, 162–180.

Dong, Y., & Li, M. (2004). Mobile communications in China. *International Journal of Mobile Communications, 2*(4), 395–404.

Ellison, N., Steinfield, C., & Lampe, C. (2007). The benefits of Facebook "friends": Social capital and college students' use of online social network sites. *Journal of Computer-Mediated Communication, 12*(4), 1143–1168.

Escobar, A. (1999). Gender, place and networks: A political ecology of cyberculture. In W. Harcourt (Ed.), *Women@internet: Creating new cultures in cyberspace* (pp. 31–54). London: Zed Books.

Ettlinger, N. (2003). Cultural economic geography and a relational and microspace approach to trusts, rationalities, networks and change in collaborative workplaces. *Journal of Economic Geography, 3*, 145–171.

Farman, J. (2011). *Mobile interface theory: Embodied space and locative media*. London: Routledge.

Featherstone, D. (2003). Spatialities of transnational resistance to globalization: The maps of grievance of the Inter-Continental Caravan. *Transactions of the Institute of British Geographers, 28*, 404–421.

Featherstone, D. (2005). Towards the relational construction of militant particularisms: Or why the geographies of past struggles matter. *Antipode, 37*, 250–271.

Fischer, C. (1992). *America calling: A social history of the telephone to 1940*. Berkeley: University of California Press.

Florida, R. (2002). *The rise of the creative class*. New York: Basic Books.

Fortunati, L. (2002). The mobile phone: Towards new categories and social relations. *Information, Communication, and Society, 5*(4), 513–528.

Froehling, O. (1997). The cyberspace 'war of ink and Internet' in Chiapas, Mexico. *Geographical Review, 87*, 291–307.

Fuller, D., & Askins, K. (2010). Public geographies II: Being organic. *Progress in Human Geography, 34*(5), 654–667.

Gergen, K. (1991). *The saturated self: Dilemmas of identity in contemporary life*. New York: Basic Books.

Giddens, A. (1991). *Modernity and self-identity: Self and society in the late modern age*. Stanford: Stanford University Press.

Ginzburg, C. (1994). Killing a Chinese Mandarin: The moral implications of distance. *New Left Review, 208*, 107–119.

Goffman, I. (1959). *The presentation of self in everyday life*. New York: Doubleday.

Goggin, C. (2006). *Cell phone culture: Mobile technology in everyday life*. London: Routledge.

Gopal, S. (2007). The evolving social geography of blogs. In H. Miller (Ed.), *Societies and cities in the age of instant access* (pp. 275–293). Dordrecht: Springer.

Gordon, E. and de Souza e Silva, A. (2011). *Net locality: Why location matters in a networked world*. New York: Wiley-Blackwell.

Graham, M., & Khosravi, S. (2002). Reordering public and private in Iranian cyberspace: Identity, politics and mobilization. *Identities, 9*, 319–346.

Graham, S., & Marvin, S. (1996). *Telecommunications and the city: Electronic spaces, urban places*. London: Routledge.

Grannovetter, M. (1985). Economic action and social structure: The problem of embeddedness. *American Journal of Sociology, 91*, 481–510.

Haarstad, H., & Fløysand, A. (2007). Globalization and the power of rescaled narratives: A case of opposition to mining in Tambogrande, Peru. *Political Geography, 26*(3), 280–308.

Hampton, K., Goulet, L., Rainie, L., & Purcell, K. (2011). *Social networking sites and our lives: How people's trust, personal relationships, and civic and political involvement are connected to their use of social networking sites and other technologies*. Washington: Pew Research Center's Internet and American Life Project.

Hampton, K., & Wellman, B. (2001). Long distance community in the network society: Contact and support beyond netville. *American Behavioral Scientist, 45*(3), 476–495.

Haraway, D. (1991). *Simians, cyborgs and women: The reinvention of nature*. New York: Routledge.

Harvey, D. (1996). *Justice, nature, and the geography of difference*. Oxford: Blackwell.

Hawken, P. (2007). *Blessed unrest: How the largest social movement in history is restoring grace, justice, and beauty to the world*. New York: Penguin.

Haythornthwaite, C. (2005). Social networks and internet connectivity effects. *Information, Communication, and Society, 8*(2), 125–147.

Herzog, H., Dinoff, B., & Page, J. (1997). Animal rights talk: Moral debate over the internet. *Qualitative Sociology, 20*, 399–418.

Hill, K. (2011). Will Facebook destroy your job search? *Forbes Magazine* (July 18). http://www.forbes.com/forbes/2011/0718/features-facebook-social-media-google-destroy-job-search.html

Hill, K., & Hughes, J. (1998). *Cyberpolitics: Citizen activism in the age of the internet*. Lanham: Rowman and Littlefield.

Huschle, B. (2002). Cyber-disobedience: When is hacktivism civil disobedience? *International Journal of Applied Philosophy, 16*(1), 69–83.

Illia, L. (2003). Passage to cyberactivism: How dynamics of activism change. *Journal of Public Affairs, 3*(4), 326–337.

International Telecommunications Union. (2010). *The world in 2010*. http://www.itu.int/ITU-D/ict/material/FactsFigures2010.pdf

Jackson, M. (2008). *Distracted: The erosion of attention and the coming dark age*. Amherst: Prometheus Books.

Jameson, F. (1984). Postmodernism, or the cultural logic of late capitalism. *New Left Review, 146*, 53–92.

Johnston, J., & Laxer, G. (2003). Solidarity in the age of globalization: Lessons from the anti-MAI and Zapatista struggles. *Theory and Society, 32*(1), 39–91.

Jones, M. (2009). Phase space: Geography, relational thinking, and beyond. *Progress in Human Geography, 33*(4), 487–506.

Jones, B., Spigel, B., & Malecki, E. (2010). Blog links as pipelines to buzz elsewhere: The case of New York theater blogs. *Environment and Planning B, 37*, 99–111.

Jordan, T., & Taylor, P. (2004). *Hacktivism and cyberwars: Rebels with a cause?* London and New York: Routledge.

Juris, J. (2005). The new digital media and activist networking within anti-corporate globalization movements. *Annals of the American Academy of Political and Social Science, 597*, 189–208.

Kahn, R., & Kellner, D. (2004). *New media and internet activism: From the "Battle of Seattle" to blogging*. Thousand Oaks: Sage.

Katz, J., & Aakhus, M. (Eds.). (2002). *Perpetual contact: Mobile communication, private talk, public performance*. Cambridge: Cambridge University Press.

Kellerman, A. (2002). *The internet on Earth: A geography of information*. Hoboken: John Wiley.

Kirkpatrick, D. (2010). *The Facebook effect: The inside story of the company that is connecting the world*. New York: Simon and Schuster.

Knudsen, J. (1998). Rebellion in Chiapas: Insurrection by Internet and public relations. *Media, Culture and Society, 20,* 507–518.

Lal, V. (1999). The politics of history on the internet: Cyber-diasporic Hinduism and the North American Hindu diaspora. *Diaspora, 8,* 137–172.

Langman, L. (2005). From virtual public spheres to global justice: A critical theory of internetworked social movements. *Sociological Theory, 23*(1), 42–74.

Lanier, J. (2010). *You are not a gadget: A manifesto*. New York: Alfred A. Knopf.

Lawson, V. (2007). Geographies of care and responsibility. *Annals of the Association of American Geographers, 97*(1), 1–11.

Lenhart, A., Ling, R., Campbell, S., & Purcell, K. (2010). Teens and mobile phones. Washington: Pew Internet and American Life Project. http://pewinternet.org/∼/media/Files/Reports/2010/PIP-Teens-and-Mobile-2010-with-topline.pdf

Li, F., Papagiannidis, S., & Bourlakis, M. (2010). Living in 'multiple spaces': Extending our socioeconomic environment through virtual worlds. *Environment and Planning D: Society and Space, 28*(3), 425–446.

Lin, J., Halavais, A., & Zhang, B. (2007). The blog network in America: blogs as indicators of relationships among US cities. *Connections, 27*(2), 15–23. http://www.insna.org/PDF/Connections/v27/20061-2-3.pdf

Ling, R. (2004). *The mobile connection: The cell phone's impact on society*. San Francisco: Morgan Kaufmann.

Ling, R. (2010). *New tech, new ties: How mobile communication is reshaping social cohesion*. Cambridge: MIT Press.

Ling, R., & Campbell, S. (2009). The reconstruction of space and time through mobile communication practices. In R. Ling & S. Campbell (Eds.), *The reconstruction of space and time: Mobile communication practices* (pp. 1–16). New Brunswick: Transaction Publishers.

Ling, R., & Donner, J. (2009). *Mobile phones and mobile communication*. Cambridge: Polity Press.

Lipshutz, R. (1992). Reconstructing world politics: The emergence of global civil society. *Millennium: Journal of International Studies, 21,* 398–420.

Livingstone, S., & Brake, D. (2010). On the rapid rise of social networking sites: New findings and policy implications. *Children and Society, 24*(1), 75–83.

Longan, M. (2002). Building a global sense of place: The community networking movement in the United States. *Urban Geography, 23*(3), 213–236.

Mäenpää, P. (2001). Mobile communication as a way of urban life. In J. Gronow & A. Ward (Eds.), *Ordinary consumption* (pp. 107–124). London: Routledge.

Marche, S. (2012). Is Facebook making us lonely? *The Atlantic* (May). http://www.theatlantic.com/magazine/archive/2012/05/is-facebook-making-us-lonely/8930/

Marston, S. (2000). The social construction of scale. *Progress in Human Geography, 24,* 219–242.

Marston, S., Jones, J., & Woodward, K. (2005). Human geography without scale. *Transactions of the Institute of British Geographers, 30,* 416–432.

Maskell, P., & Malmberg, A. (1999). The competitiveness of firms and regions: Ubiquitification and the importance of localized learning. *European Urban and Regional Studies, 6*(1), 9–25.

Massey, D. (2005). *For space*. London: Sage.

Massey, D. (2009). Responsibilities over distance. In . J. Kenway and J. Fahey (Eds.) *Globalizing the research imagination*, (73–85). New York: Taylor and Francis.

Mercer, C. (2004). Engineering civil society: ICT in Tanzania. *Review of African Political Economy, 99,* 49–64.

Merithew, C. 2004. Women of the (cyber) world: The case of Mexican feminist NGOs *Journal of Interdisciplinary Gender Studies, 8*(1–2), 87–102.

Mojab, S. (2001). The politics of cyberfeminism in the Middle East: The case of Kurdish women. *Race, Gender and Class, 8*(4), 42–61.

Moore, A. (2008). Rethinking scale as a geographical category: From analysis to practice. *Progress in Human Geography, 32*, 203–225.

Morozov, E. (2011). *The net delusion: The dark side of internet freedom.* New York: Public Affairs.

Murdoch, J. (2006). *Post-structuralist geography: A guide to relational space.* London: Sage.

Nie, N. (2001). Sociability, interpersonal relations, and the internet: Reconciling conflicting findings. *American Behavioral Scientist, 45*(3), 420–435.

O'Lear, S. (1996). Using electronic mail (e-mail) surveys for geographic research: Lessons from a survey of Russian environmentalists. *Professional Geographer, 48*, 209–217.

Paasi, A. (2004). Place and region: Looking through the prism of scale. *Progress in Human Geography, 28*, 536–546.

Pain, R., Grundy, S., Gill, S., Towner, E., Sparks, G., & Hughes, K. (2005). 'So long as I take my mobile': Mobile phones, urban life and geographies of young people's safety. *International Journal of Urban and Regional Research, 29*, 814–830.

Palczewski, C. (2001). Cyber-movements, new social movements, and counter-publics. In R. Asen & D. Brouwer (Eds.), *Counterpublics and the state* (pp. 161–184). Albany: State University of New York Press.

Papacharissi, Z. (2009). The virtual geographies of social networks: A comparative analysis of Facebook, LinkedIn and A Small World. *New Media and Society, 11*(1–2), 199–220.

Parham, A. (2004). Diaspora, community and communications: Internet use in transnational Haiti. *Global Networks, 4*, 199–217.

Pickerill, J. (2003). *Cyberprotest: Environmental activism online.* Manchester: Manchester University Press.

Pile, S. (2008). Where is the subject? Geographical imaginations and spatializing subjectivity. *Subjectivity, 23*, 206–218.

Pinkerton, A., Young, S., & Dodds, K. (2011). Weapons of mass communication: The securitization of social networking sites. *Political Geography, 30*(3), 115–117.

Porta, D., & Mosca, L. (2005). Global-net for global movements? A network of networks for a movement of movements. *Journal of Public Policy, 25*(1), 165–190.

Postman, N. (1985). *Amusing ourselves to death: Public discourse in the age of show business.* New York: Viking.

Radicati, S. (2012). Email statistics report, 2012–2016. http://www.radicati.com/wp/wp-content/uploads/2012/04/Email-Statistics-Report-2012-2016-Executive-Summary.pdf

Ritzer, G., & Jurgenson, N. (2010). Production, consumption, prosumption: The nature of capitalism in the age of the digital 'prosumer'. *Journal of Consumer Culture, 10*(1), 13–26.

Routledge, P. (2003). Convergence space: Process geographies of grassroots globalization networks. *Transactions of the Institute of British Geographers, 28*, 333–349.

Routledge, P. (2008). Acting in the network: ANT and the politics of generating associations. *Environment and Planning D: Society and Space, 26*(2), 199–217.

Rutherford, K. (2000). Internet activism: NGOs and the mine ban treaty. *International Journal of Grey Literature, 1*(3), 99–106.

SMI. (2012). http://socialmediainfluence.com/2012/03/09/the-newest-threat-to-blogging-yep-pinterest

Smith, J. (2001). Globalizing resistance: The battle of Seattle and the future of social movements. *Mobilization, 6*, 1–19.

Sooryamoorthy, R., Miller, B., & Shrum, W. (2011). Untangling the technology cluster: Mobile telephony, internet use and the location of social ties. *New Media and Society, 13*, 391–410.

Storper, M., & Venables, A. (2004). Buzz: Face-to-face contact and the urban economy. *Journal of Economic Geography, 4*, 351–370.

Stutzman, F. (2006). An evaluation of identity-sharing behavior in social network communities. *Journal of the International Digital Media and Arts Association, 3*(1), 10–18.

Swan, D., & McCarthy, J. (2003). Contesting animal rights on the internet: Discourse analysis of the social construction of argument. *Journal of Language and Social Psychology, 22*, 297–320.

Taylor, M., Kent, M., & White, W. (2001). How activist organizations are using the internet to build relationships. *Public Relations Review, 27*, 263–284.

Thrift, N., & French, S. (2002). The automatic production of space. *Transactions of the Institute of British Geographers, 27*, 309–335.

Tong, S., Van Der Heide, B., Langwell, L., & Walther, J. (2008). Too much of a good thing? The relationship between number of friends and interpersonal impressions on Facebook. *Journal of Computer-Mediated Communication, 13*(3), 531–549.

Townsend, A. (2000). Life in the real-time city: Mobile telephones and urban metabolism. *Journal of Urban Technology, 7*(2), 85–104.

Travers, A. (2003). Parallel subaltern feminist counterpublics in cyberspace. *Sociological Perspectives, 46*(2), 223–237.

Turkle, S. (2011). *Alone together: Why we expect more from technology and less from each other.* New York: Basic Books.

Ungoed, T., & Sheehan, M. (1999). Riot organisers prepare to launch cyber war on city. *Sunday Times* (August 15), 1.

Van Aelst, P., & Walgrave, S. (2002). New media, new movements? The role of the internet in shaping the 'anti-globalization' movement. *Information, Communication and Society, 5*(4), 465–493.

Van de Donk, W., Loader, B., & Nixon, P. (Eds.). (2004). *Cyberprotest: New media, citizens and social movements.* London: Routledge.

Van Zoonen, L. (2001). Feminist internet studies. *Feminist Media Studies, 1*(1), 67–72.

Vasalou, A., Joinson, A., & Courvoisier, D. (2010). Cultural differences, experience with social networks and the nature of "true commitment" in Facebook. *International Journal of Human-Computer Studies, 68*(10), 719–728.

Warf, B. (1994). Structuration theory and electronic communications. In D. Wilson & J. Huff (Eds.), *Marginalized places and populations: A structurationist agenda.* Greenwood: Westport, CT.

Warf, B. (2009). Diverse spatialities of the Latin American and Caribbean internet. *Journal of Latin American Geography, 8*(2), 125–146.

Wasley, A. (2007). Only connect. *Index on Censorship, 36*(4), 52–58.

Waters, J. (2011). Could you pass a Facebook background check? *Wall Street Journal* (July 25). http://articles.marketwatch.com/2011-07-25/finance/30745971_1_employers-pictures-and-comments-party-pictures

Webber, M. (1973). Urbanization and communications. In G. Gerbner, L. Gross, & W. Melody (Eds.), *Communications technology and social policy* (pp. 293–304). New York: Wiley.

Wellman, B. (2001a). Computer networks as social networks. *Science, 243*, 2031–2034.

Wellman, B. (2001b). Physical place and cyberplace: The rise of personalized networking. *International Journal of Urban and Regional Research, 25*(2), 227–252.

Whatmore, S. (1997). Dissecting the autonomous self: Hybrid cartographics for a relational ethics. *Environment and Planning D: Society and Space, 15*, 37–53.

Wise, P. (1997). Always already virtual: Feminist politics in cyberspace. In D. Holmes (Ed.), *Virtual politics: Identity and community in cyberspace* (pp. 179–196). London: Sage Publications.

Youngs, G. (2002). Feminizing cyberspace: Rethinking techno agency. In J. Parpart, S. Rai, & K. Staudt (Eds.), *Rethinking empowerment: Gender and development in a global/local world* (pp. 79–94). London: Routledge.

Zook, M., & Graham, M. (2007). The creative reconstruction of the Internet: Google and the privatization of cyberspace and digiplace. *Geoforum, 38*(6), 1322–1343.